Intimate Fatherhood

Fatherhood is gaining ever more public and political attention, stimulated by the increasing prominence of fathers' rights groups and the introduction of social policies, such as paternity leave. *Intimate Fatherhood* explores discourses of contemporary fatherhood, men's parenting behaviour and debates about fathers' rights and responsibilities.

The book addresses the extent to which fatherhood has changed by examining key dichotomies - culture versus conduct, involved versus uninvolved and public versus private. The book also looks at longstanding conundrums such as the apparent discrepancy between fathers' acceptance of long hours spent in paid work combined with a preference for involved fathering. Dermott maintains that our current view of good fatherhood is related to new ideas of intimacy. She argues that in order to understand contemporary fatherhood, we must recognise the centrality of the emotional father-child relationship, that the importance of breadwinning has been overstated and that flexible involvement is viewed as more important than the amount of time spent in childcare.

Drawing on original qualitative interviews and large-scale quantitative research, *Intimate Fatherhood* presents a sociological analysis of contemporary fatherhood in Britain by exploring our ideas of good fatherhood in relation to time use, finance, emotion, motherhood and policy debates. This book will interest students, academics and researchers in sociology, gender studies and social policy.

Esther Dermott is Senior Lecturer in Sociology at the University of Bristol, UK.

Intimate Fatherhood

A sociological analysis

Esther Dermott

Routledge
Taylor & Francis Group

LONDON AND NEW YORK

0182552917

First published 2008
by Routledge
2 Park Square, Milton Park, Abingdon, Oxon OX14 4RN

Simultaneously published in the USA and Canada
by Routledge
270 Madison Ave, New York, NY 10016

*Routledge is an imprint of the Taylor & Francis Group, an informa
business*

© 2008 Esther Dermott

Typeset in Times New Roman by
HWA Text and Data Management, Tunbridge Wells
Printed and bound in Great Britain by
CPI Antony Rowe, Chippenham, Wiltshire

British Library Cataloguing in Publication Data
A catalogue record for this book is available from the British Library

Library of Congress Cataloging-in-Publication Data
Dermott, Esther, 1973–
Intimate fatherhood : a sociological analysis / Esther Dermott.
    p.   cm.
 Includes bibliographical references and index.
 1. Fatherhood. 2. Fathers. I. Title.
HQ756.D47 2008
306.874'2–dc22   2007047147

ISBN10: 0–415–42261–2 (hbk)
ISBN10: 0–415–42262–0 (pbk)
ISBN10: 0–203–92706–0 (ebk)

ISBN13: 978–0–415–42261–1 (hbk)
ISBN13: 978–0–415–42262–8 (pbk)
ISBN13: 978–0–203–92706–9 (ebk)

Contents

Acknowledgements

I would like to acknowledge the support of the ESRC which funded both empirical research projects on which the book is based; also the UK Data Archive who supplied the BHPS and NCDS datasets, but who bear no responsibility for my analysis. My thanks go to the interviewees who participated in the *Men, Work and Family Life* project as well as the school principal who was invaluable in making access possible but unfortunately cannot be named, and to Michèle Smith who was the research assistant on *The Effect of Fatherhood on Men's Patterns of Employment* research. Thanks also to Jacqui Gabb for allowing me to read and reference not yet published material. I am grateful to the University of Bristol who awarded me a University Research Fellowship during which time initial thinking about the book (if not the actual writing) took place and to the Department of Sociology who granted me research leave to complete it. I also wish to thank all those in the Department of Sociology who offered me support in writing the book, in particular Jo Haynes, Ruth Levitas and Tom Osborne. To Jo, thanks also for the diversion of *La Bohème*. I am especially indebted to Jackie West for her comments on a draft of the manuscript, not only were these engaged, insightful, constructively critical, and accompanied by lots of encouragement, but were also provided on demand at ridiculously short notice. Finally, very special thanks to Rich, who has been supportive throughout.

Introduction

The setting is a seminar given by two senior male academics. The first speaker begins his talk by taking out of his pocket a bright blue child's watch, saying that he will rely on his son's dolphin watch to make sure that he doesn't go over time. The second speaker starts his talk more conventionally, mentioning his forthcoming book. After a comment from his co-presenter about his high rate of publication, he responds that any royalties will keep his children clothed and fed, adding that his productivity has gone down 'since the kids arrived'. Now if this had been a workshop on fatherhood or family life, these comments would perhaps not have seemed exceptional – but these were experts on nationalism and international migration. The incident serves as an example of the extent to which fatherhood is now pervasive as a comfortable public identity.

This increased visibility of men as fathers is part of a heightened awareness of the role of fathers that provides a rationale for sociological attention and, since Marsiglio's claim over a decade ago that fatherhood 'remains a hot topic' (1993: 484), an already substantial body of work has continued to accumulate. Yet the expansion of fatherhood studies has also revealed a diversity in fathering contexts which suggests the field is far from saturated (Lewis and Lamb 2006). However, 'because it is there' cannot alone be an adequate rationale for academic attention. It is the different, sometimes polarised, opinions about modern fatherhood, within and outside the academy, that make it an intriguing topic of study. There is general agreement that the meaning of fatherhood has altered, but there is much less consensus over the extent of change and how modern fatherhood should be understood. Questions such as what involved fathering entails, whether the absence of fathers from families is problematic, whether breadwinning is an essential component of good fatherhood and if mothering and fathering are equal, all remain key areas of debate and have encouraged the recent tendency to situate fatherhood as a sui generis topic of study within the social sciences.

In order to address the extent of the transformation in fatherhood I make a case here for reconceptualising the way in which we think about contemporary fatherhood. The concept of intimacy allows for the examination of personal relationships both in terms of orientations and tasks; that is, what is being sought from and offered in a father–child relationship as an ideal and in terms of practical caring. Adopting this approach, I hope, allows for some creative thinking around our expectations of fatherhood. A better framing of key concerns can dissolve some problematic dichotomies in discussions of fatherhood: culture versus conduct, involved versus uninvolved and public versus private. Specifically, it provides a way of resolving longstanding conundrums, such as the apparent discrepancy between fathers' acceptance of long hours spent in paid work combined with a preference for involved fathering. Nevertheless, this is a low-key argument: it does not attempt to raze previous thought to the ground, or reincarnate a theorist from another sub-discipline as providing *the* route towards better understanding, or invent a new terminology. The question being addressed is not whether fatherhood should be conceptualised as a form of intimacy but about how intimacy is done by contemporary fathers. Given the current popularity of 'intimacy' as a way to conceptualise personal relationships, this work fits within a wider body of research that is seeking to understand personal life.

The focus here is on fathers and on fathering as the object of study in itself and for providing new insights into understanding personal relationships, rather than as a causal factor in explorations of child development. One of the primary reasons for an interest in fatherhood has been the association between fatherhood and childhood outcomes. This has been dealt with predominantly, and extensively, in psychological and health literature (e.g. Flouri 2005) but has also received attention from other social scientists. The importance of fathers for child welfare is a theme to which both academics and those with political agendas and policy aims frequently return. Improving children's lives is such an uncontroversial objective that emphasising the role of fathers has provided a ready-made justification for concern with fathering. This publication, however, is not concerned with the effect of fathers' presence, their absence, or forms of involvement for outcomes for children. Therefore questions such as 'are fathers necessary?' or 'what can men contribute to family life?' are not prominent.

Fatherhood is now a controversial political issue. Any research findings are likely to be commandeered to back up particular viewpoints and justify interventions by one of the numerous interest groups, which seek to influence public opinion and policy on topics that are directly or indirectly related to men's parenting. This perhaps explains why, when presenting papers at academic conferences and even more so when engaging with the media, there is a desire from audiences to pigeon-hole research findings into one of two polarised categories: as condemning fathers or claiming that they are oppressed. When talking about the findings of the research presented here I have received accusations of doing both, so it seems important to state explicitly that my aim is to vindicate neither position. Although the nature of sociological research means that it can, and should, be interpreted for policy ends, the initial rationale for my programme of research is that developing a better understanding of contemporary fatherhood helps to explain why conflicting perspectives exist, not to pronounce on their validity.

Methodology

Arguments about the ways in which fatherhood is defined and experienced are examined in this study through looking at everyday practices. *Intimate Fatherhood* draws predominantly on two new pieces of independent but complementary pieces of empirical research and integrates these findings with other recent writing on fatherhood. The focus on 'practices' follows David Morgan's (1996) concept of 'family practices' which is defined broadly, to include not only the activities of individual fathers but also those of, for example, policy makers, which contribute to ideas of fatherhood: 'family practices are those practices described as being in some measure about 'family' by one or more of the following: individual actors; social and cultural institutions; the observer' (Morgan 1998: 19).

The two projects approached the subject of contemporary fatherhood with rather different research questions. The first study, *Men, Work and Family Life*, was concerned with exploring how men conceptualised their roles as 'worker' and 'father' and the extent to which reality matched the theory. The implied proposition from a body of existing literature was that men were now likely to face the same 'double shift' as women, as a result of current expectations that combined an obligation on fathers to be involved in childcare and to be committed workers. This possible tension provided the starting point for the project which had a specific interest in finding out how fathers managed to juggle their commitments to employment and family life. In contrast to most research, where the focus has tended to be on the transition to fatherhood and the earliest stages of parenting, these interviews captured arrangements and orientations at a later period as only fathers who had children at primary school (or, in two cases, nursery school) were included. The research adopted a qualitative approach, using in-depth interviews, in order to explore the meaning of and the rationale for particular behaviour and attitudes. Chapters 3, 4 and 5, and to a lesser extent Chapters 2 and 6 draw extensively on this material.

The 25 fathers who were interviewed were relatively homogeneous in terms of their social, as well as geographical location. They were mainly limited to white men, in their thirties and forties, who were in paid work in middle-class occupations, and lived with their female partner and primary school age biological child/ren in a single borough of South London. Further details of the sample and access are detailed in the appendix. There is probably no need therefore to emphasise that the comments made by this group of fathers should not be taken as representative of fathers as a whole. The aim towards social similarity was though intentional. The rationale for this homogeneity was in order to target a sample that might be best placed to take action towards the achievement of 'new' models of fathering: following the idea of purposive sampling, the idea was to focus research on what could be considered an 'extreme' group. At the outset it was thought that a relatively advantaged group of fathers would have more opportunities to act out their preferences. These were men who could actually make choices about how they combined work and family life (Marsiglio and Cohan 2000), but who also might mirror the particular 'career woman' dilemma of juggling commitment to work and children. A discussion session at a recent seminar prompted a pertinent comment from the chair, Rachel Thomson[1] – why should we expect the middle-classes to lead the way in doing parenting differently? It is an astute question as sociologists often seem to look towards the advantaged for social inventiveness only to be disappointed. The assumption here was not that creative parenting practices are limited to a particular family form but, because the push of economic necessity is often the reason that is given for adopting 'traditional' gendered forms of parenting, higher incomes levels might afford more possibilities. If this was not the case, there was a better chance of questioning economic rationalisations in order to better understand men's parenting identity and behaviours.

The second piece of research, *The Effect of Fatherhood on Men's Patterns of Employment,* which is discussed extensively in Chapter 2, focused more specifically on fathers' relationship with the labour market. The relationship between parenting and employment is crucial in accounts of contemporary fatherhood. A crude summary is that commentators tend to see good fatherhood either as accomplished through engagement with the labour market (as breadwinning) or achieved despite the demands of employment, which restrict time that would otherwise be devoted to children. However, there is limited published material which presents quantitative analysis of fathers' employment situation to test these theories. The thinking behind the turn towards quantitative analysis was an interest in disentangling the impact of fatherhood on men's working time from other significant factors. Secondary analysis was conducted on two existing datasets: the British Household Panel Study (BHPS) (University of Essex, 2007) and the National Child Development Survey (NCDS) (University of London, 2007). The NCDS, as a cohort panel, has followed one particular generational group, born in one week in March 1958, at regular intervals in seven sweeps of data collection. The BHPS is a representative panel study with repeated data collections at yearly intervals beginning in 1991; it follows the members of 5,500 households. Further details on each are available from the Economic and Social Data Service (www.esds.ac.uk). As longitudinal, prospective surveys, these datasets also allowed a temporal dimension to be included in the analyses. This meant that in addition to multivariate analyses of data collected at one point in time it was possible to conduct analysis that looked at engagement in the labour market at different points in time, crucially before and after becoming a father.

It is worth noting the geographical focus of the two original empirical studies on which *Intimate Fatherhood* is based. The context is primarily British and aims to capture the state of fathers, fathering and fatherhood in the UK today, where literature on fathers is still 'rather sparse' (Brannen and Nilsen 2006: 336). At the same time, the discussion also draws on literature from North America, where research on fatherhood is more extensive, along with other parts of Europe and Australia. While other national contexts can shed light on the British situation by means of contrast, conversely the UK case can help regarding broader statements about how fatherhood is conceptualised that, optimistically, will be taken up by students and academics outside as well as inside the UK.

Chapter outline

This study addresses the lived experiences of fathers and their attitudes to parenting and integrates them into a broader ideology of contemporary fatherhood. This includes bringing into the frame the role of mothers, and considering the question of who is excluded from achieving contemporary ideals of good fatherhood. Finally, it deals with the public face of fatherhood and examines both legal and policy debates, in light of new forms of contestation around paternity. In terms of breadth of material and style, *Intimate Fatherhood* aims to be accessible to higher level undergraduates with some, but not extensive, background knowledge of sociological research on family and fatherhood – there is no intention though to provide a textbook style trot through all possibly relevant material. The aim is to present the research findings as an argument which should be of interest to an academic audience, but to do so with a sufficient number of references and explanations so that those with less knowledge can still follow the argument.

Chapter 1 presents an overview of contemporary ideas about fatherhood and flags the key issues in the ongoing debate as to whether a fundamental transformation of fatherhood has taken place. The chapter suggests that there are three dominant paradoxes within current thinking on fatherhood that need to be resolved: attention and absence; creation and construction; and culture and conduct. It also details current diversity in fatherhood, from familial and household arrangements to routes to becoming a father.

Chapter 2 analyses the relationship between men's family circumstances and employment; a central element for understanding the contemporary meaning of fatherhood as it involves assessing the extent to which breadwinning retains its significance. Drawing on original findings from large-scale surveys, it is shown that fatherhood status is largely irrelevant for men's level of engagement with the labour market. Together with interview data, these findings suggest that the importance of breadwinning has been overplayed in accounts of fatherhood.

Chapter 3 examines how fathers spend time with their children; not only what they actually do, but also how they feel about particular child-related activities. It is suggested that the acts which are seen as most significant rely on building familiarity but are not necessarily time hungry. Therefore, the argument is made that there is greater potential for involved fathers to have a complementary relationship between work and family than previously acknowledged.

Chapter 4 discusses emotions in relation to fatherhood. It is demonstrated that feeling an emotional connection is important for men in grounding the relationship with their child and that displaying emotions through expressions of closeness is viewed as necessary for successful fathering. It is the physical and verbal manifestations of the emotional bond which mark out a generational shift in ideals of good fatherhood, as the existence of an emotional connection alone is not the preserve of contemporary fathers. It is also argued that an intense emotional connection does not automatically translate into taking on childcare tasks and more equal parenting.

Chapter 5 brings mothers and ideas of motherhood into the frame arguing that, especially since transformations in fatherhood have raised the prospect of gender neutral parenting and the undermining of gender inequality, a coherent understanding of fatherhood is possible only by also understanding motherhood. The chapter challenges the thesis that parents are now interchangeable by showing how fathers themselves continue to construct motherhood as distinct from, and in some ways more important than, fatherhood.

Chapter 6 discusses how fatherhood is constructed in recent government policy and the response by fathers to these initiatives. A spate of recent measures indicates a new level of policy consciousness around fathers and their families in Britain. The chapter explores the fathering practices that have been anticipated and the kinds of parenting involvement that are accommodated by these policies. The chapter places the emphasis on flexibility rather than finance for fathers' ability to achieve a good work–family balance.

Chapter 7 explores some of the ways in which contemporary fatherhood can be experienced as problematic. Fatherhood is frequently described as being in 'crisis' with men increasingly excluded from fatherhood. The chapter focuses on the situation of non-resident and gay fathers in order to highlight the structural elements which underpin contemporary ideas of good fatherhood, and its fluidity and limitations. It also examines the way in which intimacy has been constructed by fathers' rights campaigners as a demand that can be fulfilled through legislative reform.

Chapter 8 assesses the concept of 'disclosing intimacy' in the light of previous findings. This entails an assessment of: the boundaries of intimacy in talking about father–child relations; the extent to which an analysis of fatherhood can improve our understanding of the concept of intimacy and tensions within it; and how analysing fatherhood within the context of intimate relationships can add to the way we think about contemporary fathering. In conclusion, it is suggested that the concept of intimacy is useful for progressing thinking about 'good fatherhood'.

1 Paradoxes of contemporary fatherhood

Thinking about fatherhood involves thinking about fatherhood, fathering and fathers. Morgan (2003, 2004) has clarified the distinction between the three terms as referring respectively to: the public meanings associated with being a father; the actual practices of 'doing' parenting; and the connection between a particular child and a particular man (whether biological or social). This means recognising the construction of fatherhood at the level of meanings, especially the move from an emphasis on fathers as financial providers to emotional nurturers. It also involves a consideration of fathers' involvement, including the importance of pre-existing social categories as an influence on what fathers do and the extent to which various fathering practices are accommodated, promoted or challenged. Finally, it requires an acknowledgement of the diverse routes by which individual men become fathers.

A useful way of conceptualising current thinking about fatherhood is as characterised by paradoxes.[1] Three paradoxes, which, I suggest, are either explicitly recognised in the literature or are evident from competing sociological positions, are outlined here: attention and absence; creation and construction; and culture and conduct. The first paradox (attention and absence) is that, at a time when levels of father absence from the family are unprecedented (Coltrane 2004) there is increasing attention paid to fathers and fatherhood by academics, policy makers and social commentators. This dilemma, I suggest, is of a different order from the others as it is more apparent than real. The second paradox (creation and construction) is that while the tie between biological father and child is given primary status, there is also recognition that social fatherhood (without a biological link) is increasingly prevalent and that 'good fathers' are made, not born. Third, (culture and conduct) is the issue first raised by Ralph La Rossa in the 1980s, namely that while cultural representations of fatherhood suggest a new model of ever increasing involvement and a move towards equal parenthood, the conduct of fathers suggests much less change in men's activities and an obvious continuing division of labour between mothers and fathers. A better understanding of contemporary fatherhood requires moving beyond the binary positions suggested by these dominant paradoxes and towards a more nuanced approach. There is one additional tension in commentaries on fatherhood, which can be thought of as a paradox to be resolved by considering our purpose in studying fatherhood rather than empirical analysis. That is, given the acknowledgement that the social contexts in which fathering occurs and the routes to fatherhood are manifold, resulting in significant diversity in men's experiences of fatherhood, why there is still a concern to conceptualise contemporary fatherhood as one entity.

Attention and absence

Interest in fatherhood has probably never been greater, yet, as Gillis (2000) has described, the last few decades have witnessed a loosening of the connection between fatherhood and masculinity, what he refers to as a 'marginalization of fatherhood' in the West. The apparent paradox is that the two should be occurring simultaneously.

Interest in fathers and fatherhood

In 1984, Jackson titled the first chapter of his book on fatherhood 'the invisible man': in the last few decades the attention lavished on analysis of fatherhood means that this is no longer the case. Across the range of social science disciplines – sociology, psychology, history, policy, cultural studies, socio-legal, geography – fatherhood has become a mainstream concern and this has been accompanied by, or perhaps led by, attention in the popular press, in fictional writing, in books offering parenting advice, and in political debate.

As recently as the 1990s, academic writing on masculinity often excluded discussions of fatherhood altogether and texts on the sociology of the family did not automatically include references to fatherhood. For example, Morgan's important work *Family Connections* published in 1996 has a number of entries under 'mother' and 'parenting' but none under fathers or fatherhood in the index. Collections of writing on the sociology of the family would now be considered lacking if, at minimum, one chapter was not dedicated to some aspect of fatherhood. Major journals in the areas of masculinity/gender and family (such as *Gender and Society* and *Journal of Marriage and the Family*) have regular articles on fatherhood as a matter of course, while others, such as *Journal of Family History,* have had special issues focused on fatherhood, and there is also at least one journal dedicated specifically to research on fatherhood, *Fathering: A Journal of Research, Theory and Practice*. There are many research monographs and edited volumes on fatherhood that are too numerous to list, but recent publications cover a wide range in terms of discipline and methodology; from the ethnographic (Townsend 2002) to the socio-legal (Collier and Sheldon 2008), from policy focused (Hobson 2002) to edited collections (Peters and Day 2002). Research examining the situation of fathers has also been commissioned by government funded organisations such as the Equal Opportunities Commission (e.g. O'Brien 2005, O'Brien and Schemilt 2003, Smeaton 2006). Furthermore, the last decade has witnessed the publication of a number of commentaries offering overviews of the considerable research to date and setting out agendas for the future (e.g. Lewis and Lamb 2006, Marsiglio 1993, Marsiglio *et al.* 2000). It is though worth echoing Lamb's (1993) comment that the previous lack of attention did not necessarily reflect the position of fathers in society. There was a tendency in some earlier studies of fatherhood to suggest that fathering as a personal and socially recognised identity was a new invention: historical work, such as Griswold's (1993) influential *Fatherhood in America*, was important in challenging this idea. Instead the 'newness' originates from developments in sociology (and other disciplines) that now recognise fathers as an interesting social fact.

Current interest in fathers is further emphasised by the frequent presence of the topic in lay writing. The number of 'how to' books on fathering has expanded exponentially, a product of the publishing phenomenon of self-help alongside a particular demand for parenting guides. These are accompanied by both serious advice and more light-hearted reflections in popular publications, such as lists of 'Things A Man Should Know About Fatherhood', in magazines and newspapers which portray family life as not only the preserve of women and children: as just one example a current column 'Dad Rules' appears weekly in *The Sunday Times* and details everyday events in the life of a father. The subject of fatherhood has also made an impact in popular fiction with, to name just two bestsellers in the UK; Tony Parsons' *Man and Boy* (1999), a fictionalised version of lone fatherhood drawing heavily on the author's personal biography, and Nick Hornby's *About a Boy* (1998), which has a surrogate father relationship at its centre. The prevalence of fatherhood is perhaps most obvious in the mass of autobiographical accounts from the perspective of parents and children, of which Blake Morrison's *And When Did You Last See Your Father*, which recounts the relationship with his own father and inspired a raft of confessional memoirs, is perhaps the best known (see also Martin Amis *Experience* 2000, Fraser Harrison *A Father's Diary* 1985 and Fergal Keane *Letter to Daniel* 1996). This wealth of material is supplemented further by the presence of anthologies on fatherhood (e.g. Guinness 1998, Lewis-Stempel 2001).

Fatherless families, familyless men

At the same time as fathers are being 'found' as the subject of academic and popular study, the current historical period often finds men absent from the realm of parenthood. Commentators refer to the current era as witnessing a societal wide epidemic of 'fatherlessness' (Blankenhorn 1995) or the 'shrinking' of fatherhood (Jensen 1998, 1999). The evidence for this state of affairs is twofold: first, that fewer men now become fathers; second, that greater numbers of men 'leave' fatherhood, in the sense of having less involvement in the lives of their children.

The factors behind this abstention from fatherhood are related to the organisation of personal relationships. In terms of 'entry' factors, more options in personal and sexual relationships means that a choice exists either to have children or remain childless/childfree; fatherhood can no longer be automatically assumed as a life event. Commentary in the United States suggests that this avoidance of fatherhood is the choice of a particular section of society, the educated upper-middle-class (Oláh *et al.* 2002), who make up Connell's (1998) influential minority of men who exhibit 'trans-national business masculinity'. Men are having fewer children and are more likely to remain 'childfree' than their recent predecessors (Kiernan 2004), but this is often attributed to the decision-making of women and it is the issue of women remaining childless that is prominent in accounts of social change. Worries about father absence tend to focus more on men who have children, rather than on voluntary childlessness.

In terms of influences on 'exit', 'the question of the fragility of men's relationships with their children has become more pressing' (Collier and Sheldon 2006: 11). This is usually attributed to the end of the universality and permanence of marriage; significant numbers of fathers are not married to the mothers of their children and marital ties are less secure. The end of a marriage need not mean the end of parenting; in fact, as Smart (1997) has argued, the parent–child relationship has replaced marriage as the relationship of permanence (see also Chapter 7). However, the framing of the debate about father absence has co-residence as a central component: in arguing the case for the 'shrinkage' of fatherhood, Jensen (1998, 1999) notes that across Europe, women in their mid-thirties are more likely to live with children than with an adult partner, while men are more likely to live with a partner than with a child. The advent of childbearing as a dimension of serial monogamy means that children are increasingly likely to live apart from one biological parent at some point. In the UK, Canada, Australia and New Zealand around one-fifth of children live in one-parent households at any one time, a figure that rises to about one quarter in the US (Pryor and Trinder 2004). Given the tendency for children to remain resident with their mother after divorce or separation, at any one point in time there are considerable numbers of non-resident fathers, and even more biological fathers who will live apart from their offspring for some period.

The 'absence' of fathers has a number of dimensions: the physical absence of men from the households in which their children live; an emotional distance from children's lives; a relinquishing of the role of financial provider and thereby economic absence. In effect, what is usually being spoken about is the absence of fathers from the households in which children live on a permanent basis, in response to relationship breakdown. This, in turn, is viewed as impacting on the ability of men to be involved with their children in other ways. Fatherlessness, as it has been termed, has been identified as the cause of a whole range of social problems for children, from low educational achievement to childhood delinquency, gun crime to promiscuity. Just recently in the UK, incidents of youth violence have, again, been attributed to an absence of fathers. Particular concern about father absence in Afro-Caribbean families has led to efforts to promote alternative 'father figure' role models for those most 'at risk':

> And as we know – lads need dads. Of course they need their mums as well, but there is a particular point in teenagers' development, of young men, where fathers are very important and they are more likely to be absent in the case of the Afro-Caribbean.
>
> (Jack Straw, Justice Secretary, 21 August 2007, *BBC Radio 4*)

For writers such as Blankenhorn (1995) in the US and Dench (1996) in the UK, men's natural tendency towards selfishness (with the ominous prospect of 'deadbeat dads' or 'feckless fathers' becoming rampant) threatens the basis of social order, unless it is tamed by the influence of women and the responsibilities of fatherhood. 'Absent' fathers are therefore considered a social ill not only because individual children are believed to suffer without the influence of their (biological) father but because this lack of responsibility has a detrimental effect on men themselves.

Apparent paradox?

Dissecting the various aspects of the 'absence' dilemma highlights where a paradox over the absence of fathers in families and their presence in accounts really exists and where this only appears to be the case. It is paradoxical for attention on fatherhood to be increasing at a time when it is dropping in terms of importance as a social identity. However, although it is true that successful masculinity is not tied to the achievement of fatherhood, and that parenthood is less central to the construction of adulthood for men than women, it is not clear that fatherhood has entirely lost its significance. Only around 5 per cent of people across the European Union expect to remain childless and the majority of people, both men and women, think that having a child is important (Kiernan 2004). 'Fatherhood is a common life experience for nearly all men' (Dowd 2000: 22), while Townsend's (2002) study of a group of 'family' men in the US situates fatherhood as an important part of the 'package deal' of masculine adulthood (along with a steady job, being married and owning a home). Similarly, research with young men about their expectations for the future reveals trajectories which include fatherhood (Edley and Wetherell 1999); not as a considered choice but as the default option. This unquestioning attitude is, though, likely to be restricted to those who identify as heterosexual:

> Heterosexual 'situations' continue to lead a preponderance of straight men into paternity. Homosexual situations, on the other hand, currently lead most gay men to childlessness.
>
> (Stacey 2006: 48)

The second way in which absence has entered discussions provides less of an obstacle. It is completely consistent that the worry about a 'crisis of fatherhood', characterised as men failing to fulfil their duties as responsible fathers, should be accompanied by the study of ways in which fathering is conceptualised and practised. It would make sense for this concern to lead to a particular focus on; fathers who are labelled as 'bad dads' (Furstenberg 1988), the impact of absence in various forms, and research on social policies that could affect men's parenting behaviour: all of which are indeed themes in the literature. Research in this area is though preoccupied with resolving the 'problem' of modern fatherhood, and the dominance of this orientation means that fatherhood in general tends to be set up as an issue that needs to be solved.

Creation and construction

Applying the term father is 'the process of identification, of linking a child or children to a particular man, identifying the biological or the social father or both' (Morgan 2004: 382). As any student of marriage and the family will have been taught, in many societies it has been presumed that a married man is the father of any child born to his wife; marriage is taken as a proxy for a biological tie. However, this is no longer the case – as Castelain-Meunier phrases it 'the paternal link, a socializing link, is no longer guaranteed by the institution of the family: it must be built' (2002: 192). Technologies have been developed which can determine biological fatherhood, whilst at the same time the routes to social fatherhood have multiplied, so that the two often fail to coincide, leading to a 'fragmentation of fatherhood' (Sheldon 2005a). The paradox of creation and construction is that at a time when parenting by non-biological fathers is socially visible and increasingly accepted, there should be such especial attention paid to biological fathers.

Biological fatherhood

Fatherhood status has been defined in terms of a genetic connection for only a few decades (now proved through DNA testing and, prior to this development, the less accurate method of matching blood group proteins). The popularity of making sure of a genetic connection is evidenced by the inclusion of DNA testing as a stock component of daytime talk shows along with the large numbers of private companies that have sprung up to offer paternity testing services, including those that can be done in the comfort of your own home and posted off for analysis. The largest user of testing services in the UK context is in fact the state, mainly for decision making over immigration status that depends on a family link and in determining liability for the payment of child support (Richards 2004).

Even when a man has had a social role as the father of a child for many years, the dismissal of any genetic link can remove caring obligations: witness the case of one separated father who visited his young daughter, was involved in her childcare and paid child support, until a paternity test (incorrectly) revealed that he was not the biological father, at which point he refused further involvement (*The Daily Telegraph* 19/6/2001). Similarly, Smart (2006) quotes a notable English case where a father had applied for parental responsibility in relation to the children of his partner so that his status as their (social) father could be recognised. When the relationship ended he refused to pay child support and reclaimed his status as a non-father, which he could legally do since he was not biologically related to the children. Equally, a father who has had little or no contact with a child can be deemed liable for the upkeep of that child if biological fatherhood is established. One recent, high profile case involved the actor Eddie Murphy. After initialling contesting his status as the biological father to a daughter born to ex-Spice Girl, Melanie Brown, he agreed to pay child support for a child with whom he has no contact, after being threatened with legal action (*BBC* 4/8/2007). Post-divorce or separation, biological fatherhood ensures the expectation of an ongoing commitment as a father (Neale and Smart 1997) and recent legislation in the UK has ensured that unmarried biological fathers (provided they are named on the birth certificate) have parental rights. This marks a move away from what has been called the 'gooseberry bush approach' (Fortin 1994, cited in Sheldon 2005a), which solely prioritised stability of care. A genetic link is often *the* significant factor in determining whether a man should have ongoing rights and responsibilities, irrespective of any relationship that may exist between parent and child. Successful fatherhood is often based on a model of a biological link from which social activities flow or can be nurtured. This means that when fatherhood is contested, either between men who have different claims on the label 'father' or between fathers and mothers, biological fathers are given priority.

There is a belief that children should be informed about their genetic origins (Bainham 2002). In situations where there is an uncontested social father in a child's life, who has an ongoing relationship with them but is not biologically related – such as when adoption or assisted reproduction involving sperm donation has taken place – there is a strong view that children should know about the means of their conception and the identity of the man who fathered them. In line with this position, a legislative change in 2005 meant that sperm donors in the UK (following Australia and New Zealand) had their right to anonymity removed. Arguments against the change in law highlighted possible long-term consequences for a donor. Discussions about whether the decision was correct raised a concern that the number of men willing to donate sperm would go down, since potential donors would be worried about the prospect of numerous young adults turning up years later on their doorstep (see 'Hi, I'm your biological son' *The Times* 21/8/2007). The argument in favour was that children had a 'right to know'. One justification for this right was that individuals should be allowed access to information about hereditary health problems: more often, however, the rationale was not about genetic knowledge in itself but its importance for constructing an individual's identity, supposedly stymied without a biological grounding (see 'The right to an identity' *The Observer* 16/6/2002). The significance of the biological is also evident in the idea that having your 'own' (i.e. biologically related) child is considered the preferred option for the majority of people, with the possibility of adoption, for example, a distinct second best: hence the use of and demand for reproductive technologies such as IVF in the determination to have a biologically related child. Further, where donated genetic material is used in reproduction, those involved often do considerable mental work in order to align social and biological accounts (Thompson 2001), such as choosing a donor who is in some way considered biologically similar, whether in eye colour or because they are a kin relation. In one study of families with children conceived using donated genetic material, it was in situations where the *father* did not have a genetic relationship with the child that there was most commitment to secrecy (Golombok *et al.* 1999). Secrecy and anonymity are used to protect children from knowledge that their father is not their 'real' father. Although this would seem to go against the appeal to openness about genetic origins, it suggests the special status of a male biological link, even to the extent of sometimes fabricating its existence in order to construct the appropriate idea of family.

Social fatherhoods

Dominant discourse supports the claims of biological fathers (Smart and Neale 1999) and biological fatherhood seems to be given primacy. Yet, at the same time there is an increasing acceptance of various forms of social fatherhood and an emphasis on what men do as fathers, so that 'fathering is becoming an achieved social relationship' (Edwards *et al.* 2002: 2.1), which should lead to a downplaying of genetic links. It is notable however, there is still a shortage of studies (relative to the overall body of work on fathers) directly concerned with non-biological fathers.

The established route to fatherhood without a biological link – adoption – is complicated to analyse. A case can be made that the way in which biology is treated in adoption cases reinforces the importance of genetic parenthood. Biological parenthood remains the most desirable option and a genetic link continues to have some status even when legal parenthood has been transferred to the adoptive parents. Current 'best practice' advice is not only that adopted children should be told about their genetic origins but also, according to the British Association for Adoption and Fostering (BAAF) that a child may choose to keep in contact with their biological parents (BAAF 2007). Further, the impression is that work is required so that adopted children can feel 'as important' as a biological child. On the other hand, the idea that adoption arrangements should mimic an 'ideal' of a heterosexual couple with biologically related children has been challenged, most notably by the move in 2002 (which became law in 2005[2]) to allow unmarried couples, including gay couples, to adopt. Increasing acknowledgement of gay fatherhood where at least one partner is not biologically related (e.g. Berkowitz and Marsiglio 2007; Stacey 2006) is important because it not only presents an additional challenge to the actuality of having two biological parents as carers, but does so publicly; the visibility of gay fatherhood has been proclaimed as 'the decline of paternity as we knew it' (Stacey 2006). The existence of men who parent outside biological fatherhood is perhaps especially evident as step-fathering (e.g. Edwards *et al.* 2002; Marsiglio 2004), which has become more commonplace through higher rates of divorce and remarriage by men and women with children (though step-families are of course also formed through re-partnership after the death of a spouse). In Britain in 2005 more than 10 per cent of all families with dependent children were step-families, the vast majority of which included a step-father (Babb *et al.* 2006).

Another challenge to the importance of biology is through evidence about the impact of genetically related fatherhood on children's emotional and behavioural development. Comparing children born from donor insemination to those who were naturally conceived, Golombok *et al.* (1995) found no differences in the quality of parent–child relationships or in respect of children' socio-emotional development. The researchers concluded that the strong desire for parenthood was more important for positive outcomes than genetic relatedness. Looking at cases of egg donation, donor insemination, adoptive families and IVF families to compare the relative importance of genetic fatherhood to genetic motherhood also found no differences in parenting quality or the psychological adjustment of the child, although it is interesting that parents' psychological wellbeing was higher when the mother did not have a genetic link than when the father did not (Golombok *et al*. 1999). There seems little evidence that biological fatherhood, in itself, is a significant factor for children's development.

Constructing creation

Reproductive technologies and social reorganisation are responsible for increasing diversity within the category 'parent', but it is still the genetic role which often takes precedence in assigning the title 'father'. If the aim is to designate fatherhood status to a single male, and, as Sheldon (2005a) notes, at least in legal terms it is important for a child to have only one father, according biological fathers primary status seems theoretically simpler than distinguishing between potentially numerous social fathers. However, while biological fatherhood can now be proven, doing so is an unusual step, normally undertaken only in situations of suspicion or conflict. Not only is ascribing importance to biological kin a social process, but in the case of fatherhood a biological relationship will usually be assumed rather than tested.

The significance of biological ties seems to provide a retort to the idea of personal life as based on achieved relationships rather than ascribed roles (e.g. Giddens 1992, 2000): the word 'natural', sometimes used interchangeably for biological parenthood, suggests a positive and taken-for-granted status that is at odds with a supposedly choice based society. Biology is about being rather than doing, and this seems inconsistent with the idea that contemporary fatherhood is about demonstrating an active identity. Yet while biology is considered important and grounds obligations and rights, it is not sufficient: instead genetic fathers are those who should be given most encouragement to enact appropriate fathering. There is rather more attention, in both political and academic realms, placed upon the problem of genetically related fathers who are 'absent' (in different ways and for different reasons) than there is on men negotiating the role of social father (without a biological link). In the face of moves towards gender neutral parenting the elevation of genetic fatherhood reasserts the importance of men as parents.

This leads us on from how the title 'father' is assigned, to its impact on the practices of fathering. Donovan (2000) found in her study of lesbian parents that women tended to opt for identifiable male donors and so could be accused of perpetuating the idea that biological fatherhood is especially meaningful. Yet, as she points out, the women also disassociated biological fatherhood from an active parenting role. This is significant; being a genetic father need not be related to *fathering*. It raises the possibility that fatherhood is being, what we could term 'disassembled', with rights (and some responsibilities) separated from caring tasks. The real question to be addressed is not whether biological or social fatherhood is given priority but *how* biology is brought into accounts of fatherhood as relevant to intimate practice.

Culture and conduct

Whether it is viewed as positive or problematic, fathers and fatherhood have received attention because of the idea that change is afoot; something is 'going on' that is worth academic attention, fatherhood is 'in transition' (Björnberg 1992). The question remains over the extent of this transition and, in particular, whether fatherhood behaviour is keeping pace with attitudes towards fathering.

New fatherhood in theory

The cultural transformation of fatherhood has seen a move away from the good father as moral guardian, disciplinarian and educator to the single role of financial provider to a contemporary ideal of nurturing involvement and the expectation of equal co-parenting (Pleck and Pleck 1997). While nuanced accounts have challenged the temptation to overly simplify a narrative of change into neat historical segments, there is acceptance of a definite ideological shift in men's orientation towards parenthood (Furstenberg 1988; La Rossa 1988; Lupton and Barclay 1997; O'Brien 2005).

Freeman (2002) acknowledges an intense media focus on men's relationships with their children which promotes a transformed, nurturing father as the ideal. Freeman draws on a range of cultural representations which compare versions of everyday fatherhood to this ideal type; such as the 'apprentice' father who tries hard but is not yet capable of many childcare tasks, or the 'victim' father who wants to be involved but is prevented by the vagaries of influential others, or in a more positive vein, the 'celebrity' father who wears his parenthood as a badge of honour. The worlds of sport and politics are two arenas which illustrate awareness of public fatherhood. Think of the successful sports player who is pictured receiving a trophy often accompanied by a young child; from football tournaments (the captain of the winning team walking up the steps with a baby in one arm) to golf championships (the emotional last few holes of the Ryder Cup or a major championship). The celebrity dad also exists in the political realm, with politicians displaying their family credentials on election leaflets and television broadcasts. Before the current British Prime Minister, Gordon Brown, had his first child relatively late in life at the age of 50, there was concern expressed from some quarters that his lack of children could damage his popularity. The idea that a man achieves adulthood through taking on the responsibilities of a wife and child is not new (see Roper 1994 on accounts of post-war managers) – what is different is the very public nature of male parenting with children on show. Fatherhood appears in other guises too: whether speaking truthfully or not, the male politician now almost automatically use the refrain that he 'wants to spend more time with his family' to put a positive spin on a resignation or sacking because it is considered plausible. Outside of media coverage, Lewis and O'Brien (1987) noted some time ago that British public policy discourse showed signs of taking 'involved fatherhood' as the model. This cultural acceptance is also present in the analysis of social attitudes which indicate a continuing trend away from the roles of mother and father as child carer and financial provider respectively (Crompton 2006) and, among fathers, the adoption of the rhetoric of 'new' fatherhood in describing their personal orientation (Dienhart 1998) to parenthood.

These changes in fatherhood can be attributed, at least partially, to an attack on men's status as breadwinners and the ideology of separate spheres, through a restructuring of the economy and the impact of feminism. Labour markets in the West have seen a collapse in many occupational sectors previously dominated by men and a concomitant rise in female-dominated service sector industries. Higher numbers of women now enter the labour market and, importantly, maintain the role of paid worker throughout their lives, after marriage and having children. Increasingly, households are 'dual wage', and the expectation that a single male wage should be paid at a sufficient level to provide for himself and his wife and children as dependants – the 'family wage' – has disappeared. There was a belief that this change in women's behaviour would lead men to follow; as women became more like men in terms of their engagement in the world of paid work, men would become more like women in their participation in the domestic sphere, including childcare. The perceived relevance of these changes in employment for parenthood helps to explain the close link between discussions of parenthood and the agenda for a better work-life balance. The idea of men and women as equally involved in both spheres reflects both the recognition of equal competency and the rejection of the categories of worker and parent as implicitly gendered. In relation to parenthood, for example, magazine articles have shown an increased interest in gender non-specific parenting (Atkinson and Blackwelder 1993). There is though a tension in this transformation. As the debate over absent fathers showed, a different view sees increasing men's contribution to the private realm of the family as positive, precisely because they can provide something that is father-specific.

New fatherhood in practice

The extent of this alleged cultural revolution is called into question by empirical evidence which fails to detect the anticipated widespread realignment of parenting duties; in other words, the conduct of fathers does not match the cultural prescription. Fathers do not participate equally in childcare, spending less time on child-related domestic tasks than do women (Bittman 2004 (Australia), Smeeding and Marchand 2004 (US), Sullivan 2000 (UK)); 'evidence does not support great optimism about the future involvement of men in family chores and care' (Scott 2006: 14) and, furthermore, parenthood has relatively little impact on men's involvement in paid work (Dermott 2006a). Debates over time-use can be considered an example of the culture and conduct dilemma. Fatherhood is now supposed to be more about child-centred activities that entail a time commitment, with evidence that many men embrace this belief and want to spend more time with their children (e.g. Coltrane 1996). At the same time, fathers continue to devote much more of their time to paid work, with statistics indicating that men in Britain work especially long hours, and that fathers put in more hours to paid employment than non-fathers (though see Chapter 2): it could be argued that this is another instance of father 'absence'. This feeds into policy discussions around the issue of promoting better work-family balance, as does evidence about the scanty extent of fathers' leave taking. Overall there is a limited realisation of the image of new fathering into measurable caring.

Explaining the paradox

Explaining the gap between attitudes and behaviour is far from unique to fatherhood research, but it has become a significant aspect of recent study. Various explanations have been put forward for the discrepancy between the culture of fatherhood and the reality of fathers' conduct. The first is the influential proposition of the process of 'lagged adaptation', developed to explain women's continuing dominance in domestic labour (Gershuny et al. 1994). This suggests that attitudes alter more quickly than behaviour so that, over time, practice will come to resemble current beliefs. However, Himmelweit and Sigala (2004) found that mothers of young children in the British Household Panel Study who were in the contradictory position of being in employment while believing that pre-school children suffered from their mothers' working were more likely to change their attitude than their behaviour, thereby challenging the view that attitude leads and behaviour follows. Instead, they suggest that identities and behaviours adjust to each other in a complicated process of positive feedback.

The second proposition, which is not incompatible with the lagged adaptation thesis, suggests that significant groups and social structures are currently influential in restricting men's ability to fulfil their desired fathering role. Involvement in paid employment operates to restrict men from achieving their aim: the necessity of earning a wage, combined with the time greedy culture of employers and workplaces leaves fathers in a difficult situation. Some, male-dominated, industries require being away from home for significant periods (e.g. those in the armed forces, oil rig workers, deep sea fishing or high level executives with substantial amounts of overseas travel). Those in lower-paid jobs may be obliged to work long hours, while some elite workers may also face the obligation of long hours combined with extensive commuting. Further, it has been argued that employers discriminate between men and women in this regard and do not grant fathers the leeway that is afforded to mothers to accommodate childcare (Blackstone et al. 1992), even in Scandinavian countries where statutory measures and cultural climates that emphasise gender equality exist (Brandth and Kvande 2001; Højgaard 1997). Finally, incarceration is an extreme example of fathers' enforced absence from family life that has also received recent attention (see special issue of *Fathering*, imprisoned fathers' edition 2005).

Meanwhile, it has been argued that experts such as childcare workers and health professionals tend to ignore men's contribution to their children's lives (Burgess 1997) and therefore fail to encourage or nurture their involvement, while legal disenfranchisement devalues men's role as carers (Lewis 2000). Mothers are also deemed liable for the continuation of men's limited childcare as they hold a gatekeeper role within the family (e.g. Warin *et al.*1999) and can restrict fathers' level of involvement if their status of primary parent is threatened (Maushart 2002). It is argued that inequality between mothering and fathering allows the 'mothers' mafia' to assert their 'right' to do paid work on a part-time basis or take on the role of full-time mother while fathers are not able to do likewise (though see Chapter 5).

> While mothers may welcome fathers as babysitters, they may reject them as equal partners in parenthood, resenting the intrusion of males on their mother-role and unhappy about the quality of their partner's parenting.
>
> (Burgess 1997: 135)

What these sets of explanations have in common is that they describe how fathers are seeking to move on, while significant others wish to retain the status quo. These positions run the risk of portraying men as without agency, in contrast to theories of patriarchy (e.g. Walby 1990) that emphasise benefits which accrue to men when ongoing power differences between men and women are maintained. The proposal that (at least some) fathers benefit from the current organisation of childcare is consistent with the finding that fathers express limited preferences for change, indicating that there may be relatively little 'reality lag' (Hochschild 1995) between fathers' desires for parenting and what they actually do.

A different approach suggests that, in fact, initial impressions as to the extent of cultural change were misplaced, with references to new and involved fathering largely superficial, or at least overstated. Sunderland (2000) argues that parentcraft texts continue to position fathers as 'second-class' parents who tend to assist mothers rather than take primary responsibility, so that '[social] expectations themselves have a long way to go before they can be said to support fully involved fathering and shared parenting' (Wall and Arnold 2007: 523). Therefore, it is argued that taken-for-granted understandings of fatherhood may not be so far away from the behaviour of fathers as was previously believed. An acknowledgement of the limitations to the extent of cultural transformation is worthwhile, providing a counterbalance to accounts which have ignored significant elements of continuity. However, although the transformation of the culture of fatherhood to an 'involved' model is not total, there has still been substantial change. Even if this re-evaluation reduces the size of the gap between culture and conduct, there is still a rift which needs explanation. The research findings discussed in the chapters that follow interrogate the behavioural changes that are required to match the cultural prescription of good fatherhood. They also challenge the extent of the apparent discrepancy between culture and conduct by drawing attention to the plasticity of contemporary fathering with regard to practical caring, which allows the development of a close relationship that is disassociated from equal co-parenting and shared childcare. The conduct of fathering therefore may not need to change in the ways anticipated in order to conform with the idea of 'nurturing' fatherhood.

Diversity and explanation

The final paradox, which is of a different order from the previous three, concerns the fact that while fatherhood is increasingly recognised as a diverse social category there still remains a desire to apply a single meaningful label to our ideas about contemporary fatherhood. There is a tension between adequately portraying the variety that exists in fatherhood today without giving up on describing broader cultural trends.

Diverse fatherhoods

Alongside sociological categories such as masculinity and family, fatherhood too has become pluralised. Diversity has been noted in the routes men take to become fathers and the social contexts in which fathering occurs, which means that thinking of fatherhood in the singular is somewhat misleading. Research on specific groups of fathers has developed a fuller picture of how fatherhood is experienced and has encouraged leading authors to argue that a key task of fatherhood researchers should be to explore the distinctive institutional and cultural contexts that define responsible fathering (Marsiglio *et al.* 2000). The exercise of detailing the range of social situations in which fathering occurs brings to the fore the way in which decision-making about fatherhood is constrained. 'Traditional' social divisions, such as age, class, sexuality, and ethnicity, have been brought into accounts and, as Marsiglio and Cohan (2000) writing with respect to the interaction between class and ethnicity in an American context note, there are also significant interactions between key variables which situate men's parenting.

One of the advantages of emphasising diversity has been the move away from a hegemonic conception of fatherhood (white, middle-class, heterosexual, married) and the questioning of previously taken for granted ideas about men's parenthood. For example, research on gay fatherhood (e.g. Berkowitz and Marsiglio 2007; Dunne 2001a; Stacey 2006) has been important for challenging heterosexist assumptions about fatherhood, such as the construction of fathering in relation to mothering.

Age has become a controversial subject in discussions of motherhood, as the 'too old' and the 'too young' have both been criticised for being inappropriate as parents: the former for selfishly pursuing other interests before embarking on motherhood which challenges 'natural' boundaries, meaning that their children are deprived of a parent who can be actively involved; the latter for becoming mothers at a stage when they are judged to be irresponsible and unable to provide the financial and emotional resources that children require for successful development. In contrast, older fatherhood has received little attention, and is largely accepted as socially unproblematic. However, young fatherhood, predominantly through its association with young/teenage motherhood, has now gained some attention (e.g. Bunting and McAuley 2004; Fagan 2003; Queniart 2004; Quinton *et al.* 2002; Sigle-Rushton 2005; Speak *et al.* 1997). There has been particular interest in the link with poverty, and in seeking to find ways of engaging with young fathers to encourage greater involvement in their children's lives.

The shift to an involved, nurturing model of good fatherhood has been labelled a middle-class phenomenon (La Rossa 1988) with the suggestion that traditional working-class masculinity remains more strongly associated with the breadwinner model. The gap between the culture and conduct of fatherhood could therefore be attributed to the dominance of middle-class values in public arenas such as the media and among policy makers, while measurable conduct reflects not only the practices but also the orientations of the majority. There is a contrasting argument: the development of dichotomous work rich/work poor households means that fathers in financially advantaged households have less time to fulfil ideas of 'new fatherhood', while working-class fathers who are more likely to be faced with unemployment or underemployment end up contributing more to practical childcare – Brannen and Nilsen (2006) found that their 'hands on' fathers were unskilled men without qualifications. Meanwhile Vincent and Ball (2006), in their study of childcare practices, draw attention to differences among those who occupy 'class fractions' of the middle class. This discussion is taken up again in Chapter 2.

In the US, the Million Man March in 1995 explicitly linked the themes of masculinity, fatherhood and race, with a call for African Americans to be a more positive force in their children's lives (Marsiglio 1998). However, as Marsglio *et al.* (2000) note, much of the interest in ethnic diversity has focused disproportionately on men from lower socio-economic backgrounds (e.g. Jayakody and Kalil 2002). Likewise when fatherhood and ethnicity are studied together in the UK there has been a tendency to concentrate on absent Black African/Caribbean fathers, revisiting fatherhoods that are viewed in some sense as problematic, or potentially so. Reynolds (2005) argues that this labelling of fathers as 'absent' is a misnomer given the ways in which many non-resident fathers were involved with their children in the British black families she studied. With this exception, popular arguments about fathers' rights and responsibilities have not taken on a significant 'ethnic dimension' and the extent of UK research on fathering in ethnic minority groups remains relatively small, leading to calls to expand our knowledge further about fatherhood diversity with respect to ethnicity (Lewis 2000). A set of projects funded by the Joseph Rowntree Foundation (www.jrf.org.uk) goes some way to addressing this current lack of knowledge and will include reports on fathering among UK South Asians and the parenting of mixed heritage children.

Neglecting the labour market and welfare state context, in which individuals not only act out their choices but have their preferences formed, has led to underdeveloped analysis (Fagan 2001). Cross-national research can highlight the influence of legislation and social policies on the enactment of 'family'. In relation to fatherhood, studies, such as Smith's (2007) research on fathers' time use in a number of different European contexts, have provided a correction to assumptions of similarity in family practices, even within the advantaged West. Studies of fathers in a range of different national contexts provides evidence of the impact of individual policy initiatives and also how packages of policies that relate to fatherhood are made consistent with particular welfare regimes or challenge these categories (e.g. Hobson 2002).

As noted in the section on father absence, much of the interest in fatherhood has been prompted by socio-demographic changes, especially the level of family breakdown and reconstitution, which has led fathering to take place within a variety of household contexts. Research has looked at divorced/separated fathers (e.g. Arendell 1995; Bradshaw *et al.* 1999; Smart and Neale 1999), including those who as a consequence are lone parents (e.g. Grief 1985), or who are involved in shared parenting/residence situations (e.g. Masardo 2007), alongside those who take on the role of step-fathers (e.g. Edwards *et al.* 2002; Marsiglio 2004) or indeed fathers in blended families who have more than one fathering identity. Attention on all of these has, perhaps ironically, been significant in drawing attention to the way in which fatherhood is not a stand alone category but is constructed in negotiation with other relationships, including in relation to motherhood. Large scale surveys usually take the household or the individual as the unit of analysis. The advantage of household level data is that it is possible to get a sense of family relations, but the extent of fathering across households means that the household cannot be taken as a proxy for family. It is possible to use this type of data to locate fathers who are living with children that (they know) are not their biological kin, in order to get some sense of the extent of step-fathering, for example. However, the situation of non-resident fathers which is also needed is much more difficult to trace. These methodological limitations mean that there remain certain groups of fathers who are not well represented in the literature. Marriage, divorce and separation, and re-partnering mean that fathers are now more likely to experience more than one family type over their lifecourse and some recent research aims to plot the movement of men through various household and fathering scenarios (Lee 2005 cited in Lewis and Lamb 2006). This emphasises both the extent of 'non standard paternal biographies' (Lewis and Lamb 2006) and the degree to which snapshot views of fatherhood fail to grasp the often changing nature of fatherhood for a single individual.

Frameworks for contemporary fatherhood

At the same time as researchers have recognised diversity among fathers and in fathering, there remains an interest in trying to find a single term that encapsulates contemporary fatherhood. The objective in doing so is to provide some coherence to the category and to allow commentators to assess the extent of change. There are though problems with the terms that are currently in use. Both words which are employed, sometimes in tandem, to distinguish the idea of fatherhood in the current era – 'new' and 'involved' – have to do a lot of work; so that it is not always obvious what this new and/or involved fathering entails (Lupton and Barclay

1997). Other terms that have been used to describe fathering, such as 'responsible' (e.g. Doherty *et al.* 1998), tend to have more moral or political undertones that are problematic when attempting to explicate a phenomenon while avoiding a normative standpoint.

The label 'new' can perform the task of indicating fundamentally different modes of fatherhood that correspond with the modern and the post/late modern/ post-industrial periods. As such, it highlights a substantial shift in both the meaning and enactment of fatherhood: 'new' fatherhood is defined as loving, involved and non-authoritarian compared to an emotionally distant and authoritarian fatherhood of old. However, the term is problematic for a number of reasons. Because of its commonsense meaning of 'recent', 'new fatherhood' can easily become a messy category that refers, atheoretically, to anything that is going on in the present. In this sense 'new fatherhood' both requires continual re-evaluation and is composed of a mixed bag of behaviours, from changing nappies to not living with children; behaviours which do not necessarily present a comprehensible whole. Equally, if 'new' is of the moment then 'old' (or 'traditional') simply becomes a catch-all grouping of elements from the past. In accounts, which use the split between 'new' and 'old/traditional' to indicate a fundamental divide associated with the culmination of various social processes, there is a problem in marking out at what chronological point this transformation occurred. There is also the more serious issue of asserting an overly simplified dichotomy of old and new that necessarily misrepresents 'old' fatherhood as the antithesis of the new; not only authoritarian, but also unloving.

Using 'involved' instead of 'new' or as an adjunct to it, avoids reliance on a term that is defined in a temporal way. Instead, the idea of 'being involved' focuses attention explicitly on 'doing' fatherhood. It has been used to suggest a recent development which locates fathering within the private realm of the household as a counter to the historical responsibility of fathers to socialise their children into the wider world (see Tosh 1986), as such 'involved fathering' tends to refer specifically to men's (expanding) participation in childcare. The three dimensions of involvement defined by Lamb *et al.* (1987) – engagement, availability and responsibility – focus on aspects of childcare, as does Palkovitz's (1997) list of fifteen categories of paternal involvement that build on this typology. However, as with the term 'new', 'involved' is not entirely straightforward.

The concern with demarcating aspects of involvement has a specific purpose in generating measurable variables that can be used in quantitative analysis, especially in defining aspects of fathers' involvement that are relevant to child development and, more generally, in drawing attention to what men do with their children including the cognitive elements of fatherhood (Palkovitz 1997, Marsiglio *et al.* 2000). In focussing on the different kinds of fathering involvement, it has been argued that a more expansive definition is required as restricting men's involvement with children to direct care is too narrow. Morgan (1998) has challenged the idea of the parenting role as one that is entirely home centred and it has recently been argued that financial provisioning should also be considered a form of involvement (Christiansen and Palkovitz 2001), in order that fathers who are involved in more 'traditional' ways are not given the derogative label 'uninvolved'. While on the one hand it seems reasonable to recognise various forms of involvement, this development is also confusing since 'involved fatherhood' as a *form* of fatherhood was intended to contrast with the breadwinner model: by focussing on various elements of involvement the objective of demarcating contemporary fatherhood as a whole is lost.

Characterising contemporary fatherhood

Given the variety of contexts for fatherhood it may now seem paradoxical to attempt to characterise 'contemporary fatherhood' as anything but a collection of fatherhoods. The increasing diversity in fatherhood combined with the problem of finding appropriate terminology might suggest that it is time to abandon attempts at broader classification. However, there is a desire to find generalities at some level as otherwise the sub-categories of fatherhood can themselves just be further divided until they are meaningless for the purposes of social explanation. Discussions of motherhood may provide a framework; they recognise that there is a cultural norm of 'intensive mothering' (Hays 1996), but also that interpretations of this ideal necessarily depend on social context.

Morgan (1996) proposed the reconceptualisation of family studies around the idea of 'family practices', which refers not only to specific activities carried out by family members but also the wider behaviours, for example of politicians, which construct our idea of family; a term which moves the focus to 'doing' as opposed to 'being' and conveys both a sense of regularity and fluidity. In fatherhood studies adopting this approach avoids the problem of labelling particular activities as 'involved' or 'new'. The key question, which is prominent throughout the book but addressed explicitly in the final chapter, is then what *kind* of intimacy is encompassed in contemporary fatherhood and what are implications of this for our understandings both of fatherhood and intimacy.

Conclusion

It has been argued that while evidence for a transformation of fatherhood is substantial and persuasive, the nature of contemporary fatherhood remains unclear. This chapter has outlined three conundrums which have emerged from recent findings and are central in framing current debates, as well as suggesting that acknowledging diversity within practices of fathering should not necessitate giving up on deciphering the bigger picture. The remainder of the book draws on a range of empirical evidence in order to address some of main issues and suggest a possible way forward for thinking about contemporary fatherhood.

2 Fathering as breadwinning

This chapter addresses the hotly debated topic of breadwinning as a component of good fatherhood. It begins by challenging the construction of emotional/economic as a dichotomy, arguing that personal relationships often include financial exchanges, and that the presence of money need not undermine the emotional basis of a personal relationship. The chapter then provides an historical overview of the role of breadwinning, illustrating how providing financial support was seen as the key component of good fathering for most of the twentieth century. The focus then moves to contemporary life, where breadwinning has been undermined by changes in gender relations and the labour market but is still present in men's account of family life. A detailed exploration of fathers' employment situation and their attitudes to paid work, drawing on original quantitative and qualitative material, resolves some current misunderstandings about the importance of breadwinning for fathers. It is argued that breadwinning and fathering have become unshackled, but that this is hidden by the ongoing importance of wage earning for material wellbeing and male identity.

Emotions and money

The warning to avoid lending money to or borrowing money from family members or close friends is often repeated. Because intimacy and money are supposed to be diametrically opposed there is a fear that mixing the two will lead to fraught personal relationships. Intimacy often appears to occupy the realm of companionship and emotion, not finance and contracts, so the anxiety is that money will pollute the domain of the private. However, it is a fallacy to think of the intimate or emotional as operating in a separate sphere from the financial. The delineation is a fanciful one; a product of our desire to dichotomise and fit additional characteristics to existing dominant categories such as public and private. As Zelizer phrases it in *The Purchase of Intimacy*, 'far more goes on in households than coupling and caring' (2005: 212), and it is a mistake to view the family as solely the domain of sentiment. Households are the site of familial intimacy but they also operate as budgetary units. It is not that intimacy and money never mix, but that the meaning given to money within our personal relationships is complicated; within households, money transfers are commonly considered gifts or thefts rather than contractual arrangements. Much of Zelizer's text is, in fact, a discussion of the various ways in which legal cases both attempt to distinguish the appropriate use of money based on the type of social relationship, and the way in which different types of monetary exchange denote particular relationships. For example, was a sexual relationship between a man and a woman a courtship with the reasonable anticipation of a marriage as the outcome, or was it an ongoing arrangement purely for the provision of sexual services? The legal decisions which are recounted rely on how money was transferred between individuals, e.g. leaving money after each meeting was an indication of payment for services rendered, and they lead to adjudications of how contested financial commitments should be viewed, e.g. a ring was not given as a commitment to marriage, which should be returned if an engagement is broken off, but was a gift from client to prostitute.

Any attempt at a separation between the two arenas of money and intimacy is simply not possible. We may express caution about the pitfalls of lending money to relatives but we still do it, because caring about someone may at times mean caring for them through providing financial assistance. In a study exploring to whom parents turned to for various forms of support, Edwards and Gillies (2005) found that although financial self-sufficiency was considered desirable, in practice money was lent and borrowed between extended family members. They classify the small sums of money most often transferred between working-class households as 'mutual aid and reciprocity [that] was more a symbol of an *intimate connection* that made day-to-day life possible rather than barter-like exchange' (2005: 29, my italics). One of the ways of 'doing' family – something that may be constructed as a 'family practice' (Morgan 1996) – is providing monetary gifts and loans. There is evidence that parents offer substantial support to their adult children through giving them money (Grundy 2005; Nolan and Scott 2006). Results from the British Social Attitudes Survey indicate that only a small percentage of respondents agreed with the statement that, once children have left home, they should no longer expect help from their parents (McGlone et al. 1998) and young adults say they would turn first to parents and then other family members for financial assistance (Jones 2004). Further, around one-third of people have actually helped out an adult relative or friend with £100 or more in the last five years and a similar percentage had received a loan or gift; beneficiaries of help were most likely to be a son or daughter (McGlone et al. 1996). One indicator of the scale of financial transfers that are made between family members is that annual remittances from people living and working in the UK to family in the developing world amount to £2.3billion (Harman 2007). Although financial commitments between family members may, like other commitments, vary over time and are negotiated rather than defined purely by structural relationships (Finch and Mason 1993), they are very present in accounts of our personal lives.

The parent–child relationship has financial responsibility as a central component. Other discussions of financial help are largely based on exploring the situations of adults, between whom there exists formal independence and therefore some level of equality, rather than a legal requirement to provide. The obligation for parents to look after their dependent children, both emotionally and financially, is such a taken-for-granted social fact that it is rarely commented upon. Children are not expected to provide themselves with basic necessities; that is patently the role of their parents (albeit with various organisations and state agencies operating as a safety net). Therefore the entitlement of children to economic well-being is usually only discussed in the face of family breakdown or, as in the Government Consultation Document *Every Child Matters* (2003), in response to failures by social care services. Financial provisioning is a responsibility of parents – that much is clear. The issue to be explored here is whether economic responsibility is the role of *fathers* in particular. Bradshaw *et al.* (1999: 205) state that 'The moral duty on fathers (and all parents) to provide financially for dependent children is so strong that it is surely non-negotiable'. However, it is the question of whether there is discrimination between parents in this element of parental duty that is key in determining the place of breadwinning in men's parenting role.

The provider role

Historical developments, as described by authors such as Griswold (1993), La Rossa (1997), Rotundo (1993) and Pleck and Pleck (1997), mean that our current ideals of fatherhood no longer have, as central elements, the roles of disciplinarian, educationalist and moral authority. These have been replaced by a focus on the nurturing elements of parental care, especially engagement with children in leisure activities and the carrying out of practical childcare tasks. Most commentators are in broad agreement as to the decline of the former set of characteristics and, albeit with perhaps greater differences of opinion, the rise of the latter group of attributes in the construction of contemporary fatherhood.

The one major element which remains highly contested is breadwinning, that is, the extent to which an important aspect of the good father is to provide financially for his children through engagement with the public world of work. According to most historians of fatherhood the predominance of the breadwinner model was a phenomenon associated with industrialisation: prior to this the organisation of households as economic units made the idea that men alone were providers difficult to sustain.

> In a subsistence economy in which husbands and wives ran farms, shops or businesses together, a man might be a good, steady worker, but the idea that he was *the* provider would hardly ring true.
>
> (Bernard 1981: 2)

With the arrival of the machine age, employment for many took place away from the home, with the concomitant move towards a separation of spheres leaving men and women specialising in paid work and family care respectively. Although the precise timing of this change is difficult, Pleck and Pleck (1997) categorise 1830–1900 as the era of the 'distant breadwinner', while Griswold (1993) similarly situates the fall of the American family as a productive unit and the rise of the breadwinning father as a product of the later 1800s which held through to the mid-decades of the twentieth century. It was though only really in the twentieth century, when a significant portion of those in work could sustain a family on a single income, that the breadwinner model became an attainable ideal. The welfare system of the UK in the interwar period in the first half of the twentieth century was based on the model of a man earning wages which could support a wife and dependent children (Lewis 1992) (although of course, in practice, many married women did work). The piece of legislation that best exemplified the construction of men as breadwinners was the 'marriage bar', which applied across many public sector occupations and required women to resign from their jobs on marriage. While the rescinding of this policy across most occupations after the end of the Second World War did signal a shift towards greater acceptance of women's employment, it did not undermine the widespread belief that once a couple had children fathers should take responsibility for breadwinning while mothers' primary role would be childcare.

The subsequent move away from breadwinning and towards nurturing is a key component of late modern fatherhood. Men's role within the family has been characterised as moving from outside to inside the home. A trajectory sees fathers move from contributing to family life through their engagement in pursuits that take place outside the home (in particular paid work) to a situation where men fulfil their fathering duties primarily within the household, in terms of caring activities and father-child interaction. La Rossa suggests that in the US the Depression period marked a significant point for the development of 'new fatherhood', when it became possible to 'valorize identities that give less weight to financial responsibility' (1997: 13). Griswold (1993) too suggests that the origins of a new fatherhood that paid attention to involvement rather than authority can be traced to the 1920s and 1930s. However, the major period of transformation in ideas of fathering and practices of fatherhood, if not their inception, is often located from the 1970s onwards. This shift is explained by a combination of the effects of post-industrial economy, a change in gender relations and cultural processes that emphasise individual reflexivity over authority. Historical research does problematise the idea of a neat transition to a fundamentally different basis for good fatherhood; as La Rossa (1997) is keen to emphasise, the rise of new forms do not mean the complete disappearance of older ones. However, the move from provider to nurturer as the primary basis for fathering identity and the end of fathers as sole providers has been widely proclaimed: 'the position of the father as the sole provider of his family is being challenged in most cultures' (Knijn 1995: 11).

Despite this shift, a number of contemporary studies have reasserted the male breadwinner as a continuing force. This is not necessarily in a prescriptive sense as advocated by those who see disruptions to the gender divisions of the family as destructive to the moral fabric and organisation of society; those who write from this position have tended to be explicit about their preferences and rationale (e.g. Blankenhorn 1995; Popenoe 1996). Instead, drawing on empirical qualitative and quantitative evidence, it has been suggested that the breadwinner figure never really disappeared: 'Fathers' identity and role in family life is still very much tied up with a status as breadwinner' (Lewis 2000). Some have concluded that breadwinning is still an important component of men's fathering identity and even their main form of commitment to family life. Warin *et al.*, in their study of 42 men in Northern England with secondary school age children, concluded that 'Most men continue to devote themselves to "fathering" by earning money outside the house' (1999: 7, see also Hatten *et al.* 2002). In turn, this has led others to decry the sidelining of the provider role in recent accounts of fatherhood:

> providing as a form of paternal involvement in families is not adequately explored or acknowledged in contemporary fatherhood literature.
> (Christiansen and Palkovitz 2001: 102)

> many researchers have restricted their focus [to issues of interaction, accessibility and making arrangements for children] and have not considered other important aspects of fatherhood, like breadwinning.
> (Lewis and Lamb 2006: 2)

If monetary care remains the key element to good fatherhood then it must undermine the argument of a transformed fatherhood that is based on something new, such as nurturing involvement.

The meanings of breadwinning

Exploring fathers' role as breadwinners requires some reflection on the meaning of the term 'breadwinner'. Jane Hood's (1986) summary of the way in which the provider role has been measured draws attention to the need to include measures of who *should* provide income alongside who *does* provide income. Tracey Warren (2007) has recently appealed for the complexity of breadwinning to be recognised and has attempted to decipher systematically the various ways in which it is conceptualised and operationalised in sociological research. She defines two aspects that are descriptive – the extent to which men are the main financial providers and the main labour market participants – and two that relate to more cultural dimensions – the degree to which male breadwinning exists as an ideology and policy prescription and the prevalence of male breadwinning as an aspect of masculine identity. As such, breadwinning can refer to objective measurable dimensions as well as more subjective assessments of identity; it is the more subjective dimensions, Warren argues, that are usually given less attention.

If breadwinning is still the appropriate terminology to apply to modern fathering, the ideology should permeate individuals' attitudes and bear some resemblance to lived experience and measurable behaviours. Descriptions of who does provide for the household include calculations of who earns what and the amount of time that is committed to labour market participation. One way of gaining a sense of opinions about who *should* do what is through social attitude surveys, which provide evidence on fathering and mothering roles, such as when mothers should work, levels of agreement with statements like 'it is better for a man to go out to work and a woman to look after the family', the relative importance of mothers' jobs and fathers' jobs, and the ranking of the importance of financial contributions compared to men's other familial roles. This is supported by qualitative material which looks in greater depth at the significance of provisioning for fathering. Importantly, the growth of research conducted *with* fathers has meant that men's expressions of their own orientations towards fatherhood are now included within data on breadwinning. Finally, evaluating the present salience of breadwinning also requires thinking about wider political initiatives and cultural themes that might suggest the dominance of financial provisioning for achieving 'good fatherhood'.

Fathers' employment

In British two parent households men continue to contribute a larger proportion of the family income than do women: in 2003/4, 67 per cent of the total family income of couples came from the individual income of men (Department of Work and Pensions 2005). Even among dual earner couples, in only about a quarter of cases does the woman earn over 45 per cent of the couple total (Warren 2007). After couples have children, inequality in their incomes becomes more pronounced. The weekly median individual income for women relative to men is 39 per cent for couples with children, compared to 56 per cent for couples without children (Department of Work and Pensions 2005). The implication is that many women are, to a large extent, reliant on their partners' financial contributions and that this dependency is greater between mothers and fathers than between women and men in childless couples. However, given women's higher levels of participation in the labour market throughout the life course and the rise of dual income households, providing money to support family life can no longer be described as the preserve of the male parent. Female contributions to the family budget continue to increase, while those of the average male fall (Harkness *et al.* 2004). While women's economic contributions may not equal men's, they are a significant component of household income, hence the description of the one and a half breadwinner household (Lewis 2007) and women's role as at least 'component wage' earners (Siltanen 1994). So while it is true that women may often require the contribution of a male partner, it is increasingly not the case that his earnings alone can maintain a family. Therefore, contrary to the initial impression given by statistics on income, if breadwinning is interpreted as being the sole financial provider it no longer represents social reality.

Women's lower levels of pay compared to men's are a consequence both of women's shorter working hours and lower levels of hourly pay. Women's hourly pay rates are lower than men's because the types of occupations in which women tend to work are less well remunerated. Meanwhile there are high levels of part-time working among women in the UK (especially pronounced among mothers) and shorter full-time hours among women compared to men. This pattern ensures that even women who have equivalent hourly rates to men are likely to earn less in total. Among full-time employees in Britain, men average 44.9 hours per week and women 40.6 (both of which are the longest in Europe) (Crompton 2006). In households with children, the most frequent combination in Britain (40 per cent) is for couples to adopt the model of male full-time work and female part-time work, while 28.6 per cent of households have two full-time earners (Crompton 2006).[1] Using hours of paid work as a measurement of breadwinning, it appears that a pattern of male breadwinning is prominent. Despite the caveats, the disparity between men and women's working patterns suggests that men are engaged to a greater extent than women in the labour market, and therefore while men are not the sole earners, a modified breadwinner model does seem applicable to the UK. Yet it is important to be aware of what comparison is being made here. When comparing fathers and mothers it seems that breadwinning, in terms of both income generated and time spent in the labour market, is more a feature of the former than the latter – but is this really about fatherhood? If we are interested in breadwinning as a facet of *fatherhood* then a comparison needs to be made between fathers and non-fathers instead of looking only at men and women.

There is general agreement in the literature that fathers in the UK are more likely to be economically active and have higher employment rates than non-fathers as is illustrated by O'Brien and Schemilt's (2003) recent wide-ranging review of data on fathers in Britain. They found that only 8 per cent of fathers were economically inactive compared to 20 per cent of non-fathers, with a similar degree of difference in men's employment rates; fathers having an employment rate of 89 per cent, 13 per cent higher than other men: Walling (2004) reports a similar employment figure of 90 per cent for fathers with dependent children. Employed fathers also work longer hours than non-fathers. Using the British Household Panel Survey (BHPS), average weekly working hours come out at 43 for fathers and an hour and half less for non-fathers (Dermott 2006a). This is partly because fathers' employment is predominantly full-time; O'Brien and Schemilt (2003) give figures of 84 per cent and 2 per cent respectively for fathers working on full- and part-time bases (using 1995 figures). However, even within the full-time category, fathers have been shown to work longer hours than do non-fathers. La Valle *et al.* (2002) found that 30 per cent of fathers worked more than 48 hours per week and, similarly, Matheson and Summerfield (2001) reported that while a third of men with dependent children usually worked 50 or more hours per week, under a quarter of men without dependents worked these long hours. Turning again to the BHPS, 20 per cent of fathers were found to work over the 48 hours per week that are the maximum under the EU Working Hours Directive, compared to 17 per cent of non-fathers (Dermott 2006a). It is frequently noted that fathers in the UK work the longest hours in Europe (Deven *et al.* 1998). Although less well documented, there is also some evidence of a 'wage premium' that accrues to fathers (Lundberg and Rose 2000).

Fathers' employment or men's employment?

There is, though, a further consideration; comparing fathers and non-fathers makes the implicit assumption that these two groups are similar except in respect of their parental status. Yet this should not be taken for granted. One obvious variation is by age: the transition to parenthood for men is most common between the ages of 25 and 45; only 10 per cent of men under the age of 25 have become fathers but by 45 this figure has reached over 80 per cent (Burghes *et al.* 1997), with the mean age of fathers at first birth around 30 (Matheson and Summerfield 2001). Men tend to have dependent children through their 30s and 40s, a period that is also key for career progression and stabilisation. It could be that it is a focus on career development which is causing an increased level of job commitment and concomitant increased hours of employment, rather than the transition to parenthood. My analysis of the British Household Panel Study (BHPS) and the National Child Development Survey (NCDS) suggests there is some validity in this idea. The BHPS is a panel study that includes respondents across the whole age range of the adult population, while the NCDS is a cohort study, which has respondents who are all the same age.[2] Comparing the average workhours of fathers and non-fathers in both datasets resulted in a smaller difference between the two in the NCDS where age was, in effect, held constant.

In order to try and determine the particular influence that parenthood has on men's hours of work, analysis needs to take into account a range of other variables that may be confusing the results. My further analysis of the BHPS specifically allowed for this by including a range of variables that were thought to be influential such as age, occupation, educational qualifications, earnings and partner's employment status. When a multiple regression was carried out on men's hours of work, parental status was not significant.[3] In other words, fatherhood status is not a good predictor of the number of hours that a man works, once other relevant factors are taken into account. When average hours of employment for fathers and non-fathers are compared, fathers emerge as working longer, but this ignores the fact that fathers and non-fathers differ in other respects as well as their parental status. The relationship between fatherhood and longer working hours therefore seems to be somewhat spurious. Interestingly, the same analysis found that men's hours of work and their partner's working time were positively related. Men working longer hours are more likely to have partners who are working full-time than part-time or not at all. This suggests that even when men work longer hours it is not necessarily as compensation for the non-working or short working hours of their partner. Instead, the men with longer hours are likely to be part of dual breadwinning households.

More refined analysis is required in order to assess the effect of a change in parental status on men's employment. The limitation of examining cross sectional data, which is only collected at one point in time, is that it is difficult to determine cause and effect. Disentangling the order in which events happen is necessary to explain the social processes at work and there is now increasing awareness of the necessity of longitudinal data in order to examine social change (Ruspini 2000). Event history analysis is a longitudinal record of when particular events have occurred for a sample of individuals and allows the possibility of evaluating the relative importance of a number of different explanatory variables for predicting the chance of an event occurring. Using event history analysis allowed me to examine if there is any accommodation in hours of employment when men become parents. Labelling a significant alteration in work hours (5 hours) as the 'event' recognises that those who continue to be employed on a full-time basis may still have altered their working time. Modelling a downward and an upward shift in work hours, the occurrence of a new birth had a significant relationship with a decrease in working hours, and a negative, although not quite significant, relationship with an increase in work hours: fathers do make an adjustment, *downwards*, to their working time when a new child arrives. The decrease in hours that is notable here may be the result of informal reductions in working time, indicating perhaps decisions to avoid working at home in the evenings, minimising trips away, refusing additional work or being careful about keeping to contracted hours. Putting together this result with the previous analysis suggests that this alteration is not maintained throughout the child's years of dependency, as fathers and non-fathers do not differ significantly in terms of hours spent at work, taking other factors into account. As there is no reverse process, such as a dramatic increase in work hours when children are of a particular age (for example when the youngest child has reached five, school age), it is likely that men may return to their 'normal' working practices gradually over time.

If the expectation is that men should increase their hours of work as a measure of work commitment when they become fathers, in order to provide financially for their partner and children, then this empirical evidence challenges the orthodoxy of fatherhood as breadwinning. Having dependent children is not associated with working significantly longer hours, once other variables have been taken into account. Fathers do maintain full-time, and in some cases long full-time, working hours after they become parents, but this is not attributable to men's familial responsibilities. As the 'male model of employment' is already complementary to a financially responsible role, a specific 'father model of employment' is not required. Using hours of paid work as an indicator, fatherhood does not lead to a major shift in men's behaviour in paid work. Men are committed to the labour market but fatherhood is not associated with a measurable increase in this commitment; rather, men's engagement with the labour market exists irrespective of their parental status. There are exceptions, as some of the quotations in the following section indicate, but this is the general pattern. The event history analysis provides an insight into a more complex story: fathers do make some accommodation in their working time. The period around the first year after a birth is associated with some short-term decrease in working hours. This may be in line with an ideal of good fatherhood which promotes men's presence at the birth of a child and a general sense of 'being there' (see Chapter 3) but which does not undermine a strong attachment to the labour market.

Attitudes to breadwinning

An argument for intimate fatherhood needs to consider both the realm of cultural expectation and measurable behaviour. In terms of breadwinning, this translates into an examination of fathers' engagement with the labour market and attitudes towards the importance of financial provisioning: 'enactment' of the provider role means bringing income into the household but 'responsibility for the enactment' has also been noted (Hood 1986). There may be situations where the person contributing most or even all of the household income is not viewed as being the provider, despite financial reality. For example, unemployed men in a household where their female partner is employed may continue to identify with the breadwinner role (Willott and Griffin 1997). The previous section examined one measure of fathers' employment practice, namely, the time they spend in paid work. This section considers breadwinning as part of the ideology of good fatherhood through examining men's own views about their orientation to work and family.

The wider literature on the subject of financial providing presents a less than conclusive picture as there seems to be substantial evidence on which to base both an argument for the continuing importance of an ideology of breadwinning for fathering and an argument for its demise. Townsend (2002), using an ethnographic study of a community in the US, argues that while financial provisioning is only one of four 'facets of fatherhood,' it is the most important for the men to whom he spoke. Ranson (2001) found that among her sample of middle-class professional men in Canada, while there was substantial involvement in family life this was structured around paid work, leading her to reject the idea that the breadwinner model had disappeared. Studies in the UK have also argued that providing money to support children remains central to men's expectations of fatherhood. Hatten *et al.*'s report for the Equal Opportunities Commission, based on interviews with 41 fathers and three focus groups in various parts of Britain, concluded that, 'the breadwinner role still defines the way in which many men think about fatherhood' and 'the breadwinner role remains firmly etched in the minds of many fathers' (2002: 7). For the majority of fathers whom they categorise as either 'enforcer dad' or 'entertainer dad', breadwinning remained the key role.

Yet other research is either more equivocal in its findings or argues strongly against the idea that breadwinning continues to be the primary familial role for men. Thompson *et al.*'s (2005) study, a large-scale survey complemented by qualitative interviews, found that only a minority of fathers claimed being the breadwinner was the most important aspect of being a father (and Yaxley *et al.*'s (2005) complementary study of mothers found an even smaller percentage of mothers agreeing with this statement). In a study of first-time fathers in Norwich, England, 'none of the interviewees identified breadwinning as their primary role' (Henwood and Procter 2003: 345) and instead these men embraced ideas associated with 'new' fatherhood. Looking beyond research conducted in the UK, it is possible to find further support for this position. In a study of Norwegian fathers, Brandth and Kvande found that the role of provider was not emphasised and concluded:

> they [fathers] do not define a good father as a good breadwinner. This suggests that the role of provider has become secondary as an identity basis for these fathers.
>
> (1998: 299)

Cohen, whose research was based in the US in Boston, argued that although economic responsibilities did exist as one dimension of family life, less than a third of his respondents included 'providing' among a father's main responsibilities towards his children. This led him to comment that 'traditional work-centred definitions of "fathering" are inadequate for characterizing ... informants' beliefs about fathering' (1993: 19). Taken together, these findings present something of a conundrum; no sooner does one study assert the demise of the breadwinner father than another emerges to claim that its death has been much exaggerated.

The research on attitudes discussed so far is mainly based on small scale surveys or qualitative interviews, with fathers who tend to be reflecting on their own experiences and commenting on their own particular situation. Larger scale attitude surveys tend to include more abstract questions, for example, respondents may be asked to comment on their level of agreement with broad statements, such as 'a man's job is to earn money, a woman's is to look after the home and family'. These surveys reveal attitudes in the general population among people who are not necessarily parents themselves. The British Social Attitudes Survey is one example of a long running nationally representative study (it is also part of the International Social Survey Programme which asks the same questions in a number of developed countries and so allows for cross-national comparisons). Rosemary Crompton has recently reported findings from the most recent waves of BSA data. In 2002, only 20 per cent of men agreed that it is 'a man's job to earn money, a woman's is to look after the home and family', and even fewer women (15 per cent) concurred (2006: 43). This is really a measure of the conventional division of labour based on a male breadwinner, and the results suggest that while a substantial minority continue to support gender segregated roles it is precisely that – a minority viewpoint. In addition, looking at these surveys over a number of years, the trend is for more 'traditional' gender roles to have become less acceptable over time.

However, the situation is ambiguous as other responses appear to lend rather more support, at least implicitly, for the continuation of the male provider role with over half of men agreeing that 'women should stay at home when children are under school age'. Of course care needs to be taken in interpreting these findings; since this question is concerned with the actions of mothers the role of fathers is only implied. Yet, the fact that the first question (man's job/woman's job) is less clearly about the division of labour between parents than the second question (children under five) may suggest that gender segregated roles continue to be more acceptable among parents than women and men in general. The possibility of non-correspondence does need to be acknowledged: attitudes do not necessarily tally with behaviour (e.g. a female respondent may agree with the statement that women should stay at home when children are under five but actually return to work herself). Again, there may be a disjuncture between general attitudes and specific attitudes that apply to the individual (e.g. men in general should do an equal amount of housework to women, but my partner need not do the same quantity as I do). Overall, with respect to the issue of breadwinning, the results seem as inconclusive as in the previously cited literature based on qualitative research, though they suggest more of a mixed message about the role of mothers than fathers. This issue of the relationship between the roles of fathers and mothers will be returned to later on in this chapter and, in more detail, in Chapter 5.

Flintstone fathers?

The qualitative research project *Men, Work and Family Life*, which was discussed in the Introduction (see also Appendix), provides further insights into how fathers orient themselves to their employment. The study allowed men to talk about aspects of both their family and their paid work, revealing a picture which is more complex than a simple classification into either 'breadwinner' or 'involved father'.

In asking the interviewees about fatherhood, an initial question was what kind of father they wanted to be. Often the initial response was simply 'a good one', but among the comments that were forthcoming when the meaning of the term 'good' was probed, it was striking that references to earning money as an aspect of fathering were conspicuous by their absence; only two of the men spoke about breadwinning. Hugh was one of these unusual cases. When asked about how he saw himself as a father he explained how he sees his identity as located in the world of paid employment:

> I had always seen myself as a Flintstone type father, you know, out to work, out to the office, while mother stays at home and looks after the children.

His primary focus is centred on the workplace and he highlights this through referencing a cartoon based around the 'modern Stone Age family'. Perhaps in comparing his familial identity to characters in 'The Flintstones' he is also acknowledging that his viewpoint, if not quite belonging to a bygone age, is now relatively unusual. Another interviewee, Bill, also responded by characterising his role in 'traditional' terms, 'He [the father] is the provider, he is the breadwinner'. Yet while breadwinning did exist as one expression of fathering commitment on which men could draw, it commanded a very minority position among this group of fathers.

Men's comments on paid work reveal the complexity of our relationship to employment. Despite the longstanding recognition that the rewards of employment extend beyond the material – in Terkel's elegant phrase, work is a search 'for daily meaning as well as daily bread, for recognition as well as cash' (1974: 1) – writing that focuses on fatherhood tends to categorise men as instrumental workers for whom employment is simply a means to an economic end. In contrast, most of the fathers who were interviewed, when asked what was important to them about their work, emphasised the nature of the job itself and talked about their employment as interesting, or classified it as worthwhile:

> I can learn something new everyday, it is a very interesting job.
>
> (William, lawyer)

Personally it is intellectually fantastically nourishing, I have never stopped learning and it is an incredible privilege and totally absorbing.

(Greg, television producer)

It is intellectually quite stimulating, certainly gives me something to think about.

(Raj, editor)

It is teaching me new skills ... actually making a difference.

(Simon, behavioural support officer)

It's important for me to feel I am doing something like activism or supporting a cause. And technically it is really interesting.

(Gareth, IT manager for a charity)

'People's reasons for working are much more complex than would be suggested by the myth of the economic worker' (Bradley *et al.* 2000: 181), and these men did not come across as instrumental in their labour market engagement. That did not mean that economic concerns were completely irrelevant: 'work is still the most significant determinant of the material well-being of the majority of the population' (Crompton 1993: 18) as only the very few who are independently wealthy do not have to rely on paid employment to survive. A number of these fathers did make some reference to the fact that their employment supported their family as well as providing them with other intrinsic benefits. For example, William, as an adjunct to his description of why work was important to him, said 'and, you know, it does involve money'. Greg, also quoted above commenting on the satisfaction he derives from his job, similarly noted that he is in a well paid profession,

I'm just very lucky to have found something which pays well enough for us to live in comfort.

Perhaps Derek's response is the best example of how financial considerations are bundled together with other elements,

It [work] is important to me because I think it is my vocation ... It is important because it provides financially for our family to live. It is important because it is a channel for me to express my gifts and experience, my expertise. It is important because I find it rewarding. It is important because it is who I am and what I am really.

The accounts indicate how the importance of earning money is the taken for granted necessity that operates as a backdrop to working life. It appears as the reason for paid work when other, more valued, aspects have disappeared. Almost all of those who did refer to money as being the central motivation at the present time still held onto an ideal that encapsulated much more. Michael was recently made redundant and has taken another job which he enjoys much less than his previous employment. He is grateful at having been able quite quickly to secure alternative work that is satisfactory, in terms of money, hours of work and location, and therefore the job's function of paying for living costs has taken priority:

> I am very much aware that it is the finance that drives me every morning.

Similarly Duncan, who is very disillusioned with his current position, emphasises the monetary dimension as the only positive:

> [I've] got kids and family and mortgage and all the rest of it, so obviously that [money] aspect of it is quite important. I don't think that the job is brilliant, we can't deliver the service anymore, so that aspect is quite frustrating.

For these fathers, finance tended to be the lowest common denominator that was summoned as a rationale for working when everything else was absent (for a more extensive discussion of work orientations see Dermott 2002). This orientation to employment is important to bear in mind when considering when and how money was invoked as a component of good fatherhood. These were men who were earning decent salaries, just over half of whom were in the highest tax bracket, and therefore finances were one clear way in which they contributed to their families: provisioning was available as a potential discourse for them to draw on.

Even when men do have an instrumental orientation towards paid work this should not necessarily be read as a statement of breadwinning. Jim claimed that the only way in which his job is important for him is with regard to the financial compensation for his time and effort, and his only ambition regarding his work was an increase in pay,

> In the simplest way that it's important to have a job, to get money … The only thing I would like to achieve job wise is, and this sounds very materialistic, is to have a little more money, that's all really.

When asked about fatherhood, he prioritised his relationship with his son in rather different terms; 'I would want to spend time … I wanted to be around … and to take part'. There is a similar instance in the work of Vincent and Ball who quote one respondent as saying that 'Work is purely a mechanism for paying the bills' (2006: 160) and that because his income has dropped he is 'falling down' somewhat in this respect. Yet the same man also says he is 'more interested and motivated by my children than I am by my job' (2006: 160). For these two men, commitment to employment may be instrumental, but this does not equate to adopting a provider role with respect to their fathering identity.

Conclusion: earning not breadwinning

Two problems seem to confuse analysis of breadwinning; the first is the conflation of fatherhood with masculinity and the second is dealing with diversity among fathers. The task of researchers is to avoid the temptation to fall back on easy categorisations and look for more subtle arguments that can better explain everyday reality.

First, being a father can be thought of as one aspect of adult hegemonic masculinity, but the various characteristics that make up this 'package deal' (in Townsend's (2002) phrase) are not always disaggregated. Therefore aspects of successful masculinity, such as being engaged in employment (Morgan 1992) can be, unthinkingly, imposed on fathering. For an individual, masculine and fathering identities will be interwoven. Brannen and Nielsen's categorisation of the 31 fathers they interviewed as being either 'work-focused', 'family men' or 'hands-on' fathers, are groupings 'which reflect not only their identities as fathers but also their masculinities' (2006: 340). Brannen and Nilsen do also acknowledge in a footnote some element of separation between masculinity and fatherhood identities (2006: 350), however, there is the potential in less nuanced analysis to conflate fatherhood and paid work and use commitment to employment as a marker of both simultaneously. Consequently, a particular form of identification with employment can erroneously be read as a marker of breadwinning identity. When studying fatherhood it is relatively easy to avoid disentangling associations between masculinity and fatherhood. If paid working is a central component of adult male identity, it is not difficult to conclude that paid working is central to fatherhood. Fathers tend to work full-time, often long hours and view employment as important to them. Notwithstanding suggestions in the liberal press, fathers do not tend to choose to reduce the amount of time spent in work when they have children after the initial period surrounding the child's arrival. Fathers might then be labelled primarily 'committed wage slaves' with a tiny minority (statistically hard to find but with a strong public voice) of 'satisfied homedads'.[4] This simplistic conclusion is even more understandable since this was both the cultural ideal and lived reality for a significant period in recent history. For Riley the lack of a 'legitimate successor to the provider role' can be explained by a system within which 'men are left with a dichotomised subjectivity of male-breadwinner or ungendered-egalitarian' (2003: 111). As the latter is difficult to encapsulate in common-sense language that is not extremely vague, e.g. 'being involved' (which, can in turn, be adapted to include a financial provisioning role which it was supposed to supplant), the male-breadwinner image remains as a default because engagement with the labour market remains a significant part of most men's lives; it is a well-rehearsed narrative on which it is easy to fall back. Therefore when researchers do not attempt to reconcile apparent contradictions within the accounts they produce, it is likely to be the story of the provider which comes to the fore. On closer reading of Hatten *et al.*'s (2002) report, which foregrounds the continuing significance of the breadwinning role, it is clear that for many fathers breadwinning is not key. Yet the headline grabbing finding on breadwinning is more straightforward, both as a way for men to verbalise a dimension of involvement and for commentators to present an uncomplicated analysis. If men's familial role meshes with that of adult citizen, men's public and private roles are complementary – fulfilled through the same activity. While those excluded from employment face difficulties, most fathers can achieve in both realms through being a paid worker. Conversely, a retreat of breadwinning means that greater numbers of fathers must negotiate their role as fathers anew. For the majority, it is simpler to realize a good fatherhood that has breadwinning at its heart, since it remains an important aspect of masculinity. As examples from the interviews with middle-class fathers indicate, this means that the full-time employment situation for most fathers operates as a backdrop to their parenting. Therefore, fulfilling the provider role can be used as a justification for otherwise unsatisfying employment, even when other ideas of fatherhood are paramount, and the provider role may be an involvement safety net when other valued aspects of fatherhood are absent.

Second, confusion over breadwinning exists because its relevance to the idea of good fatherhood differs *between* fathers depending on their social situation. In particular, it may be that class makes a difference in this respect. This possibility is worth contemplating for two reasons; because there do appear to be class or occupational variations in the ways in which women combine employment and family life (Crompton 2006), and because some qualitative studies and some theoretical accounts of fatherhood note variations along class lines. For example, although Duncan *et al.* (2003) are eager to emphasise that their three categories of mother ('primarily workers', 'primarily mothers' and 'mother/worker integral') are not exclusive to any one class grouping, their empirical research does indicate clustering based on class (as well as ethnicity and location) in how mothers combine employment and childcare (Duncan 2005). There has been a suggestion that the ideology of 'new' fatherhood has been particularly associated with the middle-class (La Rossa 1988). The study by Warin *et al.* (1999), which found that fathers emphasised their breadwinning role, had high numbers of unemployed and low-income fathers while the research by Brandth and Kvande (in Norway), which found that fathers did not emphasise breadwinning, focused on men in professional and managerial occupations. My study, which provided the earlier quotations in this chapter, was also based on a group who are relatively financially advantaged and this is likely to have had an impact on their responses. However, the available evidence is insufficiently convincing to justify a distinction simply based on class lines with working class fathers identifying as breadwinners while middle class fathers do not. If this division was pursued, the question should be why it exists. Put simply, when money is scarce it is likely to get greater attention. For those on low-incomes an awareness of the critical importance of finances takes place on a daily basis, whereas those for whom monetary security has never been in doubt are less likely to bring it to mind in the same way. Similarly, Hatten *et al.*'s comment that 'the breadwinner role still defines the way in which many men think about fatherhood, particularly those whose partners have stopped working (or never worked)' (2002: 7) conveys an important truth; that the construction of the fathering role is intrinsically linked to that of mothering and that the absence of someone else earning money leaves the provider role available and necessary. However, as we have seen above, even doing the financial part of caring does not mean that it is seen as a requisite for good fatherhood; 'The current model of the "good father" means that earning is not automatically construed as caring' (O'Brien 2005: 25). The association between fathers and their 'traditional' role of breadwinning is actually less pronounced than the ongoing association between mothers and childcare in the home. Women's involvement in the labour market after marriage and parenthood, and especially when children are young, alongside relatively high rates of marital dissolution and repartnership, has challenged not just the empirical reality of the male breadwinner but also the cultural legitimacy of the role. Yet a belief in mothers' appropriateness for the role of carer, grounded in a legitimation provided by an emphasis on the importance of biology, maintains a widespread presence even among individuals who advocate men's greater involvement in parenting (see Chapter 5).

Accounts of fatherhood have tried to establish whether the breadwinner role is or is not still important, with a mass of sometimes contradictory evidence presented, in order either to or affirm or critique the concept of 'new fatherhood'. While breadwinning is no longer the major function of fathers, it is still present in men's discussions of their role. In an attempt to recognise providing as a valuable aspect of involvement, some authors have suggested that it should be added to the ways in which men 'do' fatherhood. This suggestion recognises the problem of some descriptions of fatherhood as stuck in repetitions of debates over which side of the traditional/new dichotomy contemporary fathers really belong. In a similar vein, this chapter has argued that one aspect of 'doing' close associations with another person may involve taking financial care of them. However, the main point is that financial provision is a component, like other forms of care, which emerges from the particular characterisation of fatherhood. Earning money, in relation to men's familial role, is primarily about being able to give children opportunities.

An awareness of the breadwinning role complicates our understanding of intimacy because it forces us to address the issue of how money is dealt with within an emotional, socially important interpersonal relationship. Breadwinning becomes pulled into current discourse on fatherhood because it has a strong currency in terms of its relevance to male adult status and appropriate citizenship in contemporary society (see Levitas 1998), as involvement with paid work remains the fundamental way in which men are viewed as being properly engaged in society (although a move towards an adult worker model means that, increasingly, this also extends to women). The association of fatherhood with breadwinning is, in actuality, not so strong. It retains a salience which fathers can draw on, because the importance of employment in displaying socially appropriate masculinity is unquestioned. These findings do not undermine the continued importance of exploring financial provisioning or the potential significance of employment for personal identity, but they do suggest that tying men's orientation to work specifically with parenthood puts the emphasis in the wrong place.

Earning money is important for individuals in order to maintain themselves and has even greater importance when dependants exist. It cannot be denied, especially in a modern consumer driven society, that the ability to participate requires financial resources and, as children are limited in their ability to provision for themselves, the legal and moral responsibility to do so lies with their parents. Increasing levels of female employment throughout the life course have challenged the idea of husbands having financial responsibility for their wives, but both fathers and mothers remain responsible for the welfare of their children. In comparing men's and women's (and especially fathers' and mothers') employment and income it is men who do more but it would be incorrect to reduce fatherhood simply to this role. The recognition of money as a resource which fathers often supply should not just be added to a list of attributes; rather the meaning of providing financially for children needs to be understood.

This chapter has evaluated the breadwinning thesis by paying attention to time spent in the labour market and the level of financial benefit, as well as subjective accounts of familial roles, examined through individuals' responses to survey or more in-depth interview data. The ideology of breadwinning can also be appraised through a consideration of more formal channels, such as governmental policy. This is an important omission in this chapter since it has been argued that 'recent laws in Britain and America have served to confirm the social construction of fathers as economic providers before all else' (Gattrell 2005: 72). Chapter 6, which examines policy and law relevant to fathers, will address this issue and challenge the argument that policymakers continue to view fathers primarily as breadwinners.

3   Fathering activities and the meaning of time

This chapter addresses the question of men's contribution to childcare, in terms of time commitment and types of involvement. Assessing the time fathers spend with their children has involved a focus on absolute measures – how many hours and minutes do men commit to children? – and relative contributions – how much time do fathers spend with their children compared with mothers and others? The chapter begins by summarising existing evidence about the amount of time men spend with their children, drawing attention to some of the methodological difficulties and substantive limitations to this approach. The second section of the chapter, drawing on qualitative interviews from the *Men, Work and Family* study, develops a typology of fathering activities in order to map fathers' childcare activities and, importantly, to highlight the different *meanings* they have for fathers. In conclusion, it is argued that while time is valued as a good in itself, the way in which times are evaluated and assigned importance is more complicated than a simple equation of 'more minutes equals better fathering'.

Fathers' time with children

Research on parents' time use has been particularly extensive in the USA but has also been conducted in the UK and other 'Western' countries (some recent reports on time use include Craig 2006a (Australia), Gauthier *et al.* (2004) (cross-national), Hook (2006) (cross-national), Larder *et al.* 2006 (UK), O'Brien (2005) (UK), Pleck and Masciadrelli 2004 (cross-national), Sandberg and Hofferth 2001 (US), Sayer *et al.* 2004 (US) and Smith 2007 (Europe)). Cross national comparisons indicate differences which are at least partially attributable to variations in state policies towards families. (Discussion of UK policy is the subject of Chapter 6.) Yet two facts emerge strongly from data across a number of countries; namely that there has been a trend for increasing amounts of paternal-child time over recent decades (in absolute terms and relative to mothers), and that fathers spend less time with their children than do mothers. 'New fatherhood' does seem to involve spending relatively more time in childcare (Yeung *et al.* 2001) but, as Smith (2004) concludes using data from 14 European states, fathers, at most, perform around 30 per cent of substantial childcare:

> Time use studies consistently show that fathers, both resident and non-resident, are spending more time with their children, albeit still at a lower level than mothers.
>
> (O'Brien 2005: iii)

> Mothers contribute disproportionately to the engaged time spent with children, although there has been some redistribution to fathers ... the average time a father spends in activities with preschoolers has doubled since 1974.
>
> (Bittman 2004: 160)

Some other tendencies are also well supported by empirical evidence: fathers undertake different kinds of childcare activities from mothers, and various socio-economic characteristics, along with the age of children, influence the quantity of paternal time and the way in which it is used. Mothers take on more primary care than do fathers and a larger proportion of fathers' childcare is secondary activity (Larder *et al.* 2006). Mothers spend more time and a greater proportion of their time in physical care; fathers spend more of their time playing with and talking to children (Craig 2006a; Lewis 2000). Although an increase in routine childcare by fathers has been noted,

> fathers selectively invest their time in the more rewarding and enjoyable child care activities while mothers tend to perform the day-to-day childrearing.
>
> (Sayer *et al.* 2004: 12)

It seems that increased childcare time among fathers is most pronounced with younger, preschool children (e.g. Fisher *et al.* 1999) and this may be responsible for an increase in fathers' involvement in daily care.

Most research suggests that class position has some impact on fathers' contribution to childcare, though what this effect is, is debated. Evidence from the US and Australia suggests that higher educated and more financially advantaged fathers are more involved with children (Craig 2006b; Sayer *et al.* 2004; Zick *et al.* 1996). Meanwhile in the UK contradictory findings have emerged. Some research has found that fathers working in professional occupations do the least childcare and manual workers the most (Fisher *et al.* 1999; Warren 2003): it has been suggested that this may be a consequence of the way in which working-class families have less synchronised time together because of the nature of employment (Warren 2003). However, analysis of the UK Time Use Survey found a different pattern, with fathers working in manual and routine occupations spending significantly less time in childcare than those in white-collar jobs (Gray 2006). Recent findings from the Equal Opportunities Commission pointed to the impact of mothers' income/class position on fathers' childcare, concluding that 'fathers are more involved in childcare when their partner has a relatively high income and is working full-time' (EOC 2003). Thus indicating the complex way in which men's own time availability combines with other structural factors, in particular their partner's employment status (see also, for Japan, Ishii-Kuntz *et al.* 2004).

Methods and meanings

Exploring how fathers spend time with their children leads us into the murky waters of methodological debate. How best to capture information about the way in which individuals spend their time has thrown up a number of issues. First, there are general methodological questions about how people remember what they have been doing and the activities they recount to researchers and, second, a more particular difficulty in assessing what counts as time with children. There are issues of categorisation: in separating out childcare from other activities such as domestic chores; in defining boundaries between work and leisure; and in making judgements about whether time alone with children should be categorised in the same way as more inclusive 'family time'. Of course, these debates can provide a useful service in calling into question the categories with which we normally operate, but they have to be resolved in some way if measurements are to happen. These pigeon holing decisions in research design, analysis and writing can also make comparisons difficult since researchers tend to settle on different options.

One solution has been the development of time-use surveys, which have become a popular and fashionable research tool. Detailed time diaries such as the UK 2000 Time Use Survey and its international counterparts have provided more exact pictures of how people spend their time. Such surveys typically ask individuals to detail every task that they do during a weekday and one day over the weekend in short blocks of time, such as 15 minute intervals. This allows researchers to find out how much time is allocated to activities, how often they occur and when during a 24 hour cycle they take place. An additional benefit, although also a complicating factor for analysis, is that respondents can mention tasks that are undertaken simultaneously – eating dinner and watching TV for example – giving researchers the opportunity to look at how activities are complementary and to explore, in more sociologically interesting ways, the social context in which activities take place, such as levels of interdependence and density of activities (Gershuny and Sullivan 1998). As a more thorough research method than those previously available for quantifying how lives are lived, they can provide insight into the amount of time fathers spend with their children and the way in which time is spent. They have contributed to attempts at deciphering how tasks are divided up within households and the multiplicities of work that may be taking place at any one point in time. In particular, time-use data has raised awareness of unpaid activities and presented a way of thinking about the totality of labour. Statements such as 'men's leisure time is longer than women's' or 'women working part-time in employment do less total work than women working full-time in employment' have been made possible by calculating 'paid work + housework + childcare'. However, by reducing activities to a calculation of hours and minutes, additive models necessarily imply that all time is equal, and so an important aspect of how we think about time – the meaning which is attributed to it – is lost.

In combination with measurements of how time is spent, surveys often ask about time preferences, which allow some insight into what is desired in terms of time use. In relation to fatherhood, results overwhelmingly indicate that fathers would like more time with children (e.g. Dex and Ward 2007) and children would like more time with their father – '90 per cent of children want to spend more time with their dad' (Fathers Direct 2001).[1] Caution though is needed in interpreting these expressed preferences. As a stand alone statistic the 90 per cent figure from the Fathers Direct survey provides evidence that time is a valued commodity and that time with fathers is seen as positive by children. Yet it is actually relatively meaningless if the issue is about how time should be *allocated* rather than as an expression of a general good. Not only is it hard to imagine the opposite question, 'would you like to spend less time with your dad?' getting more than a very few 'yes' responses, but children are likely to reply that they want to spend more time with other people as well, such as their mother and friends. Most people would answer 'yes' to the question 'would you like to earn more?' when given only that option, notwithstanding the fact that they currently have a sufficient income, may have a stronger preference for more of something else (such as time) and would be unwilling to make a sacrifice in another area to achieve it. Like money, almost everyone feels they would benefit from more time – findings from the British Social Attitudes Survey found that over 80 per cent of women and men working full time would like to spend more time with their family (Crompton and Lyonette 2007) and high levels of time pressure are commonplace (Bittman 2004) – but as a finite resource the real interest is how individuals make balancing decisions. Interestingly, analysis of the UK Time Use Survey found that only 7 per cent of fathers said that additional time for childcare was a priority compared to 36 per cent who wanted more time for exercise (Gray 2006).

The dominant method of handling time in empirical analysis of time use leads us to treat units of time equitably – any one hour is the same as any other – even though intuitively we may sense that this is not correct. Meanwhile questions about time preferences need to be understood within a broader context of competing desires. It is therefore important that studies of time are not restricted to quantitative analysis but combine this with a qualitative understanding of the meanings of time and times. As Daly points out, time allocation studies 'do not provide much insight into caretaking interests, commitments or motivations' (1996: 467). By including perceptions of time, another dimension is added to our understanding:

> the way family members talk about time serves as an important window on their beliefs, commitments and priorities.
>
> (Daly 1996: 467)

Everyday involvement

Stages of childcare

Considerable academic attention on fathers has focused on the transition to fatherhood and the first weeks, months and years of parenthood, so there is more knowledge about fathers' time commitments during this period than any other.

The earliest stage of parenthood requires coping with a set of unfamiliar tasks to which parents gradually become accustomed and also particular demands that exist for a relatively short duration: a sense of how time is used during this initial period is therefore atypical of fatherhood in general. Of course, it could be argued that, as how fathers spend time with children varies as they become older in terms of quantity, schedule, and type of activity, choosing any one stage of development can give only a limited picture of fathering involvement. The fathers who were part of the qualitative research project, *Men, Work and Family Life*, had children who were predominantly of primary school age and this certainly affected the ways in which the interviewees spent time with their children. Concentrating on fathers of children within this restricted age range is therefore by no means comprehensive, but it does move the focus away from babycare.

The structure of children's everyday lives was important in determining the ways in which fathers were able to engage with their children. Children were out at school during weekdays until the late afternoon and so beginning to spend time away from family and home; in a schedule that, at least to some degree, coordinated with the employment activity of their parents. For fathers this meant the disappearance of hours of potential childcare – one father commented with a sigh of relief that all his children now attended school and so received 'free childcare', 'in a way school is like the state nanny, I'm sure you've heard that before!'. At the same time a cluster of new intermittent engagements appeared, such as parents' evenings, which required a parental presence. As children became older many were involved in activities that were largely independent of their parents, whether after school clubs or hobbies in the evenings and weekends: Euan provided an impressive list of what each of his three children's activities added up to on a weekly basis:

> Monday night it is swimming, Tuesday night it is Mrs Marshall for Emily, Wednesday night it is whatever, Thursday night it is woodcraft [for Emily and Sam], ballet for Imogen.

Similarly, John says about his daughter:

> She has quite an active life with activities like trampolining at the recreation centre, or ice-skating or learning violin, you know, all of those are fitted in.

Children also simply spent more time with their own friends, either informally at other children's homes or their own houses, or more formally through rounds of organised birthday parties which often seemed to take up considerable portions of weekends – the 'stream of parties' as one father phrased it. This meant an overall reduction in time dedicated to childcare in terms of providing entertainment and joint activities, but an increase in other aspects of parenting such as coordinating activities, providing transport, attending performances, and feeding and looking after children's friends who might be around. At the same, the ability of children of this age to fend for themselves and coordinate their lives unaided should not be overstated. The majority of time outside education was still, in effect, family time, and for the most part parents were not yet relegated to the role of chauffeur. One father with four children ranging from 8 to 14 reflected that this role change had occurred with his eldest son and that driving him to and from events was the main way in which they spent time together, 'I do taxi service at the weekends ... it's a phenomenon of the last year or so really'. He went on to comment that for both the 12 and 14 year olds,

> I don't do much with them round the house at weekends because they've got their own rooms and their own computers and they look after themselves really ... When they were younger we did much more active things all together at the weekend. But the fact of the matter is that when they get to teenage they want to do their own things with their own friends much more of the time.
>
> (Hugh)

The types of child related activities that take place clearly alter with a child's age, or perhaps more accurately, the balance between different forms of caring activity varies over time, and this has an impact on the way in which time with children is recounted.

Fathers' accounts

The remainder of this chapter explores the different ways in which time was invoked and emerged in the accounts of fatherhood put forward by men interviewed for *Men, Work and Family Life*. Activities that are frequently categorised as childcare and are the subject of debates over gender equality, such as cooking for children, cleaning, and tidying up after children, did not dominate. The presence of these activities in more quantitative analysis is perhaps a function of the way in which both individuals and researchers tend to name and categorise what we do; prioritising the activities which take up significant amounts of time rather than the times which hold most meaning for us. These tasks were mentioned by the fathers but they were captured within accounts of daily life as a whole, and it became clear that simply mentioning making breakfast for a child or even playing football with her does not adequately portray a sense of what these activities contribute to the ideal and reality of contemporary fatherhood. Instead a sense of how time and specific times impact on, and contribute to, the constitution of father–child relationships is required. The interviewees quoted here were not asked about a range of pre-defined tasks or to estimate the time they spent on childcare or with children. In the absence of such approaches, there can be no attempt to make definitive statements about the amount of time spent by fathers or an attempt to compile an exhaustive list of the tasks that were carried out. It is possible, however, to gain some sense of the tasks these fathers undertake combined with their importance for achieving the respondents' idea of good fatherhood.

Fathers talked about spending time with children in five distinct ways. First, there was direct 'caring for' children. This fits reasonably well with understandings of unpaid work but is explicitly child related: this form of childcare consists of jobs, such as taking a child to school or finding their sports kit, which would not exist without children to require them. These tasks are referred to as 'routine caring' because they occur at specific times in a day or during the week, and were seen as distinct activities in the mind of the interviewees. These are the kinds of tasks which are often absent in general lists of housework as they only apply to households where children are present.

Second, were mentions of day-to-day chores that merge into the general category of housework, such as cooking, tidying and cleaning. These are tasks which are not necessarily related to children, and are not prominent in most existing accounts of fatherhood. However, in households where children are present, their frequency, relative importance and status as an aspect of childcare mean that they have a qualitatively different, child-specific dimension. Cleaning may suddenly become an acknowledged task once a child is born compared to the relatively slovenly existence that can be enjoyed as an adult couple, or tidiness may disappear in the face of more explicit demands on time from children.

Third, is time spent together as a family: this 'family time' covers a range of activities from going for a walk to visiting relatives to eating a meal together, but is marked out by the presence of both parents and, normally, all children. It also refers to a significant chunk of time, such as a Saturday, rather than what is actually happening, so that one period of 'family time' can contain a number of different, unrelated activities.

Fourth, there is being present at activities that involve a child – the often referred to 'being there'. This term can be taken to mean secondary activity without active engagement, for example, being in the home, absorbed in something else, but available for childcare if required either by a child or a partner. Here the term is also taken to mean devoting a period of time exclusively to participation in activity that is child related, such as a father attending a school parents' evening or going to sports day. Yet it can still be thought of as passive as it does not involve direct engagement between father and child: it is this criterion which marks out a fundamental difference between 'being there' and the one-to-one, intensive time defined below.

Finally, there is intensive time. This would come under the heading 'primary' engagement in the literature, in that during these periods children are the main focus for men. There is, though, a more specific dimension than this, similar to Craig's (2006a) term 'interactive childcare', focusing on playing together, talking, reading and teaching, and therefore involving communication on some level, on a one-to-one basis, between parent and child. This can be a considerable portion of time, if a father and child spent time together in a specific activity, but more often occurs in shorter, more intense bursts. It is the importance of short periods that have some form of interaction but are not the object of a specific activity which are given especial attention here.

It is worth noting that these categories do not map neatly onto the three-way division between engagement, accessibility and responsibility developed by Lamb *et al.* (1987) and taken up extensively since then in the literature. Nor are they an attempt to follow Palkovitz (1997) in mapping the full range of fathering involvement. The naming of accessibility and responsibility as categories of parental involvement in addition to engagement has been beneficial in drawing attention to aspects of fathering outside previously recognised child related tasks, while further analysis has provided more detailed description of what fathers do. The typology here has more in common with Gray's four-fold typology of childcare drawn from parents' comments, although the distinctions she made were based primarily in terms of what the other parent was doing (2006: 6.3). The aim here is to focus on how fathers themselves prioritise and categorise time and times.

Routine caring

When interviewees talked about involvement with their children that occurred on a daily basis, the most common stories were of a rush of activity first thing each morning to organise everyone for the day, and the set of practical, caring tasks that took place at the other end of the day in preparation for bed. Activities in the morning were limited to specific tasks that needed to be accomplished in the short period before family members left the house for work and school. Everyone has to get washed, dressed and eat breakfast, gather together all the things they need for the day and get out. There are also a number of requirements at the other end of the working day: in the evening both children and parents need to be fed, children have homework to complete and need to get washed and be put to bed. An extract from an interview with Hugh illustrates the frantic nature and numerous activities that make up the first hour of being awake in his family with four children, while Bill recounts a very similar set of activities. The subsequent two excerpts relay the similarly functional, but less harassed organisation of their evenings.

> I get up at 6.15, my oldest gets up at 6.15 as well because he likes to see me. One or other of the two boys, sometimes both, will appear by 6.30 and we'll all have breakfast. At 6.45 I make a cup of tea for my wife and we all traipse upstairs, wake up whoever is still asleep. I have a shower, my daughter runs around, she never wakes up, she never comes down, I have to wake her at 6.45, she runs round like a lunatic, I don't exchange two words with her because she's not a communicative in the morning sort of person. At ten past seven the oldest two are ready at the front door to go and catch their bus ... The two little boys will be bumbling around, my wife takes them to school about 8, and I leave the house, depending on whether I am cycling or whether I am taking the train sometime between 7.15 and 7.30. So that's the sort of intense activity of the morning.
>
> (Hugh)

> Sarah [wife] gets up at about half 6, I get up about 7 or slightly after it. I go and walk the dog, Sarah is doing bits and pieces, I bring the dog back, and by that stage Molly [daughter] is up, Sarah gets Molly hot chocolate, she

watches TV; I go have a shower get changed. Annie [daughter] sort of gets up at some stage when that is happening, she comes down stairs with me usually. I get Annie her breakfast, meanwhile Sarah has left for work, I get the girls dressed, which is not really a huge business to be fair at this stage. Then we leave here at half 8 and they get dropped off at the school at quarter to nine, I go to work.

(Bill)

Generally I will have a chance to chat to both of the younger boys and then the older two lurk around, watch the news with us, come and chat to us while we are having supper … So I'd usually see them for about an hour in the evening, sit round the telly together.

(Hugh)

I get home anytime between 6 and half 7. As soon as I get home I usually have something to eat, walk the dog again, that's his big walk … By the time I come back they [daughters] are ready for bed and I bath them, read them a story, put them to bed.

(Bill)

Morning requirements were well defined with mentions of making breakfast, helping children to get dressed and getting them ready for school dominating the accounts. Their extremely predictable nature is evident by the way in which the fathers could recite the various elements off-pat:

Make their breakfasts, do their packed lunch, that is probably about it in the morning.

(Marcus)

The morning is basically, my wife makes the sandwiches for Robbie … so Hazel [wife] would be doing that. I'd get the breakfast for them both … Between quarter past eight and quarter to nine it is just finding out where she [daughter] put her shoes!

(Duncan)

My routine is I get up first, I sort of get half dressed as it were, then I get Kari up, get her dressed. Lynn [wife] gets up and she gets the breakfast.

(Chris)

When we get up in the morning Matthew usually follows me down and I get his breakfast. He's now at the age of course when he can get himself dressed, you have to hassle him along a bit, but he can get himself dressed. One of us, not always the same one, will make his lunch, make our lunches. Then there are sort of small details, somebody hands him his toothbrush.

(Jim)

Angela [wife] generally gets the clothes out and gets them dressed, breakfast is half and half, then I generally take them down there [to school]. I get their teeth brushed, Angela puts vaseline on their faces.

(Simon)

These activities were usually described as shared between father and mother, with an 'all hands to deck' philosophy seemingly necessary to complete everything. The men appear to be both aware and involved in the minutiae of jobs that must be accomplished, whether it is handing a child his toothbrush or finding her shoes. As with family time, these are periods when tasks are undertaken as a family and the image is of relative equity amongst most couples. Only occasionally did men comment that their role was more peripheral; chipping in, as Alan phrased it, with a bit of 'shouting and encouragement' if needed.

There were also some set activities in the evenings that were frequently mentioned; getting children ready for bed, reading stories and helping with homework:

When you get home at 6 there is not much you can do, bear in mind they have got a bedtime of about 8 o'clock and even between the time you get in at 6 and 8 they have got to be, finished their food, clear up the kitchen and bathe them and get them ready for bed.

(Vik)

I often put Nicole to bed, she goes to bed about 8, read her a story.

(George)

I bath them, read them a story, put them to bed.

(Bill)

I'll go upstairs and probably sit and talk and go through the homework with the bigger one.

(Michael)

The list-like run through of precisely what happens was less evident in the fathers' accounts for this time of day and fathers were also prone to provide less detail. This seems to be related partly to greater flexibility in how tasks were managed, with a more relaxed time frame in which to achieve them. It also seems that fathers took less responsibility for providing basic necessities in the evening and so made fewer mentions of the tasks that were accomplished; most noticeably, cooking the evening meal was referred to only infrequently. In commenting that his wife had more work to do because she took more responsibility in the evenings, Duncan noted that,

The morning is a dawdle compared to the evenings because in the morning all I have to do is get them up and out, that is very regimented, it is very clear the things that you have got to get done.

Preparing food normally falls into the category of domestic chore rather than a child-centred task. Breakfast, for example, is an activity that exists with or without the presence of children and the fathers usually fed themselves at the same time as their children. However, it may well take on different characteristics when children are present and be prone to the vagaries of children's requirements. As such it emphasises the potential difficulty in determining borders between self-provisioning, childcare and housework if tasks are identified out of context.

Housework

Housework was rarely mentioned by these men as constituting part of their childcare role. The majority admitted that they contributed less to chores than their partners did:

> Sarah does all the washing, cleaning, cooking … you know I do very little it has to be said.
>
> (Bill)

> Um, I probably do quite a bit of shopping, probably 50 per cent of the shopping … Cooking, I might do a third, she [wife] would probably say less than a third.
>
> (Derek)

Even so, while it was rare for fathers to feel that housework was split equally, this should not imply that they did no housework at all; rather it was not considered within the remit of fatherhood. So George, when asked about his contribution to preparing food, mentions that, 'I'll probably cook two days a week' but did not raise this as an aspect of 'doing' fathering. Other fathers could also list, when asked, their household duties but they placed them outside the category of parenting. John was an exception in mentioning standard household tasks when talking about days when he collected his daughter from school:

> So I'd be with Kirsty [daughter] or very often with a friend [of hers as well] for a couple of hours. And it would as well, somehow, mean sorting out shopping, and then preparing the food.

While it might be expected that in practice housework and childcare would often merge, for most of the fathers the two were considered separate entities. While for mothers routine responsibilities of home may overlap with those of being a parent, these men saw the obligations of fathering as lying elsewhere.

Family time

Most of the interviewees had their paid employment concentrated into weekdays, leaving the weekends as the main opportunity for leisure time and for longer periods with children. With fewer references to scheduled activities the impression was of time that was less regimented and more relaxed.

> Weekends, it is whatever they want to do. On Saturday mornings I take them to school football, so that is a sort of regular thing … and then Miriam tends to join us with the youngest one and we tend to go over to the pub, café, have lunch there, mosey on back [home].
>
> (Vik)

> On the weekends we go for our nature rambles … I just spend time with my kids.
>
> (Joe)

> The real family time is at the weekend, it is unorganised but always the four of us [mother, father and two children].
>
> (Ivan)

Ivan emphasised the status he accorded to spending time together as a 'nuclear' family when explaining that he had explicitly told his own parents not to expect weekend visits, because he wanted to spend time with just his partner and children. This captures what is present in many of the accounts; the way in which weekends centred on joint family activities and were seen primarily as based around mother, father and children doing things together. It mirrors a recent concern in popular commentaries along the lines of, 'the family that plays together, stays together'. For example, the BBC TV programme 'Honey, We're Killing The Kids!' encourages parents to reassess their lifestyle in order to avoid long-term damage to their children's health. Alongside recommendations for healthier eating and set bedtimes, families are often requested to spend more time together and packed off to spend a Saturday horse-riding or painting or going to the zoo. The weekend is portrayed by these fathers as centred around the family and for the family, rather than as individual leisure time which compensates the worker for the daily grind of the labour market. This belief in the importance of the weekend for reaffirming family life and being viewed as a positive aspect of parenthood does seem to be a move away from a masculinity where a break from paid work is supposed to be spent with friends, stereotypically in sporting pursuits.[2]

It is notable that 'family time' could as equally be composed of doing the weekly shop as going off for a day trip to a theme park. As Simon said, 'We just go out together, even if it's shopping or something'. In fact it was the relative lack of organisation that came across strongly as is clear from Ivan's earlier comment and also in Marcus's reflection:

> We do everything together most of the time, I had never really thought about it. But we will eat, have lunch, go out – depending on the weather – go to see friends, but generally speaking it is all four of us doing it together.

It is the spending of time together as a family that is important to these fathers, irrespective of the particular activity. This family time is viewed as precious but what is less obvious is the variation between fathers in how they operate it. Categorising a day or weekend as 'family time' gives a sense of the fathers' main priority but does not provide insight into how it is managed. A comment such as 'we went out for a walk' could provoke contrasting montages of family life. The first sees a father hauled reluctantly out from behind a newspaper to accompany his family once mother has decided where to go, organised the food and made sure the children are appropriately dressed. The second has the father, also in stereotypical fashion, planning a precise but demanding route and tearing ahead, pointing out interesting features and delivering information along the way, meanwhile mother and children trail behind, nodding politely when required, but fundamentally uninterested. The third version, again a caricature but this time of contemporary family life, has the family sitting down together making a plan, responding to suggestions from all members as to where to go and what to do next, followed by a family walk with parents and children mainly focused on each other. It is somewhat unfair to draw on crude stereotypes, and for these fathers it is not in doubt that family based weekends were valued times to which they looked forward. Instead, the unsophisticated illustration is simply a reminder that the more precise activities, captured by time diary analysis for example, which might suggest gendered divisions within family time or the level of primary engagement between father and child are not readily accessible here. Instead, these comments give an indication of one aspect of a composite model of fathers' orientation towards time spent with children.

With the exception of Ivan, fathers did not dwell on the importance of carving out this time with children and insulating it from the impact of other demands. Indeed, as many men mentioned, paid work, household chores and individual preferences often did impinge on their ability to manage an unadulterated family focus. A significant number of fathers admitted to doing paid work at weekends. Shopping and cleaning have to happen at some point – a few families had paid domestic help but most did not – and with the rush of daily life weekends were often the only time available. Some fathers though did try to involve their children in these necessary tasks:

> I try and get them involved in simple things, in things like shopping and stuff like that, ordinary stuff like cooking, or gardening even.
>
> (Patrick)

As a quotation from Gareth illustrates, a preference for spending time with children may overlap with other interests, in his case involvement with football:

> We take seven kids to the football match, so there's one adult ticket and seven children's tickets and the adults share their ticket … I really like it, taking a group of kids like that to a football match.

He also refers to how this can prove a subject of tension with his partner:

> She says that I take on too many things like the football clubs and I help with refereeing … Not necessarily things for myself but things to do with the family, like organising this season ticket.

There were also reports of children going off with friends sometimes for substantial spells – 'he [son] often goes sailing on a Sunday' – and the idea of the family as a neat package functioning as a single unit begins to dissipate further as children get older and have more outside activities:

> We do most things as a family … The nine year old is more dropping her off at friends, but we would still do most things as a family. Sunday, we go swimming every Sunday as a family and we usually try and go out in the afternoon or we will be doing things together.
>
> (Michael)

> Rachel [elder child] gets invited to parties and will go off for a couple of hours every Saturday or Sunday or something.
>
> (Marcus)

So, in practical terms, devoting the weekend, every weekend, to family specific activities of some sort or another seems unlikely. While not diminishing the fact that these fathers did want to spend time with their children and for the most part did do so, it is the commitment rather than the ability for it to materialise that is most evident in these accounts.

Being there

'Being there' is continually invoked as a significant, if not the most significant component in defining good fathering that benefits children. Yet, as with the term 'involvement', meanings vary. It can refer to a physical presence or an emotional relationship, with the latter not necessarily dependent on the existence of the former. Physical presence has a range of possible interpretations from the loosest sense of not being entirely absent from a child's life to maintaining a presence in the household to a more active sense of engagement with a child: the emotional aspect can also refer to an array of possibilities, from sustaining an ongoing close relationship or simply being available as a potential source of support in extremis. Many of the fathers' initial comments about the kind of father they wanted to be centred around the idea of 'being there' – 'a father who was there', 'I wanted to be around' – and when interviewees made positive comments about their own fathers it was precisely the idea of 'being there' that was most prominent. Euan emphasised that his father was always around as a presence in the household:

He washed the dishes every night. He was a very 'there' father, he was always around.

In previous literature on fathering behaviour the idea of 'being around' has often been equated with secondary activity, or accessibility rather than actual engagement. Certainly an explanation for some of the discrepancies between mothers' and fathers' levels of involvement has been the exclusion of secondary engagement from calculations of child related activity, as this type of involvement provides a significant proportion of fathers' care (Larder *et al.* 2006). When included, the implication is that this form of involvement is less demanding and perhaps less significant, and that it comes to the fore in fathers' accounts because of the lack of more active involvement.

This type of description of 'being there' does emerge as an aspect of the fathers' accounts through comments about 'seeing' in contrast to 'communicating' or 'doing'. In similar fashion to Hugh's earlier description of morning activity, which includes walking past an uncommunicative daughter, Gareth mentions the significance of spending some time in the same physical space as his children in the morning:

I get up with her [wife] and work for a couple of hours in the morning, which means that I can see the children in the morning, not that we are necessarily very communicative then, but everybody sees one another.

Tony says that in the evenings he and his wife may not actually be engaged in what their children are doing but adds that, 'we'll both be around really'. Patrick also emphasised that even when he is not interacting with his children he remains available:

I am around the place … I don't do a hugely ridiculous amount of activities with the kids but I am often here.

'Being there' in this instance encompasses a 'milling around' in the same space. For children of primary school age accessibility is a form of reactive childcare. As children grow older and have greater independence accessibility leaves open the possibility for conversation at the instigation of the child. However, there is also a second definition employed here which involves more than just a passive sense of being on-call: from the perspective of the parent it has a child focus that involves a conscious effort, although it does not imply a joint activity or explicit communication.

He plays football Saturday mornings at school so I usually wander along, he goes off on his own, he doesn't want me to go with him, but I usually go off and watch because I quite enjoy it, a lot of other parents turn up and we have a good laugh.

(George)

While it would be incorrect to term this a joint activity, it does permit George to have knowledge about an area of his son's life. In the same way, attendance at parents' evenings at schools and, for some, participation in parent/teacher groups that assisted in the running of schools also gave important insights into the world of their child.

> Obviously there are formal parents-teachers evenings, and I tend to do that quite a lot.
>
> (Hugh)

In addition, when fathers mentioned their presence at events it was often on occasions seen as significant markers of a child's development and life experience. These were commonly events in the school calendar – school plays or sports days – or associated with children's hobbies. They occurred infrequently, perhaps only once a year, but were highly valued:

> I would say I had been to most but not all sports days, fundamentally I pitch up and I do.
>
> (William)

> I have already got down in my diary the dates of the school Christmas play and when I go somewhere and they say, 'let's sort out the date of the meeting, how about the 16th of December?', I say no, I am busy.
>
> (Derek, interviewed in September)

'Being there' is used here to convey a physical presence of fathers in the vicinity of children combined with some kind of child centred focus. For these men, managing to 'be there' for the important events is a strong signifier of the kind of involved fatherhood towards which they were aiming.

Intensive time

Time that can be clearly demarcated as solely directed towards children falls into two categories: references to play or other joint activities that involve spending time together, and time that is less clearly about a specific activity and more about communication. Playing with children has often been claimed as one of men's main contributions to parenting; the activity which holds a special place within the remit of fathering and marks out contemporary fathering from mothering (e.g. Craig 2006a; Lewis 2000). La Rossa (2005) uses the example of a father pitching a baseball to his son in the backyard, perhaps the archetypal symbol in the US of bonding between a father and son. Meanwhile, fathers in the UK drew on examples of football and rugby when they mentioned sports, alongside other play activities. There were a number of mentions of playing with children by these fathers, usually as part of evening activity:

I would see them for an hour, hour and a half before they go to bed, when they are given the chance to jump on me, and play with my rugby ball and kick that around.

(Marcus)

This evening … Joshua wanted to watch a video and Daniel was getting fed up, so I went upstairs and did a puzzle with Daniel.

(Simon)

Included within this category are other kinds of joint activity. Gareth is pleased with how he has managed to incorporate his children into one of his own hobbies, with his sons regularly accompanying him when he goes for a run:

The other thing, which is really nice, is I try to go jogging twice a week and encourage the kids to come with me, we jog round the park together.

(Gareth)

Yet, when talking about their fathering activity these types of remarks were less prevalent than anticipated based on previous literature. The reasons for this are perhaps threefold. First, playtimes were bundled up with more general 'family time' which often involved some form of activity in which fathers participated along with their partners rather than individually with children, such as going to the swimming pool together. Second, play may become less dominant in fathers' accounts as children get older, and joint interests may begin to centre more around passive forms of activity, for example, children as companions for TV viewing. Hugh's comment 'I'd usually see them for about an hour in the evening, sit round the telly together' conveys this. Similarly, George says, 'Conor stays up later now, what we usually do is we end up watching television'. Third, while activity that can be described as play is certainly a component of what these fathers do as parents, it was not to the forefront of their conceptualisation of what good fathering entails. The perhaps diminishing status of a previously key element in the creation of a distinct fathering identity can point us towards how contemporary fatherhood is constructed differently, directing us towards a recognition of communication. Play may provide an opportunity to communicate – Maureen Harrington (2006) concludes from her study that one of the reasons why doing leisure and sport with children is important for fathers is because of the opportunity for communicating and sharing – but what is striking about these men is the way in which they explicitly prioritised conversation in itself. Indeed, joint activities were valued more for the opportunity they provided for one-to-one discussion than for the activities themselves.

That communication and understanding occur in descriptions of intimacy can hardly be over-emphasised; it is listening and talking which are often centre stage, and mentions of talking to children and with children peppered the fathers' accounts. For some, this could be over an evening meal, together around the dining table:

> My wife and I have dinner together and my eldest daughter sits at the table
> with us and talks.
>
> (Joe)

> Generally I will have a chance to chat to both of the younger boys and then
> the older two lurk around, watch the news with us, come and chat to us.
>
> (Hugh)

In Gareth's case this family mealtime is orchestrated by his wife, although
appreciated by him:

> Sam [wife] has got this thing of really trying to get everyone to sit down and
> eat together, and that's very nice. So really almost every evening we sit and
> eat together, and either talk, or argue!

For these fathers eating together was significant because it provided an
opportunity to recount the day's events to each other, and so promoted regular
contact between parents and children. Conversation between fathers and children
on an individual basis was also a habitual occurrence. Gareth, who was quoted
earlier about how he encouraged his sons to participate in his regular evening
run, added 'It's good because you sort of chat when you are jogging'. Marcus
also offered up how 'general chat' with his daughters was the main activity
immediately when he came home in the evening (alongside the physical rough
and tumble mentioned previously). O'Brien and Jones (1995) found that alongside
watching TV, and doing 'nothing', talking about education as well as chatting
more generally accounted for most of the time the 14-year-olds they studied spent
with their fathers. The reports from these fathers produced descriptions of similar
types of involvement. A longer quotation from another interviewee highlights a
number of significant aspects to communication between fathers and children.

> I see my main activity in the evening, when I may or may not help with
> the bath or I may or may not help in various other ways, but most evenings
> – which is very important to me – at their different bedtimes, having read
> them a story (or maybe Felicity [wife] will read them a story), give them a
> cuddle and talk to them for five or ten minutes.
>
> (William)

For William the opportunity for conversation arises when he sees his children
just before they go to sleep. He is dedicated to a particular activity which, in his
view, underlines his commitment to be a good father; as he phrased it, 'I wanted to
be a father who built a relationship with his children', and this involves speaking
with each of his children on an individual basis. He also clearly marks out the
activity of talking to his children from other forms of childcare such as giving
them a bath. He recognises the existence of an assortment of tasks which need
to be fulfilled but these are the responsibility of his wife and optional for him,

in a way that talking to his children is not. Even reading a bedtime story, which cropped up repeatedly in fathers' accounts of the time they spent with children and was perhaps the most frequently mentioned daily activity, is not attributed the importance of a chat. However, the most striking element is the reference to the amount of time this communication takes as five minutes seems scarcely long enough to say anything at all. The implication is that such a short period of time is not necessarily engaging a child in discussion but is about checking up on the events of the day and allowing the opportunity for anything vitally important to be mentioned. Long periods of time were not set aside, but regularity, in William's case as a daily ritual, does matter.

Recognising the high value placed on communication also lends a slightly different perspective to the idea of 'being there'. The reason why accessibility is seen as so important is because physical proximity allows for talking to happen on the child's terms, being present at events is important because it builds knowledge about what is going on in a child's life and provides the groundwork for topics that might need discussion.

> It [is] important for me to make sure that I am there at the time [in the evening], so she has half an hour, 45 minutes of time and I am there available for her to question if need be.
>
> (Michael)

Conclusion: importance of time

Studying men's familial involvement invites 'a focus upon time and upon time in its plurality of meanings' (Brannen 2002). Despite this possibility, time in sociological writing on fatherhood remains situated mainly in the realms of time allocation and management. While these studies acknowledge the significance of time they do not seem to fully capture its dynamic quality. To understand contemporary fatherhood requires not only an acknowledgement of the amount of time fathers spend in parenting activities and the kinds of activities to which time is dedicated, but also the significance they are given for fulfilling ideas of good fatherhood.

There is no formal contract laid down which specifies the number of hours that someone should spend engaged in the care of their own children. However, cultural expectations suggest that the heightened desire of fathers to develop an involved relationship with their children should correlate with a greater time commitment since time is considered the 'ultimate parental resource' (Sayer *et al.* 2004: 9):

> to meet today's standards of appropriate parental behavior, both mothers and fathers must allocate substantial amounts of time to the care of their children.
>
> (Sayer *et al.* 2004: 10)

Jamieson (1998) suggests that this connection with time is inherent to the idea of intimacy since as a relationship takes time to develop, a separation between knowing and understanding on the one hand, and practical caring on the other seems unlikely. Yet the total length of time spent in fathering work was not used by these men to calculate the quality of their fathering. They did not accept that time was a useful measurement of responsibility and commitment in relation to the nurturing of children, and comparing the length of time spent in individual childcare tasks did not help in assessing how important each was considered in contributing to the overall role of 'good father'. Further to this, fathers who spent relatively less time with their children did not express feelings of guilt about being worse fathers (in contrast to evidence from research with mothers e.g. Brannen and Moss 1991 and the idea of 'intensive mothering' Hays 1996). This may, in fact, be in harmony with children's perspectives as one recent study found that there was very little difference in the scores given to resident and non-resident fathers by children in terms of involvement[3] where there was at least some contact (Welsh *et al.* 2004).

That involvement was not measured by these fathers simply in terms of time does not imply that it has no time component. The dominant impression is that a good father–child relationship is possible as long as *some* period of time is given over to it: time is not irrelevant to men's parenting. Adam's phrase 'not all times are equal' (1995: 94) applies well to fathers' childcare time. While some child centred tasks were merely listed, others were imbued with a deep significance for the fathering role. The aspects of parenting the fathers viewed as most significant indicated that 'caring about' was more important than 'caring for'; fathers concentrated on the aspects of parenting that were least 'work-like' and downplayed the requirement to perform regular child maintenance activities. This has parallels with other research: Bittman *et al.* (2004) found that parents who used non-parental childcare lowered their time in physical activities but maintained their time in activities such as talking, reading, listening to or playing with their children. It is these types of activities which were prioritised by fathers, alongside being present at important events in a child's life and achieving 'synchronised family leisure' (Warren 2003). It was key that some amount of time was available and that times of special significance could be accommodated.

It was not the routine, transferable work of childcare that mattered nor the total amount of time spent with children that counted in these fathers' version of good fatherhood – these elements therefore do not fall into the category of 'work' in Himmelweit's (1995) definition of caring activities that can be delegated to someone else – and some consequences of this finding will be explored in later chapters. The elements of parenthood most valued by these fathers were viewed as desirable because they develop and facilitate a strong parent–child relationship and the role of the emotional bond between father and child which underlies this is explored in the next chapter. It has also been highlighted that the role of 'good father' is not defined in the same way as the 'good worker', where time equals commitment. This sets up a potential difference between 'intimate fatherhood' and 'intensive motherhood', where one measure of 'good motherhood' is committing a significant amount of time to childcare; Southerton (2006) suggests that children's lives have a stronger bearing on the temporal rhythms of mothers' daily lives than they do on fathers'. In Chapter 5 the differences and similarities between the roles of fathers and mothers will be explored. The discussion in this chapter has explained why, contrary to what had been anticipated, competition over time was not a dominant theme in these fathers' accounts of their lives, as time for paid work and time for children were largely viewed as complementary. The implications of this for policy initiatives which seek to improve men's work-life balance and accommodate fatherhood through measures such as paternity leave will be taken up in Chapter 6. Finally, all of the fathers quoted here did spend some amount of time with their children on a daily basis, even if it was restricted to just a few minutes. Other fathers, for example those who are not co-resident, may find this impossible to achieve, and the situation of fathers who are excluded from this type of time involvement are the subject of Chapter 7.

4   Performing emotion

Emotion is the keystone of contemporary relationships. It is the emotional significance of a relationship which determines its importance and a lessening of emotional significance that justifies its termination. This focus on the 'interiority' of personal life is exemplified in Giddens' idea of the 'pure relationship' which has meaningfulness for the individual at its core, unsullied by either social niceties or complicated networks of obligations. Feeling a particular way is rarely viewed as wrong and in personal interactions it is emotion, rather than rationality, which is supposed to govern. In both professional and personal relationships managing the expression of our emotions may be necessary but a complete sublimation of our emotions is viewed as inauthentic. It is only the appropriateness of time, place and method for their expression which can be debated. This ability to be emotionally aware is supposedly of benefit to us as individuals, improving physical and psychological health. It is also a positive attribute in the public sphere; witness the development of the term 'emotional intelligence' (popularised by Goleman 1995) as a sought after characteristic in employees.

Recent commentaries have highlighted the emotional significance of the relationship between parent and child for men and it is this 'emotional turn' which most markedly delineates the alleged transformation in father–child relations, and is the subject of this chapter. The chapter begins by evaluating how current ideas of masculinity have embraced an emotional component before moving on to the more specific question of the role of emotion in contemporary fatherhood. The way in which emotions come to the fore in fathers' accounts are discussed, with a particular focus on child birth, bereavement and how men talk about their own fathers. It is highlighted that emotions are not in themselves a new dimension of fatherhood, but rather that emotional openness and the displaying of emotions have particular significance for our ideas of contemporary fatherhood and doing fathering.

Emotions and masculinity

The acceptance of emotion as valid alongside, or in preference to, rationality has been an especially prevalent theme in the remodelling of masculinity. It has been noted that 'researchers [in the past] studied men's lives almost exclusively in their more public dimensions' (Cohen 1993: 1) thereby ignoring the private and personal elements. It has also been widely accepted that 'conventional middle-class western masculinity tends to suppress emotion and deny vulnerability' (Connell 2000: 5). Therefore valuing emotion necessitates a reconfiguration of masculinity and any significant transformation must involve men coming to terms with their emotions (Seidler 1997). The 'new man' of the 1980s was considered at the forefront of development in gender relations because he was 'in touch with his feminine side'. This well-worn phrase implied not only accepting the principle of gender equality, exemplified for example by a willingness to take on stereotypically female work (whether in the labour market or in the unpaid domestic realm) but also an openness towards recognising and expressing emotions defined as typically feminine. It does seem the case that emotions and emotionality have become more accepted as a dimension of contemporary masculinity. Yet, at the same time it has been acknowledged, even by those promoting an alternative masculinity or masculinities, that this emotional revolution will be difficult for individual men to accomplish because it requires a radical rethinking of the attributes and displays of dominant masculinity, with many men likely to remain 'trapped in their own rationalism' (Seidler 2006: 65). Empirical research on men's emotions tends to support this perspective, as it continues to emphasise a contrast in the way in which women and men do emotion. Accounts of men's friendships, for example, tend to emphasise that they are often about doing activities, in contrast to (superior?) female friendships that centre on communicating feelings; 'many men are not comfortable forming close friendships or lack the wherewithal and skill to breach the divide' (Singleton 2003: 131). The ambiguity in accepting the 'new (emotional) man' as *the* formulation of contemporary masculinity is exemplified by the counter image of the 'new lad' which emerged in the 1990s, an anti-feminist response to the 'new man', promoted through the cultural intermediaries of magazine publishing (see Crewe 2003). As Gill (2003) has argued, both these shorthand descriptions of masculinity, the 'new man' and the 'new lad' are best understood as co-existing discourses rather than competing versions of empirical reality.

Emotions and fatherhood

By extending the field of interest in masculinity to include a focus on the negotiation of personal relationships, in place of previous attention on the more public aspects of men's lives, it is perhaps unsurprising that emotions should come to the fore; in studies of fatherhood this is analogous to the move from achieving fatherhood through engagement in the public world of work to a focus on the quality and negotiation of the father–child relationship. The discovery of an emotional dimension in sociological accounts of fatherhood also parallels a more general recognition within the discipline, where the sociology of emotions has become a significant sub-discipline in its own right. Interestingly, discussion of emotions and fatherhood, and specifically the emergence of the idea of the 'new father', seems to have provided an additional trope as a counterpoint to notions of the 'new man' and 'new lad'. Procreation is taken as evidence of a successful heterosexual sexuality, so the 'new father' avoids the criticism directed towards the 'new man' of being overly feminised. Similarly, emotionality towards your own children does not seem to be loaded with negative connotations of emasculation, perhaps because it is about the targeted expression of emotion rather than a more general heightening of it. The 'new father' provides an acceptable face of emotionality – 'the masculine new man' as McMahon's (1999) subtitle to a chapter on the new father proclaims. Fatherhood also has the potential to encourage a positive masculinity which moves away from reasserting the male dominance inherent in the idea of new lads as suggested by the title of a recent newspaper feature article on teenage fathers 'When lads become dads' (Roberts 2006). The need to encourage and teach young men to learn or recognise their emotional side can be framed as especially urgent when they become fathers, in order that they can achieve the status of 'good father'. It is the moment when men are considered especially open to this possibility. This awareness of emotional lives as within the scope of fatherhood research has led to interest in individual accounts of significant, emotional life events, in particular the birth and death of children.

Transition to fatherhood

Being present at the birth of a child has been frequently used as *the* signifier of the emergence of a new form of involved fatherhood and is often tied to the idea of a more emotionally engaged and mature masculinity. It is now commonplace, although a relatively recent development, for fathers to attend the birth of their child. In the UK in the 1950s around 8 per cent of men were present for childbirth (Lewis-Stempel 2001). This was considered unproblematic, often accompanied by the quip that it was hardly necessary as long as they had been there for the conception (Mander 2004). By the 1990s the practice had become almost universal: 98 per cent of fathers attended the birth according to National Health Service figures (2005), 93 per cent of those living with their partners who were surveyed as part of the Millennium Cohort Survey (Kiernan and Smith 2003). It is now non-attendance at a birth that requires explanation. See, for example, the comment by cricketer Andrew Flintoff that captaining the England side who were touring India when his second child was born would hopefully prove an adequate explanation for his son later in life (*The Observer* 14/5/2006).

The father's role throughout pregnancy has expanded with increased expectations around attending scans and antenatal classes: 85 per cent of fathers attend at least one prenatal appointment with a midwife, and 86 per cent at least one ultrasound scan (National Health Service 2005), but presence at the birth is perhaps the most marked and clearly measurable alteration in the practice of fathers. Although there is little evidence that fathers' presence at the birth is associated with greater involvement in childcare (Palkowitz 1985), the decision to attend exemplifies a commitment to parenthood. As a quote from the founder of Fathers Direct, Jack O'Sullivan, makes clear, being present at the birth of your child is both important for fathers themselves and sets up a connection, the first story, on which a parent–child relationship can build:

> It would be a great misfortune for a parent to miss such a great moment [birth of a child]. And to tell your children about the first moments when you held them is so poignant.
>
> (O'Sullivan in Coughlan 2006)

Witnessing the birth is often described as producing an intense, immediate and sometimes unexpected emotional response from men. As an interviewee quoted by Gattrell phrased it, 'It was obviously just the most wonderful experience ever for me' (2007: 361). In recounting their experience of becoming a father, the men interviewed for the *Men, Work and Family Life* project expressed similar sentiments. The fathers emphasised the emotional impact provided by the jolt of the new, alongside stressing the unique nature of the event, and that the immensity of their reaction was something that could not have been anticipated:

> [fatherhood] was the thing that meant changing my entire life.
>
> (Simon)

> [I]t instantly changed the whole focus of my life.
>
> (Phil)

> It was a complete shock, a complete shock actually. It was kind of fantastic and just the sort of most moving thing really … when it happened the child just seemed so fantastic, it was just such a magical, she wasn't like a human being she was like a gift from god or something, like an angel … I was so excited by the whole thing.
>
> (Raj)

Quoting one of his own respondents, 'It changes your relationship to everybody and everything' (1993: 5), Cohen states that, 'Contrary to what traditional thinking about fatherhood would lead one to expect, becoming fathers had a dramatic impact on informants' lives' (1993: 6). The period of transition to fatherhood, including but not limited to the actual birth, has arguably received the greatest attention in recent accounts of fatherhood (e.g. Henwood 2005, Jackson 1984, Lewis 1986), and this may have led to an overemphasis on emotional wonderment, associating fatherhood primarily with a happy sense of confusion. Still, there is little doubt that the immediate impact of parenthood on men that is acknowledged in these accounts is a genuine and strong emotional response.

While this initial stage perhaps produces the most striking set of comments, descriptions of intense emotion are not limited to this period. Reflecting back, now that their children are older, the fathers whom I interviewed continued to express amazement. Jack said, 'Every year of their lives from when they were born I just thought they were the greatest, but each year they got better'. These fathers also reiterated that the longer term consequences of becoming a father are incomparable to any other life experience and hardly describable. The idea that the experience of fatherhood cannot be explained to anyone who is not a father bears a similarity to the way in which motherhood is also often spoken of as an 'exclusive club' (see discussion in Letherby and Williams 1999).

> [I]t had a very dramatic effect … until you have children you simply cannot appreciate the relationship that you have with your own child. The relationship with your own child is so different from anything else you can possibly experience.
>
> (Hugh)

Quoting their own interviewees, other writers have produced a string of similar comments, 'I didn't realise how much of an effect he would have on me … I never realised how much I'd love him' (Gattrell 2007: 361). The intensity of emotion is described by one father as 'falling head over heels in love' (Risman and Johnson-Sumerford 1998: 37), which exemplifies how fathers may speak in almost romantic terms about their children (Ehrensaft 1985, 1987). Aside from the intensity of emotion expressed by mothers about their newborn babies, these comments are perhaps only paralleled by the passion with which individuals speak about the heady excitement in the early days of a sexual relationship.

Death of a child

Ariès (1962) famous historical treatise on the development of the idea of childhood argued that when many offspring were expected to die there was, and could be, little emotional investment afforded them by parents. The 'children as mere commodity' concept has been questioned with Zelizer's *Pricing the Priceless Child* (1985) arguing convincingly that there has been a shift from children as a necessary labour force who provided money for the family to children as a luxury that costs parents money. This entailed the transformation in the perception of children from 'economically useful' to 'emotionally priceless'. It is emotion which replaces money as the method of calculating the value of children. This explains why although financial recompense for the death of a child may be expected in a commercialised world, it is viewed as fundamentally inadequate in compensating for such a loss. Losing a child is seen as particularly poignant and emotionally devastating because it contravenes the idea of generational progression, 'To lose one's parent is a natural phenomenon, to experience the death of a child is not normative, and therefore viewed as "life's greatest tragedy"' (Brown 1989: 466). The emotional impact of the death of a child is therefore given particular status; witness the media attention that is given to the murder or disappearance of children as compared to adults and the sliding scale of grief with younger children viewed as more tragic because of the greater loss of potential.

Discussions of fathers' emotions with respect to the extreme case of grief over the loss of a child reflect the range of opinions on fatherhood and emotions, including continuing unresolved tensions. This subject reflects a reassessment of fathers as unemotional to emotional, underlined by a strong psychological imperative that 'doing emotion' is healthy. At the same time gender distinctions continue, both in the effect of grief and its expression, with an implication in some accounts that mothers' emotional response is more all consuming than that of fathers. Despite the acknowledgement of the emotional impact of a child's death, accepted wisdom has been that fathers are less affected by the death of a child than mothers. News stories may choose to focus on a grief-stricken father if he has lost his entire family but are more likely to show pictures of an inconsolable mother when parents have lost a child. Research has suggested that fathers have lower levels of distress a considerable time after a child's death than do mothers and experience less depression (Moriarty *et al.* 1996; Vance *et al.* 1995). This is attributed partly to an ongoing view of men as having, in general, less capacity for emotionality but primarily because their role as parent is viewed as one step removed from that of mothers and therefore the impact of any loss is reduced, especially for younger children when the maternal bond is considered most potent. In cases of neo-natal death, stillbirth and miscarriage this may be even more pronounced, justified by the idea that the development of a father–child bond develops only after birth, in contrast to the maternal bond which is considered to begin as soon as conception is recognised and builds throughout the period of gestation. Fathers therefore may see their role as principally about providing support to the mother, and are therefore emotionally present mainly through managing the grief of someone else.

Recent research on the subject of miscarriage (which in relation to men is still very limited) has suggested that men's view of their role as supporting their female partner, may lead to the (unhealthy) suppression of their own emotions (Puddifoot and Johnson 1997; Murphy 1998). Research has also suggested that men's sense of when fatherhood begins may now be earlier – because of awareness about the development of a pregnancy, which is heightened through technological innovations, and increased involvement in pregnancy, through their presence at prenatal scans and participation in antenatal parenting classes (Bronstein and Cowan 1988; Draper 2002; Johnson and Puddifoot 1998) – and that this may impact on men's response to miscarriage. Men may feel helpless and out of control (Leroy 1988) and be as, or more, upset than women, even if they are reluctant to speak about their loss (Bradley *et al.* 2002). Emotions are considered here as latent rather than non-existent and the role of professionals, and society more broadly, is to recognise them and help men to do likewise. Other findings tend to emphasise that it is *displays* of emotion which differ between mothers and fathers and that when men perform emotion differently from women they may be misrecognised as simply unemotional.

Emotions as a new dimension of fatherhood?

Taken together, the relatively new and substantial documentation of fathers' emotional response to children has been important in suggesting a shift in the foundation of modern fatherhood; away from the exteriority of public roles and towards the interiority of emotions. Yet, a certain wariness is required in specifying if and how emotion has become central to notions of good fatherhood. Comparisons between the attitudes of contemporary fathers to their paternal role and their historical peers may be problematic (Lewis 1986): given the relative lack of information on fathers' family lives in historical records it is a somewhat difficult task to assess the extent to which attitudes towards, and relationships with, children have actually changed. Indeed, available historical work has very effectively challenged the assumption that all fathers in previous generations adhered to the stereotype of limited emotional attachment. While the term 'Victorian fatherhood' conjures up images of distance and inaccessibility, Davidoff and Hall comment that the records of nineteenth-century middle-class fathers whom they studied indicate 'an intense involvement of men with their families, and a loving interest in their children's lives' (1987: 329). They quote one Birmingham bookseller who wrote that 'my children are my treasure and my happiness. I have ardently wished I might not be separated from them' (1987: 330). Meanwhile Lummis (1982), in his study of East Anglian fishermen at the turn of the twentieth century, has disputed the idea that working-class fathers tended to be brutal, drunken and aloof. These studies suggest that the idea of an emotional response by father to child as something new, may be novel only to some social researchers. Falling for the idea that it is only in contemporary society that fathers feel affection for their children is likely to be the result of the fact that a transformation in the study of families has led to an increased focus on the relationship between men and their children – an area not previously given much attention.

Simply because the emotions of fathers (and men in general) were not often recorded in the past does not mean that those emotions were absent. So it is important to differentiate between feeling emotion and talking about emotion, in order to avoid reading a transformation in expression as reflecting an alteration in feelings. However, although recognising the emotional magnitude for men of becoming a parent rightly challenges the historical image of men as unfeeling, it does not necessarily undermine the argument that emotion now functions as the basis for good fatherhood in a way that it did not in the past. A distinction needs to be made between an emotional attachment, and the suggestion that it is the performance of emotion which forms the bedrock to the contemporary concept of 'good fatherhood'. For example, breadwinning and emotional attachment are not either/or options. Taking on the role of family breadwinner clearly does not negate the possibility that an emotional attachment exists (in fact the sense of responsibility may have its origins in emotional attachment) and acknowledging fathers as emotionally engaged does not preclude the acceptance of a fathering identity based on financial provision. Yet, as previously defining characteristics of fatherhood have diminished as part of the parental role (e.g. choosing a suitable marital partner for your child), or been subsumed within a less gender specific parenting (e.g. discipline),[1] it seems that the emotional connection has been transformed from an accepted but unremarkable fact to become the central component of good fathering. Even more notably, the gradual disappearance of breadwinning as the dominant trope of fathers' parental role, challenged by transformations in the labour market and gender relations (see Chapter 2), has left space for the emotional relationship to become more prominent and sociologically significant. A warning against the tendency to argue that emotion is something entirely new to men's parenting need not mean downplaying the attention given to thinking about emotions and fatherhood. Positing that an emotional connection between father and child exists is, in any case, insufficient to imply a shift which could replace a fatherhood centred on, for example, breadwinning. Instead, it is the centrality of the emotional relationship and an openness about emotions that is at the heart of the matter.

Doing fatherhood differently: expressing emotion

In studies of fathering, a recurrent theme is men's assertion that they are doing a better job of fathering their children than their own fathers (Daly 1995). Men stating that their involvement is greater than the generation of men before them is present in literature from the 1950s through to the 1990s (Lewis 1995), and since. My study was no exception:

> If you listen to my father it was the classic, 'oh when I was young I had to walk to get to school and had gruel to eat' and all the rest of it, it was a different set up … I think he was as good a father as I was going to get, bearing in mind his background, but comparatively he is nothing like the father that I am to my children.
>
> (Vik)

> He [father] wasn't a fraction as involved with us as I have been with my children. He worked, he came home late from work, he went to sleep on the couch.
>
> (Jack)

A number of my interviewees made comments along these lines – that their fathering practices were both different and better from those they had experienced as children – and it was perhaps inevitable that interviewees would respond in this way. More interesting, is *what* is included as justification for this upward trajectory, with comparisons acting as a foil to draw out the facets regarded as most significant to the men's concept of 'good fathering'. The men's fathers were typically characterised as failing to epitomise a more 'modern' form of fatherhood and it was having an emotional bond between father and child that provided the contrast. It is the demonstration of emotion, through 'openness', that is seen as the key in both fostering and demonstrating a good relationship between father and child. A 'close' relationship constituting a positive model for their fathering was defined largely in terms of the recognition and expression of emotion. When mentions of specific activities were made they were used as a way of illustrating the existence, or non-existence, of this highly prized relationship.

Interviewees repeatedly contrasted the emotional remoteness of their own fathers to the closeness for which they were aiming, as indicated in extracts from the accounts of Phil, Simon and Gareth.

> I didn't want to be like my own dad. No, he's a nice guy and everything but he's a little bit distant with small children. He's a kind of intellectual, kind of academic guy and if people can't talk to him in long sentences with lots of subordinate clauses he doesn't tend to be that interested in them. So that excludes, obviously, children. I didn't want to be like that, I wanted to try and relate to kids on their own level.
>
> (Phil)

> My father was very remote to me when I was very little … [and] when I was starting to get stroppy [as a teenager]. I suppose, I was just, not wanting to be like that [as a father].
>
> (Simon)

> I mean I saw with my father, he was sort of very dedicated to his family but quite distant as well. I think there is something in that generation that, well, somehow people weren't quite so open as they are today in talking about their feelings.
>
> (Gareth)

Detailing what 'distant' means, Phil explains that his father was not really interested in him as a child and that this indifference was because he could not provide the type of company his father enjoyed. In contrast, he wants to engage with his child on her level rather than imposing adult standards of communication. Simon did not have a good relationship with his father either, and wants to ensure that he does not replicate the problems with his children. The same terminology of distance is encountered – his father was 'very remote'. The consequence of this remoteness was that when his father did become involved in his upbringing he viewed it as lacking in understanding. In his own parenting, he is anxious to build up a relationship so that any influence he exerts originates within a more positive context. Gareth again used the word 'distant' to describe his own father and went on to explain:

> I would say that he was close to me, but not in the way of showing emotions or talking about things, or like necessarily being very open about things. And so, I suppose, I always aspired to try to be more open with my children. I mean I'm not saying he was uninvolved or didn't care but I would have, well, I wanted to be really involved in what they do.

Unlike the previous two quotations, Gareth's statement does not present any specific problems in the relationship he experienced with his father, nor does he profess any negative feelings towards him. In fact, in this extract he uses a number of extremely positive terms to describe his father – he was very dedicated to his family, close to him, involved and caring – yet overall his father is still categorised as 'quite distant'. It seems contradictory to use the antonyms 'distant' and 'close' to describe his father in consecutive sentences but this ambiguity occurs because he is categorical in stating his father did *feel* emotion towards him but did not make him aware of this: a central plank in fulfilling the idea of being 'really involved' with his own children means being open with them on an emotional level.

In common with the more critical comments, when fathers were remembered as positive role models and interviewees intimated that they wanted to follow their example, it was the establishment of a close emotional relationship that was viewed as central. The attributes regarded as absent in the previous accounts, which emphasised the unfortunate distance between father and son, were replaced here by references to good relationships based on closeness:

> I wanted to be like the memory I had of my father because we had a very good relationship.
>
> (Greg)

> I am very close to my father and I think he's a wonderful man, and I think he always has been.
>
> (Hugh)

Derek did not use his father as a reference point, and instead offered an anecdote about two football managers to appraise potential models of fathering. Through this he illustrates the kind of relationship, or rather lack of relationship, between father and child that he wants to avoid. The invocation of the wedding day is appealing since, traditionally, it marks the achievement of full adult status and the role of the father of the bride is symbolically important in marking the transition from one family to another.

> I remember Brian Clough [who] was a prominent football manager. And he used to get a lot of stick, the fact that he would disappear off with his family in the middle of the football season at school half terms. People would say 'how can he leave his team?', when they were top of the league or got a big cup match coming up. And I remember reading an interview with him and he justified it on the grounds that he had heard Bill Nicholson – the Tottenham manager from the early 1960s – who apparently sat in the back of the wedding car, taking his daughter to her wedding, and looked at his daughter on the way to church for the wedding and [thought], I remember you being born and now you are going to get married and I have missed it all in between. And Brian Clough being determined that that wouldn't happen to him, that he would be around seeing his family growing up … [I wanted to] learn from Bill Nicholson's mistake and follow Brian Clough's example.

Derek wants to ensure that he does not miss out on significant parts of his sons' childhood so that by the time they are adults he really knows them as individuals.

He sees attending particular children's events and spending time with his family as important. These are significant times not because this is what is expected of him by peers or because there is an aim towards an equal division of labour between his wife and himself, rather they are justified because this involvement builds up enough knowledge to define the relationship with his children as emotionally close.

Jack was critical about the way in which his father had managed his family life and adamant that he wanted a very different kind of relationship with his own children. He comments that:

> In my own family, my father was very dictatorial to my mother and towards us as kids … I had things that I saw in my father's relationships that I didn't want to repeat.

The earlier quote by Jack mentioned a relative lack of involvement by his father in child-related activities, and he is keen to document that he spends more time with his children that his own father did. He also gives the impression that the activities are representative of a more essential difference in the father–child relationship. What Jack indicates is not only a greater participation in activities with his children, but also a less hierarchical relationship with them, with a move away from the authoritarian paternalism he witnessed first hand. In both these cases, the significance of daily fathering practices for achieving the goal of a close emotional relationship is again to the fore.

Conclusion: emotionality as a basis for 'good fatherhood'

> Results indicate that most men today desire and seem to have a closer relationship with their children than did their fathers.
>
> (Van Dongen 1995: 91)

Emotional closeness is positive because emotional distance in today's society is viewed as negative. In this context, emotional involvement has been seen as crucial to fulfilling the idea of being a 'good father' (Furstenberg 1995) and emotional distance one expression of bad fatherhood. 'Emotional' is though a shorthand term that requires more examination and positing simply an 'emotional connection' as the basis of a new kind of fatherhood is a vague conclusion. There is a distinct difference between saying that a father has an emotional relationship with his child (which is not specific to contemporary fatherhood) and saying that closeness and openness are the basis of good fatherhood (which does seem to be a central component to nurturing fatherhood). On the whole, the existence of some kind of an emotional connection between father and child, which is regarded as absolutely necessary, is assumed to be present. It is the demonstration of emotion, through 'openness', that is seen as key in both fostering and demonstrating a good relationship between father and child. The fatherhood which the interviewees reject is the image of the father who is reticent about expressing his feelings and is one step removed from the experiences and emotions of his child. Despite various positive qualities, the men's fathers are frequently characterised as failing in this way to epitomise a more 'modern' fatherhood. These men are aiming for a fatherhood which is based upon both the verbal and physical expression of feeling. The responses discussed here replicate the findings of previous studies in emphasising both the existence and the expression of the emotional connection between fathers and children. Julia Brannen and her colleagues (1994) found that all the parents they interviewed emphasised how close they were to their children (see also Warin *et al.* 1999). This 'good' relationship with children places great emphasis on the importance of disclosure and was based on the ability of parents and children to communicate: talking, listening and understanding.

Emotional involvement between father and child is both about men expressing their feelings and signifying the importance of their parental relationship *and* about allowing and encouraging children to express their emotions. Referring to Giddens' concept of intimacy transformed, 'it is the quality of the relationship between parent and child which comes to the fore' (1992: 98) and having this version of emotion as the cornerstone of the father–child relationship emphasises a sense of mutuality (see Chapter 8) with benefits for both men and their children. These benefits are not really about measurable outcomes, such as whether children do better at school or fathers are more responsible (although there may be some knock-on effects): as fathers want to have an emotionally satisfying relationship with their children it is much more about intrinsic gains. This could be viewed as a move towards a more individualised notion of parenting, not necessarily to the extremes of the 'pure relationship' (Giddens 1992) but, nevertheless, attributing particular significance to the father–child dyad.

The link between emotion and action is tenuous. While an emotional relationship should have some external evidence as demonstration of its existence, it is not obvious what should be expected in terms of caring activity. In other words, the link between the emotional relationship of father and child and the work of childcare is hazy. However, the importance of activities that allow the development of a relationship does fit with the discussion of activities and time in Chapter 3, which highlighted that one-to-one time in which communication takes place is seen as especially meaningful. Emotional closeness/distance is also an interesting criterion because it cannot automatically be read off from physical proximity. As is evident from the way in which men recount experiences with their own fathers, physical closeness, through co-residency, is no guarantee of an appropriately strong emotional relationship. However, since emotional closeness can be claimed as distinct this may avoid classifying men who do not have easy access to physical closeness because of the demands of work and the impact of divorce/separation as failed fathers. This issue is taken up again in Chapter 7.

5 Linking fatherhood and motherhood

In previous chapters contemporary fatherhood has been explored in terms of its relationship to money, time, and emotions. These discussions highlighted the extent to which ideas about good fatherhood have moved away from a conceptualisation of breadwinners who are physically absent from the home and emotionally distant, towards a fatherhood that is based on relationship-building. The emphasis throughout has mainly been on the father–child dyad. The problem with this account of contemporary fatherhood is that the complex network of caring relations and kinship ties within which fathers are situated has been largely ignored. In this chapter the task will be to expand beyond the narrow focus of father and child to explore the immediate context of the household, in particular, the negotiation and practice of shared parenting roles. In order to understand fathering, it is necessary to appreciate how fathers and mothers create each other (Cowdery and Knudson-Martin 2005), and it is the explicit interlinkage of mothering and fathering roles that is given priority here. The chapter begins with an overview of current similarities and differences between fatherhood and motherhood and how the influence of motherhood on fatherhood has been theorised. Following this, the main discussion focuses on how fathers differentiate between mothering and fathering and the rationales they provide for ongoing differences. It is argued that mothers are frequently viewed as retaining a unique parental status which originates in biology. However, while this has implications for childcare, it does not undermine the importance of fathers, whose parenting role is located in the individual relationship between father and child.

Motherhood, fatherhood and parenting

Asking questions about the characteristics of good parents results in quite similar sets of responses which refer to both mothers and fathers, namely, providing love, support, time, advice and good communication (Perälä-Littunen 2007). Lupton (2000) discusses how the emphasis in the accounts of first-time mothers who she interviewed was placed on the strength of the relationship with children as individuals, and the development of a bond between mother and child; in similar fashion to the way in which the fathers quoted in Chapters 3 and 4 also stressed the building of a relationship with their child. These tendencies suggest a convergence in expectations about motherhood and fatherhood with some movement towards a gender neutral concept of parenthood. The financial provision often tends to be seen as the preserve of fathers (Lupton 2000; Perälä-Littunen 2007) but is not exclusive to men, as full-time employment is also seen as an important part of good mothering for certain groups of women (Duncan *et al*. 2003) and, as discussed in Chapter 2, many mothers do make a significant financial contribution through their employment, whether working part-time or full-time. There is, though, substantial evidence that mothers continue to do more childcare than fathers. In terms of time commitment, mothers still do the 'lion's share of the parenting' (Yeung *et al*. 2001; see also Bianchi 2000; Craig 2006a; Larder *et al*. 2006), organisational issues are still ceded to mothers (Vincent and Ball 2006) and fathers are expected to make less contribution in terms of emotional labour (Lupton 2000). It is also mothers who, as a consequence of holding ultimate responsibility for bringing up children, 'bear the brunt of sanctions designed to enforce "good parenting"' (Gillies 2007: 9). So at the same time as 'culture' suggests that fatherhood and motherhood may, increasingly, be considered interchangeable, in terms of 'conduct' there is a still a significant difference. Therefore the question remains as to how these gender differences are articulated and justified.

The influence of motherhood on fatherhood

Given the close relationship between mothering and fathering, it is assumed that formulating new forms of fatherhood necessarily also involves rethinking motherhood. Second wave feminists such as Firestone (1970) and Oakley (1979) argued that motherhood was critical in underpinning gender divisions. In contemporary Western society, motherhood remains important for women as a marker of full adult status (Arendell 2000) and retains significance because of the fact that women tend to be constructed as potential mothers, whether or not they actually become parents (Letherby 1994). The prospect of a new fatherhood, which revises men's parental importance as fathers who make a greater contribution to childcare, could provide a challenge to the status of mothers and might be welcomed as a route to greater equality between men and women. Men becoming more like women with regard to parenthood could provide the other half of the transformation in gender roles, to balance women's growing similarity to men in terms of participation in paid work. This 'backdoor equality' would see an equalising of relations not through an explicit commitment to gender equality or even as a necessary response to women's expectations, but because of a desire to be involved with children in a way that was previously the preserve of women and that has been accredited little social status.

Alternatively, it has been suggested that mothers may resent the intrusion of men into their arena of expertise and therefore seek to limit fathers' parental contribution. Writers such as Burgess (1997) lay a considerable part of the blame for men's inability to be fully involved fathers, and for the continued lack of equality in parenting, on 'the mothers' mafia'. It is argued that fathers can only respond to the options presented to them by mothers whereas women's preferences over the organisation of parenting can be asserted. Other authors, who do not explicitly condemn mothers, also emphasise the level of authority that women can wield within the family. These more sympathetic explanations consider women's reluctance to concede jurisdiction as an understandable attempt to retain control over the domestic domain, given that it is one area where women can exert power, in the context of incomplete advancements in equality in other spheres. Certainly mothers can hold a gatekeeper role with respect to access to children (Warin *et al.* 1999), can be territorial about relationships with their children (Gattrell 2005), may restrict fathers' level of involvement if their status of primary parent is threatened (Maushart 2002) and often have greater access to children after divorce or separation. In contrast, Cowdery and Knudson-Martin write of how, in households where parenting is genuinely collaborative, 'mothers are comfortable letting fathers parent without monitoring or intruding' (2005: 342).

In both these approaches changes in fatherhood are used to tell us something about motherhood – either that mothers are desperately keen to embrace new fatherhood or that they are resistant to it – which are then used to draw conclusions about the possibilities open to fathers. This chapter provides a different perspective, namely how fathers view motherhood and the impact this has on their own parenting identity and practices. Qualitative accounts of modern motherhood have tended to focus on women's descriptions of their experiences and feelings, while how men (including fathers) think about motherhood is largely absent from the literature. Using the comments of my interviewees, from the *Men, Work and Family Life* project, it is possible to explore views of motherhood in conjunction with understandings of fatherhood and so develop some sense of the interrelationship between them.

Mothers in accounts of fatherhood

As other researchers have noted (e.g. Cunningham-Burley 1984), research on family life has a tendency to default to women, who are viewed as experts on children's lives. So, from the beginning of the *Men, Work and Family Life* project there was a conscious decision to try and avoid allowing mothers a gatekeeping role by very clearly presenting the research as a study of fathers and fathering. In practical terms this meant finding ways of contacting fathers directly and ensuring that they knew they were the specific subject of study.[1] There was a conscious decision not to mention mothers early on in the interviews and the one direct question asked of interviewees about differences and similarities between motherhood and fatherhood was left until relatively late.

It was therefore interesting, on listening to the recorded interviews and reading the transcripts, to note how mothers were conspicuously present in fathers' accounts of their everyday lives and that the men often presented a strong sense of partnership in their depictions of parenting. The argument that in order to understand either mothering or fathering they must be looked at in relation to each other makes particular sense in the light of interviews in which differences of opinion, relative levels of expertise, role distinctions and negotiations were openly on display. To take just one example, descriptions of daily evening activity often had as much discussion of what mothers were doing as they did of fathers. Asked about his daily involvement with his children Vik replied:

> I either do the breakfast bit or Miriam [wife] does the breakfast bit and then either I go back early or Miriam goes back early [from work] … I suppose we tend to alternate so that one of us gets to work early in the morning … and then, you know, if I am the first one in, it is picking them up after they have just been fed, bathe them, get them ready for bed, put them to bed, if Miriam is not back in time, you know, we do that together. In the morning, I tend to take them to school, I tend to be the one that does the morning bit.

This presence of mothers is evident at every stage of discussion. The following quotations, which are only a selection of the references that Gareth made to his wife, were typical of the interviews. They include comments on her interest in having children, her influence on his career development, her view on the importance of family meals and the impact of her work situation on the organisation of childcare:

> My wife Sam is 4 years older that me, so she was sort of early thirties and starting to feel, you know like, ah, she really wanted to get going in having a family.

> I spent a year or so … being part-time employed, sort of underemployed and I felt quite isolated in the end a bit depressed about that so Sam really made me go into a computer retraining course.

> Sam has got this thing of really trying to get everyone to sit down and eat together, and that's very nice.

> Sam works part-time so there's always complicated arrangements about all sorts of things.

On other occasions, for example when fathers could not remember a piece of family information, such as how long they had taken off work as paternity leave, they would often suggest that their partners would know this detail. In most cases, where interviews were conducted in the interviewees' homes in the evening, mothers were also physically present. For the most part there was relatively little interaction, just an awareness of them in another room with a brief hello and goodbye but there was considerable variation to this model. In one instance, the partner of the interviewee was in the next room but the open plan nature of the living area meant that conversation carried and the father would occasionally call out for confirmation of something he had said or to ask a question. On that occasion the father being interviewed suggested that we all go to the pub after the 'formal' interview and so the three of us continued discussing parenting issues there. At another interview I was invited to have dinner before the interview and chatted to Greg and his wife who was pregnant with their third child. While the concern to focus on fathers meant that mothers were not directly participating in the interviews, these kinds of interactions provided some sense of the family atmosphere, which provided additional context in which to consider the comments made about motherhood.

This presence of mothers, both physically and in the stories that fathers told, is also interesting because of the contrast it provides with research on mothers, which has emphasised the relative absence of fathers in women's accounts. Heather Elliott (2007) who has recently researched transitions to motherhood, has commented that in her interviews with women, fathers were fleeting presences who flitted into view and then disappeared (both physically and metaphorically); the same was not true here.

'It's all just parenting' or 'gender makes a difference'

Turning to what fathers said about motherhood, when asked directly about differences between mothering and fathering, men's responses varied, including both absolute denials of any distinction and strong opinions that very real differences did exist. One group of fathers were adamant that it was all 'just parenting':

> Oh, I don't think there need be any at all, at all ... I prefer to use the word parenting, the whole shebang altogether, it involves everything. I don't think, in and of themselves women have a particular way of bringing up children, it's highly cultural and it's variable.
>
> (Ken)

> This is quite naïve but I suppose I don't really feel that there should be differences between mothering and fathering, I think there is parenting.
>
> (Jim)

> I don't feel it is that gender specific, what I do.
>
> (Raj)

These comments echo findings that a belief in distinctive roles for men and women as breadwinner and homemaker respectively is diminishing (Crompton *et al.* 2003) and that there is uneasiness in attributing separate characteristics for good fathers and good mothers (Perälä-Littunen 2007). There is a hint however, even in these quotations, that while distinguishing fatherhood and motherhood may be undesirable, in practice differences may still emerge. Raj's remark that what *he* does is not gender specific leaves the impression that he believes gender distinctions do exist for most others and that it is his situation which stands out. Indeed Raj is in the relatively unusual position of being separated from his partner and caring for his children on a 50/50 split basis.[2] Both Jim and Raj also say that they 'feel' gender should be irrelevant with respect to parenting, which may suggest that they are less convinced that this is the case in reality, especially combined with Jim's opening phrase that this is a 'naïve' belief.

Others were certain that gender *was* significant. George and Euan were typical of this group in talking about the importance of gender specifically in relation to parenting, while Jack's opinion about differences between fathering and mothering originate from a more general belief in gender difference.

> There are still I think quite distinct roles that are being played by both mother and father, in this family certainly.
>
> (Euan)

> Yes, in the sense that what Ruth [wife] does, she does almost naturally without thinking, she's very good at [it] ... The kids need a mother more than they need a father ... More people are like that than otherwise ... I think [with] most of my friends that are parents the mother is more important than the father.
>
> (George)

> I think, it is my own belief, that the gender makes a big difference, in everything. I think that men and women are different ... I think you can see big differences in behaviour and attitudes of kids which show that a mother has a different effect on kids than a father.
>
> (Jack)

Alustaari's study in Finland (2003, cited in Perälä-Littunen 2007), showed that mothers were given the status of primary parents not only by mothers but also by childcare professionals, in advice literature and by fathers as well. The fathers quoted here also seem to be making reference to the heightened importance of mothers, possibly because they are reflecting the reality of who does more childcare in their own homes. However, these responses are interesting given that, as we have seen, these men did not hold 'traditional' views about fatherhood as centred, for example, on discipline or breadwinning and instead considered their emotional relationship with their children as fundamental. Embracing a version of fatherhood that is constructed around newer ideas of involvement seems somewhat problematic when it is matched with the continuing prioritising of motherhood. This shift in some of the gendered assumptions surrounding parenthood accompanied by a recognition of ongoing differences perhaps explains why the majority of fathers were either circumspect or uncertain:

> Broadly speaking, yeah, I see it as parenting. Although, there are definitely, there are different things that we give to the children. Well, I don't know how much of it is personality and how much of it is, you know, gender, I don't know. Ermm. I don't think I can answer actually.
>
> (Tony)

I think she [wife] sees there are differences between men and women, which probably I think there are as well. But if you're just talking about how people relate to one another then I don't really see different roles for the parents. I mean she has some things that she does, that are more to her personality rather than because she is a mother or, it's difficult to unscramble those things.

(Gareth)

These interviewees wanted to maintain that, while there may be an underlying difference between men and women as parents, this does not undermine the fundamental equality of fathers and mothers. While mothers may be seen as having closer emotional ties with children and doing more in terms of practical childcare, men still need to be considered as parental peers. The interviewees, for the most part, seem uncomfortable with a partition of distinct parental roles, hence a return to the phrase that, 'it is all just parenting'. Instead the differences in what they do compared to the mother of their child are ascribed purely to the 'personality' of individual parents. This is similar to broader accounts of housework which also see tasks divided up along lines of personal preference: although it might appear that gender is what makes the difference, the comments posit that divisions should be understood at an individual level:

You know you read in these surveys in the paper where it says women still do 90 per cent of the housework or whatever – that the traditional roles haven't changed … to a certain extent [that] is true in our household, but what underlies that is a sort of barter system that goes on … I think it's more important that people are comfortable with what they are doing, rather than trying to make a statement out of it. Sam [wife] goes, 'you know, we really need these shelves in the bathroom so I'll do the washing and tidy the kitchen if you put the shelves up', and it's sort of quicker for both of us that way because I can put the shelves up more quickly than she can. Although the roles remain allocated in the traditional ways I suppose it doesn't necessarily reflect an unfairness.

(Gareth)

Explaining the distinction

A better understanding of these, somewhat confusing, accounts is possible once the rationale behind what the fathers said is explored; that is, how their views on the similarities and differences between fathers and mothers were justified. When fathers acknowledged some kind of distinction between mothers and fathers, they referred to biology, personal preference, and the influence of social forces in order to explain differences in levels of everyday engagement in childcare and orientations to children between mothers and fathers.

Biology as trumps

The most frequently voiced reason to explain the contrast between mothering and fathering was the existence of a biological imperative towards a particular division of labour. Cowdery and Knudson-Martin (2005) found that among the couples they labelled as 'traditional' or 'gender legacy' (in contrast to the progressive 'postgender' group) there was a belief that mothers were uniquely connected with their children. Among the fathers I interviewed, Hugh epitomised this viewpoint. He took a liberal position in stating that the family is a private site and that he would not want to tell anyone else what is the 'best' way to approach raising their children. Yet, as his final sentence indicates, he also believes that the division of labour which he and his wife have adopted, where he takes on more financial responsibility while his wife is in charge of most domestic matters, is the most 'normal' form of household organisation:

> I think that the way which people bring up their children is entirely up to them and I have no views, I really genuinely have no views as to whether it is better or worse. I am a traditionalist in the sense of what I, we, have done for ourselves. I also believe there is a strong evolutionary impulse to do what we have done.

While Hugh uses the idea of evolution – a primordial drive – other respondents were more specific in defining the distinction between fathers and mothers as resulting from the early period of child development, due to women's role in childbirth and breastfeeding and a concomitant psychological attachment.

> The mother is really the point of contact with the child, particularly in the first nine months, a year say. The father really has pretty limited input ... particularly if she [the mother] is breastfeeding. I mean you can change the odd nappy and things like that, give your wife a bit of respite, particularly if the child is difficult ... but there is a pretty limited amount that you can do.
>
> (Bill)

> Obviously fathering and mothering are not the same and clearly at different stages of the child's development they are not the same. I don't think I, I can't be as close to a small child as a mother is, it's very obvious for her, in times of deep distress it will be the mother that they ask for.
>
> (Michael)

Opinions of this kind resonate with the majority view that it is women who should stay at home when children are young (Crompton *et al.* 2003; Scott *et al.* 1998); an opinion which is held most strongly by men (Calderwood *et al.* 2005; Crompton *et al.* 2003; Scott 1999). A particular, unique maternal bond is invoked and used to illustrate the 'naturalness' of a division of labour between provider and nurturer. This is unsurprising given that comparisons with the natural world are commonly invoked at the popular level to justify dominant practices and, with respect to reproduction, the tendency towards the 'predetermined nature of caring and femininity' (McKie *et al.* 2001: 241) is especially notable. However, although the move from biological fact through psychology to social prescription is strong (Phoenix and Woolett 1991), it can be problematised. Two examples from the interviewees illustrate this point. The way in which biology is manipulated into the realm of the social is perhaps best indicated by the comments of George. As quoted above, George believed that in the lives of his children, his wife was a more important figure than he was and he went on to locate the source of this difference as originating in 'the fact of giving birth'. Employing a similar turn of phrase to a number of other interviewees, the importance of mothers was grounded in the act of childbirth which engendered, in his view, a special connection. Yet, this was a rather surprising pronouncement from George, given that his wife had not given birth to their two adopted children. When presented with this apparent contradiction George insisted that, nevertheless, there was a singular bond between his wife and their adopted children, grounded in the biological fact of motherhood. Although George claimed that it is giving birth which leads to a distinctive mother–child connection, he in fact articulates the way in which women as potential mothers (Letherby 1994) are considered to have an intrinsic maternalism which is triggered by the mere presence of children. This illustrates the way in which biology can refer to specific biological processes such as gestation and childbirth as well as chosen practices that are specific to one sex such as breastfeeding; but there is space too for biological associations to be made which draw on more general allusions to womanhood and, through their absence, to manhood. It is also noteworthy that some fathers who mentioned biological differences were dismissive of the impact of biology and early parenting practices on the forms of parenting provided by mothers and fathers in the *long* term.

> With the exception of the first year in the child's life I don't think I do see much distinction really. There are distinctions in the first twelve months.
>
> (Derek)

Derek acknowledged that in the early period of a child's life the roles of mother and father were not the same, but felt that this was a clearly demarcated stage, one that did not have later repercussions. In contrast Bill used the initial phase of intense mother–child activity as the rationale for his view that 'the mothering role, is, the traditional mother'. The biological appears definitive and so can be presented as responsible for the origins of difference, but as Derek's comment indicates it is still open to interpretation.

Personal preferences

Some interviewees personalised the division between mothering and fathering: they rejected broader explanations in favour of arguing for individual (or household) agency over parenting decisions and their consequences. These men were less likely to accept the idea of a maternal instinct – at least not one that is stronger or more significant than a paternal instinct. By declining the influence of the 'natural', expressed through biological processes and personality traits, these fathers were able to foreground the role of choice. For this group of men, fatherhood and motherhood are relatively malleable and can be adjusted at will according to the preferences of the individual or couple. These comments do not help address the sociological question as to why public and private dimensions of family provision tend to be gendered but suggest a way for individuals to assert control of the way in which they organise what mothers and fathers do in their own families, through drawing on a discourse of choice. For these men divisions between mothering and fathering emerged from the particular preferences they had in respect to caring roles. Importantly, this decision-making was presented as a joint activity which corresponded with their partner's preferences as well as their own.

Phil states that what marks out the difference between his own and his wife's connection with their child is the fact of the division between his full-time work and her part-time employment.

> In our own particular situation there is that difference because she [wife] just spends more time with her [daughter] … my wife knows her better than I do … she effectively spends three or four times as much time with her in a week as I do, so there is a difference.

William also asserted that some kind of inherent difference was not the correct way of framing issues of mothering and fathering but argued that distinct roles could emerge, by virtue of taking on different familial responsibilities that developed forms of knowledge and skills.

> I'm not certain it is the right question [are there any differences between mothering and fathering?]. By which I mean, do I think there are fundamental differences between being the anchor at home and the provider outside home? I think there are differences. In some sense I am recasting the question, I'm not saying it is a mothering/fathering role, the father could be at home and the mother could be out at work … I think either could do both jobs.

Simon was also adamant that it was the 'doing' of care that marked out types of relationship, rather than distinctions based on sex. He explicitly refused the notion that breastfeeding surpasses anything else as *the* method of building a strong connection between parent and child.

> You know there is research galore about bonding and mothers who stick the kids straight on the breast as soon as it is born but there is no mention of the father's role in all of that, and you look at the man the next door but one and he is the one that has bonded with that child. You can't tell me it is a gender issue, it is a primary care giver issue.

Time, in these accounts, was viewed as instrumental in determining parent–child relationships. The men believed that the substantial amount of time their partners spent with children was responsible for any dissimilarity between their partners' parenting and their own, and, by extension, this situation results in women in general doing more childcare than men. Lynn Jamieson writes that 'knowing and understanding take time' (1998: 166) and it is this motto to which fathers adhered in explaining the primacy of mothers over fathers. Mothers *became* more significant because of their time commitment and therefore this was something which could be altered through adopting different practices. It is important to remember that fathers for the most part were happy with the amount of time they had together with their children and were not envious when mothers, commonly through part-time employment, had more time with children than themselves. Neither did the men speak about mothers' greater time with children as having a negative impact on their own relationship. Phil, whose partner had opted to work part-time in order to spend more time at home with their daughter, saw the amount of caring that his partner provided as contributing to a close mother–child relationship, and contrasted this with the lower level of closeness that existed between him and his child. Yet he did not see himself in competition with his partner over this or feel that he was losing out: closeness could be evaluated as existing to a greater or lesser degree but this was not a contest with a winner and loser. So, in contrast to some previous accounts, fathers did not consider themselves reluctantly pushed out by mothers' high level of involvement.

Social forces

Other interviewees focused on how accepted ideas about gender lead to assumptions about mothers and fathers, while making the point that these are not always typical of everyday practices. These were the group of fathers whose initial response had been to make strong statements rejecting gendered roles: they held the view that motherhood and fatherhood were fundamentally the same, and drew on the idea of 'social influence' to explore and explain observable differences. Changes to mothering and fathering roles were, for this group, less fluid than for those who emphasised personal choice. They could be adjusted, but only in the face of societal obligations about gender appropriate parenting behaviour. Raj makes a distinction between, on the one hand, societal ideals (which do discriminate between fathering and mothering) and, on the other hand, his own orientation and behaviour (which do not).

> I don't feel it is that gender specific what I do really … I mean obviously the way society is structured there is a big difference between mothering and fathering but I don't think that there are essential differences. That fact, that you were a man or a woman, if you were put in the same situations I think it might end up looking very similar actually.

Following on from his claim that 'there is parenting' (rather than fathering and mothering), Jim talked about how,

> society sometimes imposes roles … there is this notion that somehow mother equals parent, and society looks to mother to do things, 'get your mummy to make that for you [for school]' 'get mummy to bring that tomorrow' rather than 'get you mum or dad' or 'ask your mummy or daddy' … There's a certain amount of stereotyping.

Both men go on to explain how they account for the fact that for men and women rarely end up in similar situations and how stereotypes are reinforced. They suggest that employment is the crucial factor and illustrate how their own circumstances have been influential in challenging commonplace ideas.

> Working patterns I think can maybe reinforce the stereotype, but because of the sort of hours that Claire [wife] would work, to some extent we're interchangeable.
>
> (Jim)

> To me that is the difference really with mothering and fathering … dads are often at work, they come home and they do a lot of fun things with the kids or they have a lot of energy whereas the mothers [are] just sort of bored and knackered and they just, sort of, look miserable! And that is just circumstances that create that situation, I don't think that is about gender at all, I don't think that is about mothering or fathering. And I think once you find, I have been doing what a lot of mothers do, you know I feel I am much more like them in a way.
>
> (Raj)

Jim and his wife both worked similar full-time hours and he described how they shared care for their son, in a quite formalised way.

> What we do is we have sort of two nights on, two nights off … But there are nights when one of us has to go out so we try to balance it out … So that's sort of a normal school/work day, so we try our best to share it.

Raj's paid work was on a part-time basis. He lived separately from the mother of his children and shared their care on a 50/50 basis with his ex-partner, taking full responsibility for their care for half of the week.

> In my office the other lads will have a bit of, it will be laddish sort of comments that I get, you know, they are all very nice about it, but it is seen as a very odd thing for a man to be doing all that with their kids, or a bit unusual anyway … I get the feeling, where I work, for a woman to go part-time when she has had a child people are quite sympathetic and fully

understand that, and it must be hard for them because people immediately then think, 'right she's not moving anywhere, that is as far as she is going' and that must be hard for them. But I suppose what is hard for men is it is such an exceptional situation. I don't know how common it is but it doesn't feel very common where I am.

These fathers had experienced expectations that mothers should take priority in childcare and felt a dissonance between these widely held assumptions and their own, relatively untypical, circumstances:

People make a whole set of assumptions … I'll give you a simple example … when I go away for four weeks, it's basically expected that Carol [wife] will do just fine. When *she* goes away for two or three weeks I get patted on the back, 'can we help with anything?' … they are slightly concerned and amazed that I'm not falling apart. And they [friends and colleagues] don't make those assumptions about her, or any other women – they can manage … even modern fathers are expected to have a harder time of it.

(Ken)

This view suggests that expectations about what is appropriate for mothers and fathers are based on observations and extrapolations from current patterns; what is common to the majority is assumed to be normal and differences in mothering and fathering behaviour are assumed to be innate.

Negotiating attitudes and behaviour

The relationship between attitudes and behaviour is complex. Himmelweit and Sigala (2004) have discussed the feedback effect between behaviour and identities; behaviour does not simply follow on from a set of beliefs, instead views are moderated in the light of circumstances and actions. This process is also evident within these accounts. As a one-off interview the comments could only reflect the interviewees' opinions on mothering and fathering at a particular moment. Yet, there were insights into how opinions about differences in parenting roles between men and women may be adjusted over time to correspond with the performance of parenting; to support a coherent worldview in the face of changing circumstances. Phil has moved from believing that there are no really significant differences between fathers and mothers to a situation where he thinks there is something that sets them apart from each other. Intellectually, he seems to want to adhere to a doctrine of similarity which he associates with equality, but his first hand experience of parenting has challenged this.

I would like to say, if you had asked me ten years ago I would have said there is absolutely no difference whatsoever … but now I do genuinely feel there is some kind of difference, I don't know what it is, whether it is biological or whether it is societal, I really don't know [laughs].

The process of how expectations affect preferences, which in turn influence individual behaviour and how these, in circular fashion, are reinterpreted into expectations, is evident in the remarks of Euan. He begins by saying that it is the difference in work schedules that has affected the way in which he and his partner parent, since he has a job which means he works away from home for significant periods while his partner works from home on a part-time basis.

> The advantage with Susanne's [partner's] work is that it is part-time and can be scheduled around other things, commitments with the kids, my work and such, and she has a certain amount of control over that … I have much less control over mine, I have to be more at the beck and call of my employers when they need me.

The differences between fathering and mothering within his household have developed, to a certain extent, from his particular employment circumstances as a self-employed cameraman who spends periods of time away on location, and his explanation foregrounds his obligations to paid work. It is interesting, though, how Euan characterises their respective employment positions. Susanne, who is also self-employed, is depicted as having a flexible job while Euan is portrayed as at the whim of his clients. Despite noting elsewhere that his self-employed status does have considerable flexibility – he chooses whether to accept or turn down work and in the periods when he is not on location he works from home and has authority over the scheduling of his tasks – overall Euan emphasises his lack of control, in contrast to that of his partner.

Euan does acknowledge that it is not simply particular attributes belonging to their respective jobs which have affected their decision-making. First, there is his very strong commitment to work, which he expresses in terms of a vocation:

> I can't be who I am without my work, that is fundamental … I have chosen to do this work, in a way I would also say that it has chosen me, therefore I am defined by it.

Meanwhile, the decision to have children is framed as being driven by his partner,

> I guess I was persuaded by my partner that we, she, should do these things [have children].

Combined with a preference that children should be mainly cared for by their parents rather than paid childminders, his partner's decision to spend more time at home can be constructed as the only viable option to achieve these priorities.

> We probably made a self-conscious decision when the kids were born that Susanne [partner] wanted to spend more time with them as a mother, in being part of their upbringing, rather than go down the road of hiring a nanny and only seeing them at bedtime.

The option of Euan taking on a significant portion of the childcare is not mentioned – the options lie either with the mother or a nanny; following the discourse that a mother providing one-to-one care in the home is the best option and, if not available, should be mimicked in paid forms (Vincent and Ball 2006).

An association might have been anticipated such that those espousing a gender neutral position – who considered mothering and fathering as interchangeable – might also behave in this way, taking an equal part in childcare and avoiding the division of tasks along stereotypical lines. Meanwhile men who asserted strongly differentiated roles for mothers and fathers could be expected to practise this themselves. The fathers who strongly denied the existence of intrinsic parenting differences between men and women did tend to say they took on a considerable portion of childcare and all had partners who worked roughly equivalent hours to them. These men described gendered parenting roles as socially imposed and constraining, as they had the experience of facing social assumptions about men's and women's responsibilities that did not resonate with their own organisation of family tasks. For fathers such as Raj, who through separation from his partner had taken on half the childcare and the full range of caring activities, an alteration in responsibilities may have been influential in his construction of fatherhood and motherhood as equivalent to each other. However, there was not a reciprocal relationship for men who viewed mothering and fathering as in some way distinct.

Among both the majority who were uncertain how to attribute the influence of gender and those confident about a division between the social roles of motherhood and fatherhood, a range of levels of involvement in childcare were found, and while some of the partners of these men worked on a full-time basis, others were part-time and a few did not have paid work.[3] Even among those who saw biological factors as suggesting a strong orientation towards a gendered division of labour, individuals and couples were spoken of as being able to opt for the parenting roles they preferred in the free market of parenthood. Of course, they may have chosen to express their position in this way in order to avoid making the claim that their own decision was in some way superior. Alternatively, as they were not personally confronting social expectations, they may have been blissfully unaware of limitations that others experience. In general, for these fathers, the pre-eminence of mothers over fathers grew out of a shallow sense of biological difference, reinforced by daily practices and couched in terms of choice.

It is perhaps initially surprising that there was little consistent pattern between attitudes to gender differences in parenting, the interviewees' opinions on good fatherhood and their own fathering behaviour. Despite a predominantly coherent view of what constitutes good fatherhood, the men were engaged in various levels and kinds of parenting activities. However, the key to understanding the level of variation is recognising that while strong views about motherhood may correspond to a set of behavioural expectations, contemporary fatherhood does not equate to childcare tasks in the same way.

Conclusion: mothers and fathers

Some recent scholarship on fatherhood has focused attention on the benefits for child development of the presence and involvement of fathers (measured by, for example, educational attainment, language development and psychological well-being) (e.g. Flouri 2005; Lewis and Lamb 2003; Pleck and Masciadrelli 2004). The results of such academic research have been taken up in the political sphere where the importance of fathers is frequently emphasised as a necessary complement to motherhood. Introducing a review of the effect of fathers' involvement, entitled 'What Good Are Dads?' (Lewis and Warin 2001), the sponsors of the research, Fathers Direct (a UK government sponsored, national information centre on fatherhood) comment on their website, www.fathersdirect.com, that 'father involvement can be vital to children, improving educational achievement, social skills and cutting criminality'. Similarly:

> An involved father figure – preferably the child's natural father because they are more likely to provide continuity and to take real pride in the job of parenting – can do much to influence his children's behaviour.
> (Matthew Stannard, *Families Need Fathers* 29 April 2002)

The significance of fathers is repeatedly mentioned in public debates over wide-ranging issues, from gun crime to shared residency orders. As such, a case for the *unique* contribution of fathers to family life is highly visible in current discussions. Having men and women perform distinct parental roles, however they are conceptualised, makes it easier to assert fathers' particular importance for children.

Yet, attempting to separate out a specific sphere that is exclusively the domain of fathers seems difficult on the evidence available from the interviews. Only two fathers adhered to a straightforward delineation of parental roles and used the kind of terminology for fatherhood that was notably absent from other accounts. Bill said 'I have always been the breadwinner' and:

> I've a pretty conservative outlook on life … father [is] the head of the family…the mothering role is well, you know, the traditional mother … The mother is really the point of contact with the child.

Bill's quotation sees women and men making different but equally important parental contributions; mothers providing nurturing, time and daily care, while men provide discipline, financial support and play. However, almost all of the fathers interviewed rejected this 'traditional' version of male involvement and did not replace it with a new version that retained a unique role for fathers. The rejection of a 'different, but equal' ideology, with separate spheres of influence, negates the exclusivity of the fathers' role. When combined with evidence both that involved parents of whatever sex can provide a secure basis for successful child development (Tasker and Golombok 1997), and that the absence of a parent may not, in itself, be an important feature of separation for children's development (compared to the financial benefits of being in a dual parent household) (Rodgers and Pryor 1998), a substantial degree of merging between the roles of father and mother presents a strong challenge to the position that it is fathers per se who are a significant ingredient in children's lives.

The comments in this chapter indicate that mothers, however, do retain some areas of maternal expertise and often a higher status than fathers as care givers, so that a gender neutral parenting where mother and father are truly equivalent is not entirely plausible. Cowdery and Knudson-Martin (2005) posit that a belief in mothers as uniquely connected with their children is important for explaining the ongoing gendered division of parenting. The comments made by the fathers in the research discussed above to some extent parallel this belief in a maternal bond and its significance in the construction of separate parenting roles. Pre-given rationalities based around biological and psychological dimensions which gave mothers the principal parental role were emphasised in many of these accounts and tended to emerge in some form even when the fathers were reluctant to give them too much status: fathers pursuing an egalitarian approach to household work still felt they had to address the issue of biology. Fathers who cited biology as the explanatory factor behind differences in mothering and fathering normally considered it as something with fixed repercussions, leaving it outside the realm of choice and social influence. The influence of biology was exacerbated by caring practices which, in turn, ensured that mothers spent more time with their children than fathers did. The majority of these fathers tended to be in agreement with culturally dominant ideas of good motherhood that emphasise a maternal bond which then becomes translated into the 'intensive mothering' noted by Hays (1996).

While these fathers discussed factors that prescribed the role of mothers, they made no mention of equivalent biological forces that affected men. The compliment to the nurturing mother could be considered the breadwinning father but the interviewees did not refer to any biological urge or psychological necessity for fathers taking an instrumental, provisioning role. Nor did any interviewees refer to a nurturing role for fathers emerging specifically from the genetic tie with their children or from early interactions such as being present at the birth or feeding. Fathering is constructed as more variable than mothering and is not bound by involuntary biological impulses or practices contingent upon this biology. The perception of mothering as in some way pre-set is influential in delimiting male as well as female parenting, through restricting the latter and leaving the former relatively fluid. While mothers' care of children is 'expected and universal', as through expertise or obligation, they have little choice about opting out, that of fathers is 'optional and limited' (Daly 1996: 473).

These findings seem to leave fatherhood with nowhere to go. On the one hand, a traditional gendered division of parenting roles no longer exists, ending the distinct public sphere role of fathers. On the other hand, mothers have not been entirely displaced from the role of nurturing parent. In replacing previous forms of fatherhood with one based around relationship building, the dividing line between mothering and fathering becomes blurred, but mothers are still seen as the more important parent in this regard. This would seem to leave fathers as, at best, secondary parents. However, although fathers are not seen as 'complementary' to mothers by providing something which is gender specific, neither is it true that they are seen as reserve parents. Fathers add something else to the parenting of children through the individual relationship they have with their child. By emphasising the personal relationship between father and child, fathers' parenting is exclusive and, therefore, fathers remain the parental peers of mothers. The suggestion that fathers no longer have a clearly defined role is only true if the focus is on the *work* of childcare. This view of fatherhood and motherhood does not imply gender equality or a revolution in the domestic sphere. It remains true that 'becoming a mother markedly increases and cements the difference between the sexes' (Craig 2006c: 136) as 'Men who choose to be involved fathers do not necessarily have a motivation to become equal partners' (Björnberg 1995: 42).

It has been argued that as mothering is the parenting norm, this is the standard against which fathering is measured (Ambert 1994). However, the kind of fatherhood which these fathers seek to practise does *not* position fatherhood as second-class to motherhood. Neither does it necessarily involve thinking about fathers as excluded from their desire for a more equal position. Men, like George who commented that his children 'always turn to her [his wife] before they turn to me', tended to speak about the primacy of the mother's role without rancour. Examining fatherhood in relation to motherhood indicates how intimate fatherhood does not challenge the primacy of the mother–child bond. Contemporary fatherhood manages to avoid the two horns of the dilemma through constituting itself as being primarily about the negotiated, individual relationship between father and child. However, there are some structural requirements that exist as a basis for this contemporary version of good fatherhood, and the circumstances of men who are excluded from achieving it are the subject of Chapter 7.

6 Policy

Defining and accommodating fatherhood

Previous chapters have focused on the pertinent aspects of fathering identity and practices as expressed by individual fathers and available as measurable behaviour. This chapter explores a different resource for understanding the construction of fatherhood, namely recent UK legislation and policy that is relevant to, or directed at, fathers. The last two decades have seen major developments in family policy as a response to changes in the organisation of family life and the ongoing political desire to influence both the structure and operation of families. New statutes, together with new interpretations of existing legislation, have altered the classification of who should be considered a father. The question of *who* is a father is addressed in this chapter through a consideration of the regulations put in place to establish fatherhood where children are conceived using reproductive technologies and an examination of some recent high profile court cases which have clarified how fatherhood should be defined. Meanwhile tensions exist in the policy arena as to what factors should ground the rights and responsibilities of fatherhood. The overall direction in which family policy is heading has been assessed elsewhere (see for example Dey and Wasoff 2006; Lewis and Campbell 2006; Smart 1997) and analysis here centres on policies which are especially illustrative of the conceptualisation of good fathers and fathering. The objective is not to examine in detail the wording and legal interpretation of individual pieces of legislation, rather the focus is on initiatives in a broader sociological context, including their reception. The chapter addresses two sets of government policy which are crucial for understanding how contemporary fatherhood is interpreted and accommodated. The controversial Child Support Act is examined in order to address the question raised at the end of Chapter 2, that is, whether fathers are primarily economic providers in the eyes of the state. The second set of initiatives discussed here are collectively referred to as 'family-friendly policies'; examining their introduction and take-up allows for an assessment of the extent to which fathers have been encouraged to balance work and family, and how men have responded to these measures.

Who is a father?

In terms of defining who is a father the legal position is complicated as biology, social relationships, the intention to create a child, and marital status to the child's mother are all relevant, depending on the issue at stake. The criteria vary depending on whether the concern is to allocate child support, to determine contact orders or to establish parental responsibility. Since the biological and the social (in its various forms) do not always coincide in simple fashion, the result is necessarily a continuing process of debate and clarification. The ongoing development of reproductive technologies has been one catalyst for legislative debates. For example, the regulations laid down by the Human Fertilisation and Embryology Authority (HFEA) define a man as the father of a child born using IVF in a complex way. If he is married to the mother he is the father of the child unless he did not consent to artificial insemination. If he is not married he is considered the father if he underwent treatment together with the prospective mother (see Sheldon 2005b). Therefore marital status and the intention to father a child are both given a role in the definition. A high profile case documented in the UK press in recent years brought this debate to public attention. It concerned the situation of Natallie Evans who become infertile due to cancer treatment. Prior to her diagnosis she had been in a relationship and together the couple had fertilised eggs stored for future use. Now recovered, Ms Evans wanted to have these embryos implanted in order to have a child, but in the meantime had split up with her partner, Mr Johnston, who did not want the implantation to go ahead. After taking the case all the way to the European Court of Human Rights in April 2006 and then to the Grand Chamber in the spring of 2007, the decision went in favour of Howard Johnston on the basis that consent was required from both parties at each stage of treatment. However, as Mr Johnston and Ms Evans were not married, and Mr Johnston clearly disputed rather than consented to treatment (at least at some stage), whether he would have been considered the legal father under UK law if Ms Evans had been granted leave to use the embryos and a child had been born as the result is contestable. Ms Evans made clear that she was not asking for financial or other support and there are precedents in which biology is not used as the criteria for legal parenthood (see Sheldon 2004 on this case) but Mr Johnston's lawyer did make reference to the ongoing responsibilities which he would be obliged to fulfil. Interestingly, the comments of the protagonists and media representations framed the case in terms of Natallie Evans' right to have a biological child – 'This is my only chance to have children' (*The Daily Telegraph* 15/9/2002), 'All I was fighting for was my right to become a mother' (*The Daily Telegraph* 11/4/2007) – versus Howard Johnston's right not to have one – as he stated after the final court ruling 'I want to choose who with and when I start a family' (*The Daily Telegraph* 11/4/2007). Howard Johnston's description of the good father he would want to be draws on normative ideas of choice and involvement in the upbringing of a child (Carsten 2007), but it also illustrates how these commonplace ideas of fatherhood rest on the premise and taken-for-granted significance of the biological.

An earlier court case indicates how the significance of biological fatherhood holds even when the father in question was not alive when conception took place. The case of Diane Blood concerned a widow who won her court case to be allowed to use the sperm of her dead husband in IVF treatment. Although she was initially refused the right to use the sperm, as it had been removed without her husband's explicit written agreement when he was in a coma, this decision was later overturned and she was allowed to have the procedure outside the UK. A few years later she returned to court in order to have her husband's name on the birth certificates of her two sons (*BBC* 28/2/2003). For the purpose of this discussion what was interesting was the way in which her argument was centred on her 'right' to have a child that was genetically related to her late husband. While the children born to her would have a father who was biologically known to them but otherwise absent (Carsten 2007), her situation received almost universal sympathetic media attention.

The 'biological' has become more complex in relation to motherhood, with genetic and gestational mothers both having a claim on the term biological parent. In the UK the gestational mother is legally the mother of the child, leading to problems with managing surrogacy. Meanwhile the advent of DNA testing has simplified knowledge of genetic fatherhood. In the UK, until 2003, the legal status of unmarried fathers was uncertain as men's parental responsibility was defined solely through their relationship to the mother of the child; *pater is est quem nuptiae demonstrant*. The rule which defined that a man married to the mother of a child was automatically considered the father of that child was a way of defining familial relations long before paternity could be established as biological fact. The continuation of this law into the contemporary period, however, meant that whereas a married father gained 'parental responsibility' – this includes the right to be consulted and make decisions over issues such as education and medical treatment as well as the responsibility to provide care – through the fact of his marriage, unmarried fathers could only be granted this status by the mother, even if they could prove a genetic link. The change in law in 2003 ensured that as long as a father was named on a child's birth certificate he would now automatically have parental responsibility status (although the listing of parents' names on a birth certificate does mean that mothers who are not married to the father of their child still retain some degree of control).

The entrenchment of the significance of biological fatherhood is also evidenced in current debates about the status of sperm donors. Men who donate sperm have historically been ensured anonymity. In 2005 this guarantee was removed in the UK, so that any children born from donor sperm would have the right to request knowledge about their 'natural' father. Worries were expressed from some quarters that the change in law could reduce the number of individuals willing to come forward as donors,[1] even though under the new regulations donors do not have legal status as fathers, with concomitant rights and responsibilities for children. However, the argument which won the day was that children were entitled to know something about their biological parent, to know 'where they came from'. Indeed in both donor and adoption scenarios where the social parent or parents are not genetically related there is strong encouragement to provide children with information about their biological parentage.

Smart argues that the emphasis on the lifelong link of genetic parenthood has created a 'new marriage contract' which operates even after divorce. This arrangement ensures that after the end of a relationship, a 'clean break' is no longer possible if the couple have had children, since this would result in children losing contact with one of their biological parents (usually the father). She quotes from a case of contested contact where the right of a child to know the identity of, and potentially have a relationship with, his or her 'natural father' takes precedence over the argument for preserving an ongoing stable family unit. The end of marriage as the relationship of permanence has seen instead the rise of the 'ongoing parenting arrangement' (1997: 318) as 'what seems to matter is the question of biological parenthood' (1997: 320).

These examples indicate a certain complexity in definitions of fatherhood which link to wider debates about the meaning of 'family' and discussions of 'who counts' as kin. There is a tendency in the way in which individuals negotiate the label of father to revert to the biological as the template, though individuals and legislators must wrestle with reinterpreting the authority of a genetic link in ways that make social sense. Nomenclature is complicated as there is both a strong sense of 'real' (i.e. biological) connections and a recognition that practices (i.e. 'doing' family) also define relations. Ryan-Flood points out that, with respect to her study of lesbian parents' negotiations of fatherhood, the 'significance of biology to kinship was both destabilized and reinforced' (2005: 189). As earlier research suggested, family obligations are negotiated rather than being simply dependent on given kin relations (Finch and Mason 1993). The importance of biology is intertwined with the implicit heterosexism of fatherhood (Collier 1999), even though challenges to this have been made with the formal granting of parental status to gay couples through adoption and through donor arrangements (e.g. Stacey 2006). While other ways of being a father are not always viewed as inferior, and are clearly on the rise (see Chapter 1), there does appear to be a default definition that is in operation in legislation which assumes both that a genetic link exists between parent and child and that this biological link deserves to be nurtured, and is significant enough to often trump other forms of fatherhood. If the question 'who is a father' is relatively straightforward, the question of 'what is fathering?' is more complex in legal and policy terms.

Breadwinning and policy

The British welfare state has historically been based on a strong male breadwinner model (Lewis 1992). Its institutionalisation during the twentieth century was illustrated by trades unions' argument for a 'family wage' to ensure that working men were paid a sufficient wage to support their wife and children (accompanied by their acceptance of a lower rate of pay for women workers). Since the passing of Equal Pay Acts in the 1970s and 1980s the idea that the work women do is of less value than that of men has diminished. Public declarations as to the benefits, indeed the necessity, of employment for all citizens – 'Working parents can give their children a higher standard of living and provide role models for adult employment' (Government Consultation Document, *Supporting Families*, 1998) – has undermined the idea that men alone should be engaged in waged labour. Recognition of the economic costs of excluding women from the labour market has resulted in the move towards an 'individual adult worker' model, in theory if not necessarily in practice (Lewis 2001), with employment as *the* route to recognition as a full citizen (Levitas 1998). Therefore, as was argued in Chapter 2, financial provisioning is no longer the especial preserve of the father. Yet, the introduction of the UK Child Support Act in the 1990s, could be argued to reflect the continuing priority given to men's breadwinning role in the family, for it endorses the position that while men may not be responsible for supporting their spouse, fathers do have an obligation to look after their children financially. In 1991 (following similar measures in the US and Canada), the then Conservative government passed the Child Support Act which required non-resident fathers to provide economic support for their children.

The Child Support Act: reinforcing breadwinning?

Before the 1991 Child Support Act was passed, discretionary maintenance for the up-keep of children could be awarded by the courts to the resident parent; now the Act made it clear that all non-residents parents should pay if at all possible. While the arrangements were based on the apparently gender neutral concepts of parental earnings and residency, as fathers' incomes tend to exceed that of mothers, and most lone parents are women, it was men who, in the main, would be targeted for payments. A key concern for the government was the issue of absent or 'feckless fathers' – 'no father should be able to escape from his responsibility' (PM Margaret Thatcher, 17 January 1990) – one which echoed the equivalent furore over 'deadbeat dads' that existed in the US. Whilst ability to pay was taken into consideration in calculating the amount a non-resident parent should provide, the existence or non-existence of a relationship with the child was not. The Child Support Act was not a 'pay to play' mechanism whereby contributing financial resources resulted in an entitlement to access. As such the move to introduce the law was part of a 'fundamental moral view that biological parents should be responsible for children throughout their lives' (Bradshaw *et al.* 1999: 124) and this was expressed through accepting the financial burden of children. This perspective was not restricted to the government who preached the importance of 'family values', as there was cross-party support for the introduction of the measures. There seems therefore a clear case that the ideology of father as breadwinner continued to be widely accepted, at least as recently as the 1990s.

Yet this construction can be challenged. The legislation appears to have its origins in an ideology of parenthood, and especially fatherhood which emphasises financial provision, but it also has a wider political context which influenced its birth. While the rhetoric was of bringing feckless fathers into line, the political reality was a need to reduce the level of benefit payments being made to single mothers by finding someone other than the state to stump up the cash. Given the increasing numbers of lone mothers reliant on benefits combined with the low level of maintenance payments decreed by courts, moving the financial burden from the public pocket to the private individual was a priority in order to cut public expenditure. In the late 1980s and early 1990s there was a moral panic around lone mothers, especially teenage lone mothers, with the belief that 'irresponsible' young women were using pregnancy as a route to government 'handouts' and to secure council housing. This view was epitomised by Peter Lilley at the Conservative Party Conference in 1992, where he infamously stated, in a Gilbert and Sullivan pastiche, that the list of problematic benefit claimants included, 'young ladies who get pregnant just to jump the housing list'. Additionally, while in practice it was most frequently men who were pursued for payments, in theory non-resident mothers were also included in the remit, so the measures were primarily designed to solve a budgetary problem. It might even be suggested that if the breadwinning ideology required government measures to enforce it, then this in itself is an indication of its waning power.

While this legislation did have widespread political support initially, it also provoked strong resentment and challenges. By the late 1990s a review of UK child support stated that the Act had,

> become notorious; viewed as a failed policy initiative ... created in indecent haste ... and designed to cause far more problems than it solved
> (Ceridwen Roberts, Director of the Family Policy Studies Centre, in foreword to Barnes *et al.* 1998: 5)

Some of the anger about the legislation was directed at the level of mismanagement in the Child Support Agency (CSA), the body set up in 1993 to administer the new system. The CSA seems to have been a disaster from early on and now seems to be in its death throes, as assessments have highlighted problems in calculating the levels of payments, failure to produce compliance from many fathers who were not previously contributing, long waiting times for assessments, and high annual running costs. An evaluation in 2004 described it as 'a failing organisation which is currently in crisis' and, despite receiving more funds, problems have been ongoing. The government admitted to a backlog of 300,000 cases with £3 billion uncollected and only a minority of cases receiving maintenance (John Hutton 24 July 2006) and after review it will be replaced with a new agency, the Child Maintenance and Enforcement Commission (C-MEC). It appears, though, that a key issue in the reorganisation of the agency will not be the principle of paying support but encouraging more people to use direct maintenance payments between ex-partners that are less expensive and time-consuming to manage (Bell *et al.* 2006a; Bell *et al.* 2006b). Despite numerous problems with the execution of the Act and the running of the CSA, there were reasons for a hostile reception that lay with its content rather than implementation. Many single mothers were unhappy with the Act, as a father had to be named in order to receive benefits and informal arrangements were bureaucratised (meaning that if a woman refused to name someone her welfare support could be cut). However, the Child Support Act provoked especial criticism from fathers. If being a father was solely, or even predominantly, about financial providing then this legislation should surely have proven unproblematic since it is precisely these terms in which fathering is being defined, yet complaints were many and vociferous.

Some men resented the decision to include a retrospective element to the Act, which meant that individuals who had negotiated a divorce on the basis that any settlement reached at that time was a once and for all payment – a 'clean break' in popular parlance – could still be pursued for claims. A further complaint was about how levels of support were calculated. This was especially prominent in cases where both the father and mother had repartnered. Fathers resented the money paid out to their ex-partner citing the financial responsibilities they had to their new family. In cases where their ex-partner had a new husband or partner this was exacerbated by feelings of unfairness; the case was made that 'she' would be benefiting from two sources of income. These could be thought of as challenging the way in which payments were assessed rather than the notion of financial provision per se. Yet, comments also indicate that breadwinning is subject to conditions rather than accepted automatically. Financial support from fathers is dependent on advantageous personal circumstances (when fathers can afford it), is balanced against other priorities (supporting a child living with a previous partner child versus providing for a current household), and takes into account other financial factors (ex-partner's income or potential income) which allow it to be seen as manageable and fair. As one father in Bradshaw *et al.*'s study said,

> I mean to be honest I felt once she had remarried and they were both working and I was out of work I thought hang on a minute, why should I have that uh responsibility for [daughter's] you know basic needs when she [mother] has chosen to take – she remarried, they have got two loads of savings – why am I still having to pay so much?
>
> (1999: 197)

Fathers also often protested that they had no control over how the money they were being asked to provide would be spent; that in effect it went to the mother rather than directly to children:

> you don't see any – there is no feeling at all – or there is nothing there to say that you contributed towards paying for that.
>
> (Quoted in Bradshaw *et al.* 1999: 216)

Again the issue could be considered one of how money was transferred to and used for the children it was supposed to be benefiting; who gets to control the spending of the money. Linked to this, fathers often describe how they wanted to be able to buy gifts for children directly rather than take on the role of invisible benefactor. This is therefore not just about providing financially, with the personal knowledge that you are doing so; it refers to the need for some kind of reciprocal acknowledgement. Fathers want their children to know that they are providing for them, and handing over money personally to them or giving presents provides this visibility. This would seem to suggest that there is a dimension to breadwinning which is not about, or nor only about, fulfilling the idea of good fatherhood through ensuring that children have material goods, but that is a symbolic part of a broader sense of 'caring for'.

However, the key concern voiced by fathers was that men who were not entitled to see their children, or had only very limited access to them, were still expected to pay a financial contribution. The argument was that, in effect, fathers were not 'getting anything' for their money. Payment suggests that some goods should be received in return, in this case in the form of parent–child contact time, or that if fathers were doing their bit by contributing financially, then it was unfair if mothers restricted access and retained complete parental control. This interpretation was especially prevalent in comments expressed by irate fathers and the fathers' rights groups that sprang up to represent them – 'It's wishful thinking for policy makers to imagine that child support and contact are unrelated' (John Baker, Chair of *Families Need Fathers*, 9 February 2006).

This might seem a relatively straightforward equation; contributing money is one form of involvement and as such should be recognised, with associated parental rights. However, it does not get to the heart of the issue. What was being contested was not payment in itself but about providing financially without the context of a broader father–child relationship. For many fathers who had enduring relationships with their children this financial enforcement was felt as harsh, with their value as a parent reduced to only one dimension. For fathers who had no contact the idea of monetary contributions in a relationship vacuum felt antithetical. Arguments can be made about the importance of ongoing responsibility towards the product of any sexual liaison, but this legislation disaggregated a monetary contribution from an intimate relationship. The formulation dismisses fathers solely as breadwinners, not involved fathers who contribute financially as part of an overall package. It was this apparent separation of money from care that provoked outrage from many men, with banners in protests at the CSA reading 'Dad Tax: I am Innocent' (Westwood 1996). Interestingly, in Norway, a recent change in the calculation of child support includes a deduction in the amount non-resident parents pay related to higher levels of contact time (Kitterød and Lyngstad 2007), indicating that the argument has not been restricted to the UK.

The Child Support Act raised great consternation among fathers and mothers for a number of reasons and debate over this law can be seen as indicative of current contestation around the breadwinner role. While making monetary contributions remains an important component of responsible parenting it is not only the responsibility of fathers, and the requirement emerges from an engaged caring role rather than being an inherent constituent of good fatherhood. To return to Zelizer (2005), within family groups the transfer of money needs to be constructed as a gift. As a gift, it is representative of a broader relationship that cannot be defined purely in monetary terms. So the Child Support Act enforced breadwinning model jarred with men's ideas of good fatherhood and their rebuttal of the notion that breadwinning is seen as *the* fathering role. Hobson and Morgan comment that in social policy discourse 'the question of who pays for the kids is now paired with who cares for the kids' (2002: 2); it was the separation of these by the Child Support Act that provoked anger.

Family-friendly policies

The 'being there to care' criterion of good fatherhood, absent from the CSA, is present in other policy discourses around family life. Before 1997 the UK had no explicit commitment to work–family balance policies (Lewis and Campbell 2007), yet their introduction may be a lasting legacy of New Labour. Within documents and speeches, family-friendly measures have been promoted both as good for the family and good for the economy. Two themes are therefore evident in government sources that discuss the rationale behind the introduction and extension of family policy measures. First, children need the involvement of both their parents and so fathers (as well as mothers) are entitled to time for parenting. Second, citizenship is anchored in employment, so mothers (as well as fathers) are expected to be engaged in paid work. For parents, emotional responsibility is required *along with* financial responsibility:

> Effective families – families which are good for children – also require a new sense of emotional as well as financial responsibility in men. Children need time as well as money from their parents.
>
> (Blackstone *et al.*[2] 1992: 11)

> Parents, both men and women, need time with their children and time to create a supportive home in which their children can thrive.
>
> (Government Consultation Document *Fairness at Work*, 1998: 31)

> Employment is not just the foundation of affordable welfare, it is the best …
> pro-family policy yet invented.
>
> (Labour Party Election Manifesto 2001: 24,
> cited in Lewis and Campbell 2007)

Reviewing the impacts of developments in legal provisions for new fathers, a paper from the Department of Trade and Industry on paternity leave again reflects on the two concerns to which they see new policies contributing: promoting greater levels of father involvement in care and encouraging women to return to the labour market:

> These rights promote the involvement of fathers in the care of their young children … The introduction of improved paternity rights and benefits therefore reinforces strategies promoting labour-market participation among mothers.
>
> (Smeaton and Marsh 2006: 76)

It is emphasised that children require time, while reinforcing the accepted knowledge that they also require money (and hence parents who earn). The time demands of parenthood are considered to be in potential competition with the demands on time from the world of paid work, but there is no suggestion that this should lead parents to choose to devote their time to one area or the other. Instead, work and family must be made complementary and so the aim of government is to make responsibilities at home and work easier to reconcile.

> The White Paper sets out policies that will enhance family life while making it easier for both men and women who work to avoid conflicts between their responsibilities at home and at work.
> (Margaret Beckett MP, then Secretary of State for Trade and Industry publishing *Fairness at Work*, 21 May 1998)

It might be argued that the gender neutral term 'parent' or references to mothers and fathers is more a gentle acknowledgement of male parents than an explicit effort to engage with fathers' needs and encourage greater involvement in childcare, since in practice work–life balance measures are often directed at and taken up by mothers. Yet recent statements seem to suggest more strongly that a concern with fathers is at the heart of the agenda: 'It will enable employed fathers to have a greater involvement in raising their child in the first year of the child's life' (DTI 2007: 10), and at the EU level it has also been noted that fathers' use of leave has received considerable attention in recent years (Deven and Moss 2002).

Fathers' leave taking in the UK

There are a number of specific forms of leave and other policies which are designed to accommodate work–family balance (or at least are promoted with this aim). These are: the gender specific maternity and paternity leave; parental leave; leave to care for sick children; family tax credits; access to flexibility over hours of work; and childcare support. Of course, a whole range of other policies also impact on individuals' decisions about employment and childcare, for example minimum wages that push up earnings among the lowest paid, but this chapter focuses attention on the main forms of leave taken by and directed at fathers – paternity and parental leave – as well as the issue of employment flexibility.

The UK has in place a system which allows for maternity leave of up to 52 weeks (with a paid component followed by a number of months' unpaid leave), paid paternity leave of two weeks, and unpaid parental leave of up to 13 weeks in total with a maximum of 4 weeks to be taken in any one year, available until a child reaches school age. The introduction of paid paternity leave is recent, since 2003, and parental leave is also relatively new, established in 1999 in order to comply with an EU Directive. This is generous compared to the US where there is no legal requirement to allow parents time away from work for childcare, and Australia which also has only unpaid leave provision. It is, however, less generous with respect to fathers than many other EU countries, not only Scandinavia (including Sweden which has led the way in leave arrangements) but also countries such as Belgium, France and Italy. The UK is unusual in other ways compared to its EU partners. Parental leave in the UK is restricted in how it can be used (unpaid and without the option to take the leave in a continuous block) (Deven and Moss 2002) and has received little publicity. The UK has gone down the gender specific maternity/paternity route rather than promoting the gender neutral parental leave option. In most other European countries, while a 'daddy quota' available only to men may exist, parental leave allows flexibility in dividing time between parents. The government has published a consultation document (DTI 2007) on a proposal which would move closer to the European model, allowing fathers to have an additional 26 weeks of leave if and when the mother returned to work, which will 'enable an equal division of paid leave if the parents so choose' (DTI 2007: 4). However, this proposal is in the early stages of discussion and, at the earliest, would not come into force until 2009.

Paternity leave

Paternity leave allows fathers to be present at the birth of a child and at home for a period immediately afterwards. It can be paid or unpaid but usually refers to a relatively short amount of time lasting from a couple of days to a few weeks. The British allowance is relatively meagre compared to most other West European countries, granting two weeks of paid leave, paid at the level of maternity pay (currently £112.50 a week) although its introduction did mark a significant change in policy. Some employers go beyond the legal obligation and grant longer periods of leave and/or higher levels of remuneration, especially within the public sector.

Figures for the years immediately after the introduction in 2003 disclose high numbers of fathers taking paternity leave (among fathers who are co-resident with the mother of their child). Thompson *et al.* (2005) suggest a figure of 94 per cent and Smeaton and Marsh (2006) found that 93 per cent of employees and 83 per cent of self-employed men took advantage of the new entitlement. The vast majority of men in the UK actually took some time off after the birth of a child even before paid paternity leave was introduced (Smeaton and Marsh 2006); Forth *et al.* (1996) suggest a figure of 93 per cent during earlier 1990s. Famously in 2000, when the Prime Minister Tony Blair became a father for the fourth time, there was public debate as to whether he would follow the Finnish Prime Minister in taking time off and he duly did take two weeks of unpaid leave.[3] Even in the United States, where there is no legal requirement on employers to allow leave, research suggests that some new fathers may still take a few days away from work (Pleck 1993; Seward *et al.* 2006). One way of managing this is to make use of paternity leave provided by employers on a voluntary basis – two-thirds of fathers claimed to be eligible for such schemes before the statutory right was introduced in the UK (Smeaton and Marsh 2006). Most others make use of annual holidays with smaller numbers taking time off in lieu, making informal agreements with their managers or even using sick leave. Indeed these alternative forms of managing leave do not disappear even when a legal entitlement is available (Thompson *et al.* 2005). (As noted above, since 1999 fathers have also been entitled to unpaid parental leave, but this has had a very low take-up rate.) It seems that 'being around' at the time of birth, not just for the birth itself, has become commonplace so that not taking leave is exceptional and requires an explanation. In fact, the figures for men who spend time away from work during this early period may be even higher considering that some fathers will not require leave, for example a school teacher whose child is born during the summer holiday period.

It was therefore not surprising to find that most interviewees in the *Men, Work and Family Life* study (all of whom had children before the right to paternity leave had been introduced) had taken some time off. The majority placed great significance on the initial period and viewed the days and weeks immediately after a child's birth as an important time to be at home. They tended to have taken one or two weeks, mainly as annual leave.

> I think that those first days are really important, for everyone, and I think it would be really sad to miss out on that time.
>
> (Gareth)

> It would have to be a pretty big thing not to take time off when children came.
>
> (George)

> For the first one I took three weeks, for the second one I took a week I think … They were a very rich and positive time.
>
> (William)

In welcoming time at home, fathers saw leave as allowing for an emotional space. Time with their child was certainly seen as allowing the process of developing a relationship with their son or daughter to begin, but was perhaps as much about negotiating their own emotions around the new identity of 'father'.

> It is that emotional stuff that paternity leave would have given me, would give all fathers.
>
> (Simon)

> Immediately there was like this bonding thing going on … You know your kids are only, you have only got that one chance really, and you want to spend some time with them and develop a bond with them I think.
>
> (Raj)

The majority welcomed paternity leave but showed little interest in an extension of this right. It was perhaps surprising, given these men's commitment to involved fatherhood, that there was relatively little sense of unfairness over current legislation and any demand for longer paternity leave or paid parental leave. The idea of having planned periods at home in order to be with children, except for around the period of the birth, did not really register as an advantage. Instead it seemed that a relatively short period of time was sufficient to orient themselves to their new or additional fathering role, acknowledge its emotional impact and establish a bond. Of course this was not the only viewpoint presented. For some of these fathers there was a sense that having a longer period of time at home in the early stages would have been preferable:

> I think to go back after five days is quite hard actually … to do five days [full-time work] was quite a lot really, it was a bit too much when you have just got a new baby and all that to deal with.
>
> (Raj)

> I was probably still in a bit of a headspin when I came back to work, I don't think two weeks is enough after the birth of a child really to get yourself back into a normal state.
>
> (Phil)

These men were mainly recounting the arrival of a first child, when the overwhelming nature of the change meant that returning to the obligations of everyday working life had been a difficult experience. It was the act of establishing a new identity and a relationship with their child that mattered most to fathers; the difference was the length of time men felt they needed to achieve it. In other words, this leave was, in keeping with their wider understanding of fatherhood, about a focus on the father and child and was not for establishing equal caring status with the mother. As discussed in the previous chapter, the importance of mothers, especially in the early stages, tended to take precedence over fathers. A small number of other fathers were more dismissive of the need for paternity leave; not only had they tended to take a short period off work themselves but they did not really see what this period achieved, or rather, when pushed they conceded that the mother might need some assistance early on, but they did not see time as necessary for the father–child relationship. It was not sought by fathers because it was not seen as needed by babies.

ED: Did you have time off work when your children were born?
MARCUS: I really can't remember, probably not. I may have taken a couple of hours off.
…
ED: Would you have liked to have had some time off?
MARCUS: I'm not sure really.
…
ED: On the questionnaire you suggested that men should get one week paternity leave.
MARCUS: Maybe men should get a week off but I am not sure … I am not so sure if I would want to take a week off, I'm not sure how beneficial that would be.

Unpaid leave

> That's generous, I don't think. Thirteen weeks unpaid leave, that's a real chocolate fireguard ... the useful thing would be paid leave.
>
> (Jim)

The reason put forward for reluctance among fathers to take paternity or parental leave is often financial. The main reason that fathers give for not taking their full *paternity* entitlement is money – though it should be noted that the majority of men who take paternity leave (70 per cent) are paid in full for the entire period (Smeaton and Marsh 2006). There is obviously logic in this, since statutory paternity pay of £106 will be a major drop in income for many fathers, and this will be especially noticeable at a time when mothers are on maternity leave. Take-up rates of *parental* leave have been extremely low since its introduction, a meagre 3 per cent of men in the first year (Government Consultation Document, *Work and Parents*, 2000) and 8 per cent in 2005 (Smeaton and Marsh 2006); and these figures refer to men who take *any* portion of parental leave not necessarily their entire quota. This is usually explained as a rational and entirely predictable response to the fact that it is unpaid – as noted by Deven and Moss (2002), the UK is unique within the EU in not paying any portion of this leave (the other reason that tends to get mentioned is that fathers are unaware of the existence of parental leave). The Commons Select Committee on Social Security concluded in its report on the issue of remuneration for parental leave that, 'it is clear to us that if parental leave is unpaid take-up among fathers will be particularly low' (1999).[4] The Income Data Services commented in similar fashion that 'While parental leave is unpaid ... take-up by parents is likely to remain limited' (2000: 1). The overall assessment has been that men are willing to take leave when finances allow but that parental leave, and to a certain extent paternity leave, is simply an unaffordable option for British fathers.

Achieving a successful work–life balance often seems to centre on achieving an equilibrium between finances and time, as everyone would like more of both. If the aim is a greater contribution to childcare in the early period, then that is likely to be partnered with some reduction in income – as is the case for most women who take maternity leave. At the same time, for many people living without their current level of income would be difficult to sustain, even for a relatively short period of time. For those least well off, the consideration may be simply one of surviving whilst for those with higher incomes, continuing to pay mortgages and maintain living standards may be more possible but still feel like a difficult option. It is intriguing to note, however, that when the incomes of fathers who claimed not to be able to afford to take all their leave were compared, there was no significant difference between income groups (Smeaton and Marsh 2006). There was also no association between the use of (unpaid) parental leave and income. Although larger numbers of men are encouraged to take leave when it is paid, evidence from other countries is that the majority of men still fail to take substantial amounts of time. This evidence suggests that other factors are also at play in men's decision making. On its own the issue of payment cannot explain the reasons for men's ambivalence in accepting parental leave and this is sometimes recognised: 'paying parental leave does not in itself guarantee take up amongst fathers' (New Ways to Work 1999). The impression from my interviews with relatively advantaged fathers was that money was generally not a central feature of how fathers talked about leave or how they justified their views on it. The concept of parental leave was rejected by a few fathers because it was unpaid, but most would not have considered taking it up in any case. The qualified welcome for the legislation was often phrased in general terms rather than more personalised replies: the idea of leave for parents was seen as a 'good thing' in a political sense but had little resonance with their own lives.

> It sounds very civilised. These are the things that would be in an ideal world ... these would be the moves that will progress society.
>
> (Euan)

An extended period of parental leave was not viewed as something especially desirable because it was simply unnecessary for their construction of fathering: a financial sacrifice was therefore not required rather than impossible.

Workplace flexibility

> For decades now women have been calling for a better work-life balance to help them be the productive workers and good mothers that they want to be. But men have been excluded from this process. Now fathers too are calling for a fairer deal.
>
> (Margaret Hodge, then Minister for Employment and Equal Opportunities, November 2000)

As Margaret Hodge's quote suggests, fathers' desire to be more involved in childcare was anticipated as providing a substantial group of male workers who would support reductions and alterations in the organisation of their working time. Yet, this does not seem to be substantiated by available empirical evidence. Within the UK the part-time employment route has developed as a common option for mothers who want to maintain a presence in the labour market (Crompton 2006) but fathers have neither followed suit, nor do they appear eager to do so: fathers are not becoming more like mothers in this regard. My analysis of men's preferences over hours of work using the BHPS indicated that while around a quarter of men wanted to work fewer hours, less than 1 per cent wanted to increase their hours and the remainder wished to continue with their current hours of work. When factors associated with a desire for an increase or decrease in hours were examined further, neither fatherhood status nor having become a father in the past year were significant. Similarly, the interviews in the *Men, Work and Family Life* research produced little evidence of any preference for reducing hours of work and certainly no indication that fathers wanted to move to part-time employment.

Broadening the picture, in analysis of the BHPS (see Dermott 2006a) I found no indication that fathers were more likely than non-fathers to make use of flexible forms of working. However, narrow, formal measurements that are available in these large-scale surveys potentially fail to capture the extent of flexibility in work practices. There are likely to be substantial informal arrangements in place. These may be at their own discretion in the case of individuals in senior, relatively autonomous positions. Hugh, as a partner in a law firm, did not need to consult anyone else to take some time off – 'if I want to take an hour off to do something else I'll take an hour off to do something else'. In settings where some level of approval is required, semi-formal negotiations may take place. Rosemary Crompton quotes one employee, Charles,

> My immediate line manager is one of the ones without children, and he can be quite difficult ... But then his manager has two kids and she's more understanding ... so what we tend to do, we tend to bypass him and go straight to her!
>
> (2006: 107)

Additionally, the category of flexible employment is a broad one. It includes both employee controlled flexibility, such as flexitime, and forms of flexibility that are under the jurisdiction of the employer, such as shiftworking. The latter are for the benefit of employers rather than employees though they may still prompt creative ways of managing work and family. Finally, the formal versions of employee-led flexibility are available only to a small proportion of the population who tend to be in particular occupations and employment sectors, so that take-up rates are skewed by availability. For example, there are few policies to improve work-life balance in the male dominated construction industry (Dex and Smith 2002). One of my interviewees recounted his amazement at finding out that a fellow trainee on a football refereeing course, who was a train driver, would not be able to pursue the next qualification because it would involve taking a day off work, which he did not have the flexibility to schedule. Whether or not the situation of his friend is accurate, the level of surprise indicates how low level flexibility may be taken for granted among those that have access to it.

Flexibility has been claimed as 'key for working fathers' (Thompson 2005: x) but, despite some caveats about the way in which this concept is measured, it does not appear that fathers are queuing up to make use of what is currently on offer. In 2002, as part of a raft of measures designed to introduce more family-friendly working, the government introduced the right for parents with children under 6 or disabled children under 18 to request flexible working as part of the Employment Act.[5] The law is relatively weak in that an employer need only 'seriously consider' any request, nevertheless the shift should not be underestimated as it did introduce a new right. The main form of request has been for a reduction in working hours and, unsurprisingly, the number of requests by women has far exceeded those by men; only 10 per cent of eligible fathers have submitted a request. However, it is important to avoid thinking that a 'female model of balance' is the only way to combine work and family: other forms of flexibility may be preferred by fathers, such as those which are less visible and less amenable to current policy thinking. The vast majority of interview respondents in my study acknowledged that there were occasional points when competing demands were difficult to reconcile. Jim was one of the fathers who located the root cause of his problems in achieving a successful work–life balance in the rules of his employment which, even though they included formal flexitime, were still too rigid to accommodate all aspects of family life.

> Something we really must do is the 'meet the teacher' day, you know, when you go along for 10 to 15 minutes … we [wife and I] took a half day for that last year because we could only see the teacher between 2 and 4. Well, flexitime doesn't start until four so I had to take time off to go … there isn't the flexibility to say, 'yeah, pop off for an hour, work that time again, I know you'll do it'.

Using the words of another interviewee, tensions occur on the 'micro-level' rather than the 'macro-level'. When asked what he would like to change to ease any work–family conflict, Simon also responded with a relatively minor alteration to his work schedule. The flexibility to get into work slightly later two days a week would allow him to participate in a part of his children's lives that at the moment he has to miss.

> I would just like the flexibility to take them to school, occasionally. When I first started this job and didn't have much work on at the beginning I took [son] to school a couple of days and it was fabulous being in the playground with the other parents, it was lovely, just dropping him off. So I would like to be able, actually I would love to be able to start late, say if we started at ten o'clock some mornings, say a couple of mornings a week, so I could take them to school.

This wish makes perfect sense for the fatherhood that dominated in these men's accounts. Being able to have a direct sense of children's lives is important and being present at the school gate can provide an element of that. What is most interesting is that because this involvement is seen as achievable through actions which take up only small amounts of time, these fathers' comments were about tinkering at the margins of their work obligations. Interviewees did welcome some minor changes to employment practices but were not interested in a wholesale revision of their working lives, which would mean challenging a work culture based around full-time employment. Measures such as allowing some variation in the times at which people came in and left work, and a limited degree of homeworking were viewed as acceptable and perhaps desirable: these were often already used on a limited and informal basis. Concepts such as part-time working, job sharing and capping the number of hours individuals could work were both more controversial and less popular. They were viewed as unnecessary for their personal needs and seen as interfering in the smooth running of businesses and organisations. In other words, interviewees generally accepted the status quo;

flexibility to which they were already accustomed was appreciated but extending it much further was rejected.

What these respondents really welcomed was the possibility of leave which could help avoid occasional conflicts raised by the spontaneous demands of family life. The concept of parental leave did not always make sense to fathers and when asked to think about how it would work for them, responses tended to involve 'emergency' situations, such as a child's illness, instead of the regular care for which it is intended. These comments correspond with Smeaton and Marsh's (2006) results. On closer inspection of the survey results provided by the small number (8 per cent) of men who said that they did take parental leave, the majority did not use it for its designated purpose of spending a significant period of time in childcare (to 'enable parents in employment to look after their newborn child for a certain time' ILO Recommendation No. 165, quoted in Deven and Moss 2002: 241). When asked the main reason for using parental leave most responded that they took it for a short period of time, either because of a child's illness or because their partner was ill. Only a quarter said that it was an opportunity to spend time at home. This finding and the comments below suggest that emergency family leave may be the initiative that is really valued by fathers:

> That should be built into legislation, for emergencies … If your child is ill or something they [parents] should be able to take time off.
>
> (George)

> If a child is ill, you see, I think it would work.
>
> (Greg)

> One morning the telephone rings at half 8 when you're about to leave, the childminder says 'there's been an accident, I can't look after Matthew today', and there's nobody to look after him. Under those circumstances we can get leave … I thought that was quite a good scheme.
>
> (Jim)

What interested these fathers most was the idea of some flexibility to take time away from work for short periods, either for scheduled events such as the school play, or for occasions which could not be planned for in advance, such as a child's illness. This accommodation suggests a realisation that mothers will not, and perhaps should not, be automatically responsible for all childcare tasks, alongside the desire to be involved in activities which are important in a child's life. However, employment need only adapt to the family in unusual circumstances as normally it can exist in a straightforward fashion alongside the demands of children.

Conclusion: time and money

Lewis (2002) concludes that throughout the 1980s and 1990s in Britain, policy towards fathers was noteworthy for attempting to counter negative aspects of contemporary fatherhood, specifically a concern with absent fathers, rather than a positive, enabling approach to encourage greater involvement from men. She argues that the British response to changes in family life has been 'to reinforce men's traditional obligations to maintain' (2002: 148). This chapter has argued that although financial provisioning for children continues to be a concern (especially given relatively high rates of child poverty) this is not constructed as the role of fathers per se. The Child Support Act may have sought to re-impose breadwinning on non-resident fathers but it was strongly opposed when detached from other elements of a parenting relationship. Other policy initiatives such as tax breaks to encourage single mothers to re-enter the labour market also highlight that the role of earning money to provide for children is increasingly seen as the task of parents, not just fathers.

There is evidence that policies are increasingly oriented towards allowing men additional time with their children, even if most family-friendly policies continue to have women as their main target. Forms of flexible working, as currently devised, are recognised as mainly of use to mothers who combine labour market participation with most of the work of childcare. The idea of taking leave which is time delimited and for a specific child-related purpose – whether the birth of a child or an illness – fits with an ideal of good fatherhood that is based on a strong relationship between father and child, not a gender equality model of parenthood. This corresponds with an emergent picture of fathers in contemporary Britain who are keen to spend time at home with their family after the birth of a child, and so make use of paternity leave or its equivalent. It also fits with fathers who accept that tasks such as a child's illness should not necessarily fall on the mother and so are eager for measures such as emergency leave that formally allow them to do this, when informal procedures are not available. This version of new fatherhood can also explain men's reluctance to take up some other 'flexible' working options such as part-time employment, as these more radical alterations in employment are simply viewed as unnecessary.

7   Fragile fathers

The fatherhood which has been documented in previous chapters appears relatively unproblematic. This is not to suggest that men's parenthood is always experienced as easy but, for the interviewees in the *Men, Work and Family Life* study, present day-to-day difficulties do not present insurmountable problems in achieving 'good fatherhood'. Neither does quantitative analysis indicate significant tensions between men's preferences and practices. The picture thus far is therefore at odds with the idea of fathers as confused about contemporary fatherhood, which has men drowning in a myriad of possible parenting options. It also does not tally with the image of fathers as being stretched to the limits, with men pulled in opposite directions towards employment and childcare and failing to achieve a parenting ideal that is overambitious in its scope. Most significantly, it does not match the impression given by some commentators that fatherhood is facing pressures which have made it a less secure identity and who describe the 'ominous' 'decline of the father' (Popenoe 1996).

Neale (2004: 10) has defined two aspects to father–child relationships: 'mechanics', meaning level of contact, division of care and residency arrangements, and 'intrinsic', elements which are based on quality and relate to its emotional core and everyday conduct. While these are intertwined, the first is only a means to an end, in that it allows the personal relationship to flourish. The purpose of previous chapters has been to tease out various dimensions to the father–child relationship, focussing predominantly on its intrinsic nature. The concern in this chapter is with the structural requirements that underpin the successful enactment of contemporary fatherhood. In other words, this chapter discusses the plasticity of 'good fatherhood'; exploring whether fathering is now individualised to the extent that it is adaptable to all parenting situations, or if there are limitations to its pliability. To do this there is a focus on fathers who are considered to be, in some way, 'fragile', that is, fathers for whom temporal, financial, biological or emotional links with their children are either non-existent or under threat. Young fathers, step-fathers, gay fathers, non-resident fathers, divorced or separated fathers and incarcerated fathers can all potentially be included within this category for disparate reasons. Men who are unemployed or those with extremely long working hours might also be included, but the focus here is on fathers who in popular discussion are presumed to be in some way problematic.

Although there are a number of characteristics which potentially place men in the category of 'fragile father', the chapter concentrates on the situation of two groups that are of particular significance to current debates, non-resident fathers and gay fathers, since it is the demise of the nuclear family based on heterosexual marriage which has caused most consternation among social commentators (e.g. Blankenhorn 1995; Dennis and Erdos 1992; Popenoe 1996). The rise of so-called 'fatherless families' created by the impermanence of couple relationships, which means that relatively high numbers of men live apart from their children, has been characterised as an acute social problem. This concern is rooted in a belief that a 'traditional' family form operates best as the foundation block for society combined with a specific concern for children who are left without the influence of a male role model. The increased visibility of gay fathers provides another attack on the alleged bedrock of 'the family'. Not only do gay fathers challenge the conventional family model of two parents of opposite sexes but gay male parenthood is even more controversial than lesbian parenting because of a cultural nervousness around men and young children that is exacerbated by homosexuality (Weeks *et al.* 2001). This chapter will explore both the difficulties and possibilities faced by non-resident and gay fathers and use these two examples of fragile fatherhood to argue that while paternal intimacy is fluid there are also obstacles to its accomplishment. However, it is further suggested that these barriers are not insuperable as they depend on a set of assumptions about how contemporary fatherhood should be achieved that does not always hold true.

Non-resident fathers

Although over 80 per cent of fathers in the UK with dependent children do live with all of their own biological children (Clarke *et al.* 1998), this means that a significant minority, one in six, lives apart from some or all of his biological children (Burghes *et al.* 1997). It is, though, difficult to estimate accurately the number of non-resident fathers in the UK: official information about men who are fathers but do not live with their children is not regularly available (Matheson and Summerfield 2001). Most national surveys do not ask men if they have ever fathered a child because of problems with validity – men may not know – and while household surveys provide information about fathers who live with their children and those who live with children who are not biologically related to them, information about non-resident fathers is often omitted. Determining the reliability of men's knowledge about their children who are living elsewhere, through cross-checking between households, has not been a major priority. Interest in non-resident fathers has often originated from a child-centred perspective with calculations based on the number of children who do not live with their parents, rather than the number of parents who do not live with their children: it has been estimated that between a third and a half of all children will experience a period of not living with both parents during their childhood (Bradshaw *et al.* 1999). Non-resident fathers are also are hard to track through official databases because they are less likely to be the beneficiaries of state support than lone mothers and using lone mother households as an approximation underestimates the true figure of non-resident fathers as many lone mothers repartner and are removed from the category. Although not all lone mother households have a non-resident father elsewhere, there are overall more non-resident fathers than lone mother households (Bradshaw *et al.* 1999). Bradshaw *et al.* (1999) suggested that the total number of non-resident fathers could range somewhere between 2 and 5 million men; Hunt and Roberts (2004) estimate 2 million.

The percentage of fathers living with all their children is much lower in the US than the UK – it has been estimated that over half of American children will live apart from one of their parents (usually the father) (Kiernan 2004). Living with *some* biological children is, however, more common for American fathers, due to higher rates of divorce, repartnership and step-parenting (Clarke *et al.* 1998). There are also marked differences in rates of co-residence between fathers and children by ethnicity in the US (Clarke *et al.* 1998). Although non-resident parenthood has grown in the UK, its extensiveness in the US, along with its socio-demographic profile, goes some way to explain why there has been more academic and popular attention directed towards it than has been the case in the UK (e.g. the widespread debate on solving the 'problem' of fatherlessness). While there are clear differences between the UK and the US, the UK does have the highest rate of lone parenthood in Europe and has been considered more similar to the US, if less extreme, than its European neighbours (Clarke *et al.* 1998; Kiernan 2004).

The most common route for men to become non-resident fathers is through the break up of a household through divorce or separation, where the children remain living with their mother. Non-resident parents do include a very small, though possibly increasing number of non-resident mothers (Kielty 2005) but the overwhelming majority of 'lone parent' households are headed by women, meaning that 'non-resident parents' are nearly all men. Less attention is paid to those children born to parents who are not living together at the time of their birth and who therefore begin their life without the presence of a resident father – it has been estimated that in the UK this was the case for 15 per cent of children born in 2000, a higher figure than across most of the rest of Europe (Kiernan 2006).[1]

Involvement

Along with the problems in assessing the numbers of non-resident parents, there are also difficulties in securing an accurate picture of the level and type of involvement which non-resident fathers have with their children. There are some fathers who have no contact at all with their children and others who see their children on a daily basis: there are men who have an intimate knowledge of their children's lives and those whose involvement is based solely on financial support.

One broad generalisation is that the majority of non-resident fathers do have contact with their children. While between one in ten and one in three fathers have no contact at all with their children, a conservative estimate is that around half have frequent and regular contact. Bradshaw *et al.*'s (1999) study of over 600 non-resident fathers found relatively high levels of contact. Almost half of the fathers they questioned reported contact at least once a week and almost 70 per cent had contact at least once a month; 21 per cent of these fathers said that they had not seen their child within the last year. Burghes *et al.* (1997) also reported that 50 per cent of non-resident fathers see their children every week and 70 per cent reported some ongoing contact with children. One cohort study, which reported even higher levels of contact, found that some type was taking place for 82 per cent of non-resident fathers, with over half having contact on a monthly basis or more frequently (Dunn *et al.* 2004). Calderwood (2004) has suggested a bimodal pattern with men either tending to have no contact or frequent contact: 36 per cent of non-resident fathers had no contact at all but 49 per cent saw their child at least once a week (14 per cent every day). Although variable, these figures are roughly in line with results from Norway (57 per cent of non-resident fathers had seen their child in the last week and 77 per cent in the last month) (Skevik 2006). In contrast, in the US the majority of separated fathers have little or no contact with their children at all (Seltzer 1991).

The variations in the British figures can be explained partially by who is asked about contact: resident mothers tend to report lower levels of contact between children and non-resident fathers than do non-resident fathers. In a study for the Office for National Statistics (cited in Wasoff 2004), 77 per cent of non-resident parents said that they saw their children once a month, but only 60 per cent of resident parents said that the non-resident parent had this level of contact. Similarly, Bradshaw *et al.*'s (1999) study of 'absent' fathers which involved interviewing men found much higher levels of contact between men and their children than did a previous study of lone mothers (Bradshaw and Millar 1991). This may be due to a desire by mothers and fathers respectively to understate and overstate non-resident fathers' level of involvement. However, it may also reflect genuine differences in interpreting the term 'contact' with non-resident fathers perhaps more likely than resident parents to include forms of contact beyond face-to-face interaction. Many surveys do not distinguish between different kinds of contact, and those which do vary in their method, so this non-standardised approach may also contribute to differences in the figures. The ONS survey (Wasoff 2004) differentiated between face-to-face contact and contact defined more widely, to include, for example, phone calls; unsurprisingly, lower figures were produced when contact was restricted to face-to-face interaction. Also surveys may tend to capture formal arrangements rather than actual contact, and since the majority of separated couples do not have a court order regarding contact and either have informal arrangements or claim to have no agreement (Hunt and Roberts 2004), these formal assessments may be inadequate. Even when formal arrangements are in place, a non-resident parent can have additional, flexible contact (especially if the relationship between ex-partners is amicable), which is not captured in all surveys.

Given the wide variation in the extent of contact between non-resident fathers and their children, attempts have been made to determine what factors contribute to making contact either more or less likely. Lewis *et al.* (2002) quote two instances of non-resident fathers whose cohabiting relationships had ended and now had no contact with their children. In the first situation the father had moved with his new partner from the UK to Australia, while in the second, the father had been excluded from contact after a legal dispute over residence. This example illustrates that there is no single factor that can explain levels of contact between non-resident fathers and their children; nevertheless a number of factors appear influential. Fathers seem to be more likely to have contact with their non-resident children if they live alone or just with a partner, if they are in employment, if children are young, if there are low levels of conflict between ex-partners, if they live close to the residence of their child and if the separation was recent (Bradshaw *et al.* 1999; Wasoff 2004; Welsh *et al.* 2004). These factors also mean that oversampling of particular groups of fathers may affect results about levels of contact.

Involvement or non-involvement in the context of non-resident fathers usually refers to whether men have personal contact with their children. However, as Christiansen and Palkowitz (2001) have highlighted, involvement can also be defined to include financial support (see Chapter 2). Personal contact between a father and child and the provision of financial support often go together (Bradshaw *et al.* 1999; Kiernan 2006; Seltzer 1991) although whether there is a causal relationship is not clear. However, for some men with no contact, involvement may be restricted to paying child support; as one man phrased it 'my responsibility to him [son] now is purely a financial one' (Bradshaw *et al.* 1999: 193).

Difficulties of non-resident fathering

'Becoming non-resident creates particular problems for parenting' (Wilson *et al.* 2004: 3). It often seems taken-for-granted that non-resident fathers have a more difficult parenting task then those who cohabit with their children. Accounts are available which reveal the problems men face, to the degree that negotiating the relationship is so practically difficult to manage and emotionally draining that they may even give up maintaining a parenting relationship with their children (*Families Need Fathers* cited in Bradshaw *et al.* 1999). However, it is not assumed here that all non-resident fathers necessarily face difficulties or that some men will not, in fact, find parenting easier as a non-resident father than as part of a cohabiting couple. Instead, the focus is on fathers who do wish to remain involved on some level and the form that problems take if and when they do emerge.

A reading of research conducted with non-resident fathers indicates three main concerns that reflect uncertainty about their fathering. First, fathers speak about problems in their lack of a regular routine (Bradshaw *et al.* 1999; Simpson *et al.* 1995; Trinder *et al.* 2002); the absence of daily contact which provides them with information about the minutiae of everyday events and a sense of continuity. When fathers do have contact, often at weekends, time is spent in a whirl of joint activities, and with fathers attempting to catch up on what has gone on during the rest of the week. This creates a sense of discontinuity in men's parenting, and their lives in general (Bradshaw *et al.* 1999). Second, fathers often express the feeling that they have no control either over their own parenting, because it is often very clearly prescribed in a time delimited way, or over the parenting of their children in general, as mothers, with whom children spend more time, have a greater influence than they do (Smart 1999). For non-resident fathers, relationships with their ex-partners are important in determining the relationship they have with their child but interactions often involve men 'having to "perform" in a role imposed upon them' (Wilson *et al.* 2004: 3). Finally, when an ex-partner or wife has a new relationship, especially when it is a cohabiting one, fathers may reflect anxiety over the existence of a competing male role model (Smart and Neale 1999).

Carol Smart (1999) who has written extensively on post-divorce parenting, argues that a major reason why men experience difficulty in negotiating their new identity as post-separation parents, is that they no longer have mothers to act as facilitators to their parenting relationship. Drawing on the work of Kathryn Backett (1987), Smart draws attention to the way in which, prior to divorce, 'a father's relationship to his children may thrive simply because of his wife's mothering skills' (1999: 102) and therefore, when this support is removed, men's parenting requires radical transformation. Smart appears to suggest that two types of problems can emerge. The greater amount of responsibility that mothers, as resident parents, have over children translates into a certain degree of power *vis-à-vis* fathers. Mothers have day-to-day knowledge about when events occur (such as dentist appointments) and what practical activities need to happen so that everything runs smoothly (such as making sure that sports kit is washed on a particular day) and fathers resent this if it means that mothers remind them when and how things should be done. The other aspect is that mothers are no longer available to mediate the relationship between father and child, to fill in the gaps in fathers' knowledge about what is going on and to take over the work of childcare so that fathers have time available for the more enjoyable aspects. So fathers allegedly have issues with mothers' active control in one area and the absence of their management role in another.

The idea that it is mothers' responsibility/control which makes it difficult for fathers to negotiate their parenting when they are outside a cohabiting relationship does correspond with the finding that non-resident fathers are concerned that they have less input into their children's upbringing. The issue is not simply a relative lack of control that is imposed by circumstances but one that is caused by the particular way in which mothers can assert control over fathers. As Smart suggests, the pre-eminence of mothers' parenting may often be highlighted by divorce or separation rather than caused by it. However, the issue is perhaps more complex than she suggests, as, for fathers, the fact that the image of equal co-parenting is destroyed may be as much of a problem as ceding practical control to mothers. Moreover, the suggestion that mothers' role as mediators can explain the feeling of discontinuity is less persuasive. While Smart is correct that continuity for fathers is often provided by mothers who 'fill in the blanks', there is an additional element in that being around on a daily basis (even if for fathers in full-time work this is restricted to a short period in the early morning and some time in the evening, perhaps as little as the 10–15 minutes that one of my interviewees spoke about) does permit a grounded knowledge of a child's daily life. Finally, the worry about another man replacing the non-resident father in a child's affections and taking over the fathering role seems less about mothers as the figures who 'hold all the cards' (Smart 1999: 109) than about the downgrading of the father–child relationship. Overall, although non-resident fathers' recognition of a new form of parenting inequality between mothers and fathers is present as a tension, the move from a supportive co-parenting relationship to one marked by competition over parenting exacerbates the problems of non-resident fathers rather than causes them. The concerns expressed by non-resident fathers, especially when placed alongside comments of fathers who are co-resident with their children, indicate the significance of time. While resident fathers did not flag time as a central concern in their accounts (see Chapter 3), the difficulties of maintaining a close relationship based on scheduled, delimited periods and over a distance, are evident in the comments of non-resident fathers. This is felt acutely, given the contrasting position of resident mothers.

Backett (1987) makes the case in her study of parenthood that fathers' parenting does not operate as an independent relationship but is mediated by mothers. The interviews from the *Men, Work and Family Life* research (discussed in Chapter 5) parallel this view, but only to a degree. It is clear that fathers often have much less contact with children than do mothers, that being a father is not defined as taking on half the childcare and that this situation is one with which fathers are comfortable. However, the difference between our two studies, conducted 20 years apart, is that Backett suggests that even when men do have considerable contact with their children the relationship between father and child is still not direct, as fathers rely on mothers to interpret children's needs and wants for them, thereby guiding their parenting. This is different from the fathering relationship that was sought by my interviewees, for whom the contemporary ideal of good fathering centred on the development of a close, dynamic relationship between father and child. Here the actions which exemplified the intimacy of fathering were talking and listening to children. These were meaningful not only because they were often enjoyable in themselves but because they reinforced the one-to-one relationship between father and child. It seems that it is the loss of this direct father–child relationship, which for non-resident fathers must be largely negotiated through the mother, that is the root cause of sadness and anger. However, for fathers who successfully negotiate their new situation, the physical detachment which demands that more work goes into maintaining the father–child relationship can potentially lead to a stronger emotional attachment (Bradshaw *et al.* 1999; Smart 1999). Thinking about non-residency as problematic because it provides a challenge to the father–child dyad also makes greater sense of the debate over paying maintenance. For non-resident fathers the imposition of this financial obligation is often a contentious issue, witness the heated debates over the imposition of financial obligations by the Child Support Agency (see previous chapter). However, relatively few men express the view that they should have no financial obligations (Lin and McLanahan 2007), rather it is the context in which it takes place that poses problems. While some reluctance to pay is attributable to the control which mothers are able to assert over how the money is spent, and Bradshaw *et al.* (1999) note that mothers do play a central role in the men's negotiation of their commitment to provide maintenance, fathers see financial support as part of the package of involved fathering rather than just a stand alone financial commitment. The correspondence between paying and contact is not viewed as an equation whereby contributing money equals entitlement to time so as much two important indicators of an ongoing relationship.

Fathers' rights

The situation of fathers post-divorce or separation has become a topic of public debate and highly politicised, at least partially because of the impact of fathers' rights groups. Such groups are certainly not representative of the interests of all fathers or all organisations promoting fatherhood, nor do they even necessarily correspond to the interests of all non-resident fathers. Within the US, fathers' rights groups are mainly concerned with the legal rights of divorced upper- and middle-class fathers and even have an ambiguous relationship with other organisations within the broader category of the 'father responsibility movement' (Gavanas 2002: 220). However, examining the arguments these groups put forward about the current position of fathers and the changes which they hope to initiate at the legislative level exposes the way in which non-residency is constructed as problematic, because it is viewed as marking the loss of the intimate father–child relationship.

Fathers' rights groups

Fathers' rights have had increasing public prominence in the UK in the last few years. Fathers 4 Justice,[2] with its commitment to direct action, has, since its launch in 2002, had a major impact on raising the profile of fathers as an interest group. Its founder, an ex-marketing executive, organised a campaign which garnered media attention and public awareness through a series of publicity stunts, including scaling the walls of Buckingham Palace, throwing flour filled condoms at the Prime Minister in the House of Commons, invading a live television programme, and numerous other events in which members, usually dressed up as 'superheroes' have closed roads and bridges (e.g. 'Aggrieved dads stage bridge protest' *BBC* 2/2/2004). This organisation (now joined by a splinter group, Real Fathers 4 Justice[3]) is not the only fathers' rights organisation in the UK – Families Need Fathers[4] founded in 1974 has a much longer history – but the aims of Fathers 4 Justice, if not its methods, are representative of those of other fathers' rights groups, both within and outside the UK (Collier 2006: 55). Groups with similar aims exist in a large number of other countries, e.g. Canada, Australia, USA, and across Europe (Collier and Sheldon 2006). In essence their focus is on the status of fathers after divorce or separation and particularly the legal treatment which fathers receive, based on a strongly held belief that fathers are the new victims of family law (Collier 2005).

The approach taken by fathers' rights groups has been itemised as consisting of five components: adopting a language of equality, an appeal to formal legal rights, the construction of fathers as victims, a conflation of the interests of fathers and children and a concern to protect the heterosexual family (Collier 2005: 514, Collier and Sheldon 2006: 15). Fundamentally, the argument made is that fathers are equal parents with mothers and so the demise of a relationship between mother and father should not diminish the status of the father–child relationship. Fathers therefore have the right to maintain contact with their biological offspring and should be facilitated in doing so by resident parents (mothers) and the legal system. This viewpoint is expressed in the primary objective of ensuring that equal/co-parenting should be the default position in childcare arrangements post-divorce: both Fathers 4 Justice and Families Need Fathers have declared that there should be an automatic right to a 'meaningful, loving relationship' and that shared parenting should become the normal order of Family Courts. Shared parenting in this context means that there should be a physical split in terms of time spent with each parent so that children have two homes which they move between.

The rationale behind this demand for a change in law (one which, despite some public sympathy, seems unlikely at the moment) relies on a particular formulation of fatherhood, one that is centred on a strong emotional tie, has a biological link as its foundation, views fathers and mothers as equal parents but does not rely on an equal division of childcare to demonstrate this, and constructs mothers as influencing fathers' involvement with their children. Richard Collier has described the actions of Fathers 4 Justice as driven by an emotional imperative, dealing with 'anxiety, anger, compassion, disgust, enmity, fear, guilt, hate, humour, love, pleasure, remorse, resentment, sadness, shame' (2005: 520). Fathers' rights activists emphasise the love of fathers for their children and the sadness of men who are restricted in the level of contact they are permitted: Bob Geldof, who has become a vocal supporter of fathers' rights, has claimed that 'the love of a man for his child … is the real love that dare not speak its name' (2002). This emotional component is also evident in the accounts of 'personal tragedies' which are used as illustrations by Fathers 4 Justice of the impact on individual men of legal restrictions which reduce their ability to engage as fathers. In fact, it is the strength of their emotion which underpins the claim that their case is genuine. Other commentators have argued that anger may be the primary emotion of these fathers:

> men involved in the fathers' rights movement are angry men: angry about paying out what they consider to be huge sums of money in child support, angry that they have limited access to their children, and angry with the whole divorce and child custody process.
>
> (Bertoia and Drakich 1993: 597)

and suggest that legal environments are often the location for playing out the anger that exists between ex-partners (Smart and May 2004).

The assumption of an entitlement to contact with children is grounded in the importance of a biological link between father and child: biological fathers who are not granted formal parental responsibilities are often considered to have been treated unfairly. Biology is frequently used as a way of choosing when there is competition between men over responsibilities and rights and so is important in distinguishing the significance of *the* father from competing father figures in a child's life: the original Fathers 4 Justice manifesto (2003)[5] declared that one problem they wished to counter is that of 'children growing up with multiple surrogate fathers but being denied access to their natural father'. Boyd (2006) also mentions how, in Canada, prioritising biological fatherhood over the social role of parenting has been used as way of arguing that fathers have an inalienable right to involvement. Starting from this basis allows fathers to assert that they have an equal parenting status with the biological mother of a child. This biological basis is then translated into the right to a 'meaningful relationship' between father and child.

> All I want is good access so that I am not a visitor. I want to have the freedom to phone them, and I want the freedom for them to phone me. I want to be able to see them when I want to without asking permission all the time.
>
> (Cited in Bertoia and Drakich 1993: 600)

> I can't go up and see him any time I want to, it's got to be done through an appointment, so where does your parental rights come into it?
>
> (Cited in Smart 1999: 109)

Importantly the language of formal equality is used to argue that fathers should not have to negotiate with mothers in order to see their children as, irrespective of residency arrangements, equality of parenting is viewed as translating into an *independent* relationship between the child and each of his/her parents. This is consistent with the 1989 Children Act which introduced the idea that the parenting relationship did not end with the dissolution of a marriage or a separation. Instead, the presumption is that there will be an ongoing relationship between parents and children, with both parents encouraged to share in the upbringing of their children. Fathers are engaged in a struggle for recognition of their parenting status (Smart 2004a) but equal rights do not necessarily map onto an equal responsibility for childcare. Bertoia and Drakich (1993) concluded that the majority of the Canadian fathers they spoke to who were members of fathers' rights groups did not embrace the idea of seeking sole custody, nor did they really want to have shared 50/50 parenting. The majority did not want to have responsibility for childcare half of the time, but wanted to be able to choose their level of involvement.

> Joint custody doesn't have to be fifty-fifty. You can have a joint custody arrangement where you only see the child ten, fifteen, twenty percent. But at least you have an input into the child's life.
>
> (Cited in Bertoia and Drakich 1993: 602)

> Coparenting implies that it is not one person cut off.
>
> (Cited in Bertoia and Drakich 1993: 603)

Fathers' rights groups argue that it is the *principle* of 50/50 parenting that is important, even if in practice most fathers would not avail themselves of this right. 'The amount of time the children spend with each parent will need to vary' but 'The parents should be of equal status in law'(*Families Need Fathers* 2007). The goal, in fact, seems to be a continuation of the model of motherhood and fatherhood that normally exists within marriage, where mothers have greater responsibility for childcare while fathers contribute some help. It is certainly true that fathers' groups are rather less concerned with challenging the ongoing inequalities that exist with respect to childcare within couple relationships (for example there has been little focus on promoting flexible forms of working among fathers or encouraging men to take on a greater proportion of childcare tasks) than they have been with asserting men's rights after the breakdown of relationships.

Collier (2005) has suggested that there is some ambiguity over the 'meaningful relationship' that is sought for fathers by activists. However, examining the complaints of those who feel they are excluded from involved fathering through non-residency alongside the version of contemporary fatherhood put forward by resident fathers, shows what is being mourned is the loss of the father–child relationship based on Jamieson's (1998, 1999) idea of 'disclosing intimacy', which revolves around knowledge and understanding. Prioritising this type of parenting relationship means that 'fatherhood is participation in the life of your children on a day-to-day basis' (Municio-Larsson and Pujol Algans 2002: 208) to which most non-resident fathers do not have access. The value placed on the emotional father–child dyad means that it is not necessarily the loss of an actual relationship but the potential for one that is most keenly felt.

Gay fathers

Gay fathers are similar to non-resident fathers in that their structural positioning means they could be considered 'fragile'. However, an interesting difference is the way in which non-residency or variable levels of contact are more often viewed as an opportunity for creative approaches to social parenting that expand the options available to fathers than as a blow to the concept of fatherhood.

In what has been termed the 'gayby' boom, 'increasing numbers of non-heterosexuals are opting for parenthood' (Weeks *et al.* 2001: 159). While there has been increasing media attention encouraged by high profile cases and legislative change, there is still little academic study on gay fathers (Dunne 2001a). The overview of fatherhood research by Marsiglio *et al.* (2000) does note non-heterosexual parenting as one example of current cultural diversity in fathering contexts, but the references are limited to two studies: one on gay male stepfamilies (Crosbie-Burnett and Helmbrecht 1993) and the other on the impact of gay fathers on child development (Patterson and Chan 1997); in stark relief to the extensive list of published research on other sub-groups of fathers. The extent of gay fatherhood is itself difficult to enumerate, not least because research suggests that a proportion of these men may not be open about their sexual identification and/or continue to live within heterosexual relationships (Dunne 2001b). More recent studies tend to concentrate on the routes by which gay men become parents – the transition story – and on more general accounts of the way in which procreative identities are negotiated alongside sexuality (Berkowitz and Marsiglio 2007; Dunne 2001a; Stacey 2006). A better sense of the everyday parenting of gay fathers, although from the standpoint of mothers, may actually be gained from some accounts of lesbian parenting (e.g. Donovan 2000).

In terms of categorising the routes by which gay men become fathers, a distinction can be made between men who have fathered children within heterosexual relationships and those who have pursued fatherhood *as* gay men, either as an individual or part of a gay couple. There is a second distinction between biological and social fatherhood which maps imperfectly onto the first division, in that while the men in current or previous heterosexual relationships are normally biological fathers, this is the case for some but not the majority of men who opt for planned gay parenthood.

Surrogacy is difficult in Britain since it is illegal to pay egg donors or surrogate mothers more than their expenses so the possibility of gay male British couples achieving parenthood through surrogacy in the United States has gained high levels of public attention and comment (e.g. 'Gay couple become fathers' *BBC* 12/12/1999, 'Gay British men pay fertility clinic £33,000 for designer babies' *The Times* 25/3/2007). However, while surrogacy is easier to navigate in legal terms in the US, it remains hugely expensive and is therefore limited to an elite group of the very affluent (see for example 'Eddie and Charles' interviewed by Stacey 2006: 34). Since 2003 fatherhood has become more accessible for gay men in the UK via a different route, as gay couples are now allowed to adopt as a couple. Finally, some gay men become fathers through donating sperm either to single women or lesbian couples (Donovan 2000; Dunne 2001a). As with any group levels of involvement in fathering vary, and since the data available is mainly small-scale getting a sense of the overall picture is difficult. However, available accounts do suggest that gay men who co-parent with either a male or female partner may be more engaged in childcare than is typical for fathers as a whole (Dunne 2001a).

Difficulties of gay fathering

Views within the gay male community and heterosexual society have broadened to include the possibility of gay fathering. However, the availability of parenthood as simply another choice should not be overstated; ambivalent attitudes 'continue to prevail with regard to gay fatherhood, both within the non-heterosexual communities and in wider society' (Weeks *et al.* 2001: 160). Research documenting narratives of fatherlessness among gay men has found expressions of regret and sadness about what has been seen as a lack of opportunity for parenthood (Dalzell 2007), and in the US gay men still presume that fatherhood is not an option (Berkowitz and Marsiglio 2007). Procreative identities are not taken-for-granted among gay men and becoming a father must be negotiated, in the sense of decision-making over the route to parenthood and the type of parenting relationship that is desired and possible. In one example of the difficult choices that can be required in order to achieve fatherhood, Stacey (2006) documents how Californian regulations for potential foster carers resulted in one gay man ending his relationship so as to be able to pursue his 'passion for parenthood'. While negotiation does entail a greater freedom to think through preferences and re-think accepted ways of 'doing' fathering (Dunne 2001a) it also demands more planning and self-monitoring (Weeks *et al.* 2001).

In the everyday management of family life parenting may not be experienced as a problem, but when tensions arise in the nexus of intimate relationships, these men run the risk of being excluded (see for example 'Sam's' story in Weeks *et al.* 2001: 177). In some ways this pattern is similar to that experienced by those in 'traditional' parenting relationships whose contact with children may be severely diminished when the parent–parent relationship breaks down. However gay fathers in this situation may be in an even more tenuous position. Although courts are now less likely to make decisions based on the idea that non-heterosexuals are intrinsically deficient as parents, the ongoing association between gay masculinity and ideas of risk to children may still be influential, so that for gay fathers who were previously in heterosexual relationships, their sexuality may be used as an argument against gaining contact. Further, some gay men who are highly involved as social parents have no biological or legal status as fathers; this means that they may not have either the fallback of a biological connection or legal parenting responsibility on which to base an entitlement to involvement. Gay men who have organised their fathering involvement differently from the model of heterosexual co-residency may encounter incomprehension and are likely to have to explain and justify their own parenting model.

Conclusion: tensions and opportunities

In the discussion about fatherhood in previous chapters, the argument has been that contemporary fatherhood is fundamentally concerned with the development of a strong, emotionally open relationship between father and child rather than the work of childcare. Defining fatherhood in this way gives tremendous leeway in fathers' childcare activities; the important theme of 'being there' implying a psychological attachment and a willingness to prioritise children when required rather than a constant presence. In particular, time was not used as a proxy for men's commitment to parenting. Accompanying this, most concern about men's parenting has been directed towards categories of 'absent fathers' who are physically isolated from their children.

It might seem initially that, as the core of intimate fathering does not rely on carrying out a large proportion of childcare tasks, non-resident fathers could keep the same fathering ideals and achieve them in the same way as those who live with their children. However, while substantial stretches of time devoted solely to children are not deemed necessary, it appears that involvement in the minutiae of daily activity is significant. The aspect of 'being around', even if it is only being present in the same building, is itself judged to allow the development and enactment of the father–child relationship because the father can take a more active role when either he or the child wants it. Non-resident fathers do not usually have access to this. This chapter has therefore highlighted the extent to which contemporary fatherhood continues to rely on the intact family unit and the importance of co-residency in allowing the development of an involved, but not necessarily intensive fathering. The fathers' rights group approach to the dilemma of non-resident fatherhood has been to argue for maintaining the same fathering relationship post divorce/separation as existed for men when they were part of a co-resident couple. Given that the alteration in the context of fathering makes this difficult, involved fatherhood often becomes constructed as a demand that can be realised through legislation reform rather than a personal relationship. However, the contrast between the situation of non-resident fathers and gay fathers highlights how fragile fatherhood has less to do with 'moral' ideas of parenting (the heterosexual, biologically related father) than access to the 'mechanics' of fathering which allow it to be performed. Gay fatherhood, because it is outside conventional opposite sex co-residential unions, can often offer alternative expectations and possibilities for constructing fathering identities. This means that even when non-resident divorced or separated fathers and gay fathers have similar levels of fathering involvement the meanings afforded to them are different.

8 Discussion

Aspects of intimacy and fatherhood

It has been claimed that theorising about relationships currently has 'sociological street cred' (Smart 2004b: 1037). While the study of family life has a long tradition as a significant sub-discipline within sociology, it seems that courses and texts on 'personal life' are now taking its place. Taking the place of family is perhaps overstated, rather it is that research on personal relationships has subsumed more 'traditional' family studies within its broader remit. This has allowed for greater diversity in what is studied, reflecting the fact that 'more and more people are spending longer periods of their lives outside the conventional family unit' (Budgeon and Roseneil 2004: 127) and providing the opportunity to move away from rigid, normative depictions of family life. It has also encouraged studies on more 'conventional' family life to reassess the framing of their research agendas. This chapter highlights key aspects to intimacy that are central to contemporary fatherhood and, drawing on the findings discussed in previous chapters, suggests how an understanding of fatherhood contributes to wider debates about the meaning of intimacy.

Defining intimacy

There is 'a new story of the nature and significance of intimacy' (Jamieson 1998: 2) which is increasingly used to encapsulate changes in the way we think about and perform our personal relationships. Tracing the history of personal relationships, Jamieson (1998) documents a trajectory: from a pre-modern period with intimacy as a minor consideration relative to the hardships and traditions in a stratified, community based society; through a modern period that had the family/household as the centre of society along with a heightening of intimacy; to the current 'postmodern' period in which the achievement of 'good relationships' is what matters, with a concomitant diversity in how personal lives are acted out. Jamieson is not entirely convinced about this neat storyline and the extent to which the new form of intimacy really represents reality, but she echoes Giddens' view that,

> Intimacy is above all a matter of emotional communication, with others and with the self, in a context of interpersonal equality.
>
> (Giddens 1992: 130)

As she summarises it:

> intimacy is increasingly understood as representing a very particular kind of 'closeness' and being 'special' to another person founded on self-disclosure. This self-disclosing intimacy or self-expressing intimacy is characterized by knowledge and understanding of inner selves.
>
> (Jamieson 2005a: 2411)

This new stage in our personal lives is associated with the arrival of what Anthony Giddens has termed the 'pure relationship', which is a

> relationship entered into for its own sake, for what can be derived by each person from a sustained association with another, and which continues in so far as it is thought by both parties to deliver enough satisfactions for each individual to stay within it.
>
> (1992: 58)

The development of intimacy and its academic treatment have been thoroughly examined elsewhere (see Jamieson 1998 and Gabb 2008). The discussion here is more selective. Using the work of Giddens and Jamieson as starting points the purpose is to consider five themes which are prominent in discussions of intimacy; sexuality, reflexivity, equality, fragility and communication, as well as the meaning of time (which is often assumed to be significant but less often explored directly) – in relation to our understanding of fatherhood.

Sexuality and embodiment

In everyday usage the word intimacy is often a synonym for a sexual relationship and academic analysis too often still begins with the couple: 'Intimacy is bound up with sexuality and (hetero) sexual relationships' (Gabb 2008). Indeed, it was a concern with the interiority of couple relationships which prompted sociologists to move into the arena of sexual relationships that had previously been the preserve of psychologists and psychoanalysts. During the 1980s and into the 1990s, research on the way in which individuals negotiate their sexual relationships became increasingly important and sexual relationships became a focus of inquiry into modernity. In Giddens' (1992) *The Transformation of Intimacy* (subtitled 'sexuality, love and eroticism in modern societies'), it is the remodelling of relationships between *sexual partners*, of whatever sex, that is used to illustrate the revolution in intimacy which he believes has occurred.

However, although relationships between sexual partners have often been used to explore the dynamics of intimacy, sexuality is not intrinsic to 'disclosing intimacy'. Giddens himself claims that,

> The transformation of intimacy is about sex and gender, but it is not limited to them ... what is at issue here is a basic transition in the ethics of personal life as a whole.
>
> (1992: 96)

It has been suggested that the study of personal lives needs to decentre conjugal relationships and explore the lives of those at the 'cutting edge' of social change outside the narrow remit of sexual partnerships (Roseneil and Budgeon 2004). In particular, it is friendship which has been highlighted as offering most potential for exemplifying the 'pure relationship' in practice, and research on personal lives has recently witnessed particular interest in friendship and non-sexual relations (e.g. Jamieson *et al.* 2006; Pahl 2000; Spencer and Pahl 2006). The relationship between father and child is also outside the sexual couple relationship, and this too provides important insights into the pure relationship.

Yet the continuing centrality of sexuality in discussions of intimacy is indicated by its impact on how we think about non-sexual relationships. As Jamieson (1998, 1999) has noted, the (sexual) couple continues to be treated as the most significant personal relationship in both public stories and everyday practices. For example, close friendships, especially if they are cross-sex or if neither individual has an ongoing sexual relationship with someone else, often need to be clarified to outsiders. Even when dealing with personal relations where sexual contact is explicitly defined as outside the bounds of the relationship, such as between a father and child, the association between a close personal tie and a sexual relationship is awkward to separate: fathers who are highly involved run the risk of being accused of relationships that are 'too close'. One study of primary care giver fathers highlighted how fathers, in entering unusual territory, both literally and metaphorically, were forced to consciously recognise their masculinity and became aware of the way in which they were sometimes viewed as a potential (sexual) threat by other parents (Doucet 2006). One father spoke about the reluctance of parents to allow their children to sleepover at a house with only an adult male present ('I read it as parents being cautious': 2006: 706) and another, of his decision to behave in a way that completely avoids the possibility of any misconceptions ('I have purposefully not had anybody [children's friends], especially girls, to sleep over': 2006: 706). In facing continual messages about the manifold risks that children face, parents are put on high alert about possible dangers which may partially explain the kind of reactions to which these fathers felt susceptible. However, the default position which associates intimacy, especially physical intimacy, with a sexual partnership is also responsible for the difficulty fathers face in their parenting.

Self-reflexivity

Proponents of reflexive modernity, such as Giddens and Beck, point to reflexivity as central to the 'project of the self', suggesting that in contemporary society individualised responses to circumstances are foregrounded. It is this emphasis on self-reflexivity which provides a backdrop for the emergence of a transformed intimacy around the 'pure relationship' based around the ideals of autonomy and democracy. Older traditions no longer hold weight and individuals instead get to produce their own guidelines for living. An increased range of social possibilities means that life-style options have to be negotiated and re-negotiated, producing a 'narrative of the self' (Giddens 1992: 75). In terms of personal life, a diminishing of certainties around how relationships *should* operate is associated with the requirement to be more creative in how we think about ourselves and how we construct our relationships. The dynamics of contemporary life mean that individuals increasingly encounter challenges to the idea that personal life is experienced as distinctly mapped life stages and this disrupts previous understandings of 'the family'. This results in a breakdown in the uniformity of social categories (such as 'father'). In relation to fatherhood then, a Giddens-like version of reflexivity would see men constructing their fathering in diverse ways in response to their *own* biography.

Increased reflexivity is frequently theorised as the societal response to a diminution of the determining influence of structural forces on behaviour: reflexive modernisation describes 'the ever increasing powers of social actors, or "agency" in regard to structure' (Lash 1994: 111). This has led to Giddens' version of reflexivity being criticised for overemphasising agency and the associated possibility of social transformation. In the face of empirical social descriptions, which reiterate the continuing existence of longstanding social divisions, identities and codes of behaviour, it seems that the impact of self-reflexivity/agency has been overstated: Jamieson's (1998, 1999) specific attack on a reflexive modernist analysis of personal relationships provides an example of such a challenge. Her critique of the transformation of intimacy argues that personal relationships display rather more evidence of significant ongoing power relations than the influence of creative individual choice.

While it is mistaken to exaggerate the extent to which choice is everything, recent decades have witnessed a relaxation of the social prescriptions surrounding personal relationships. The accusation of an ungrounded reflexivity can be addressed through a rapprochement between structural elements and the agency of individual actors. This reintroduces structural elements by emphasising the importance of individuals' social location as the starting point for reflection and reinvention:

> Whilst many people do have new spaces in which to act and new levels of autonomy, it is a mistake to interpret this as a 'retreat' of social structural forces and a concomitant freeing of individual agency.
>
> (Irwin 2005: 179)

As Irwin states, there is a need both to recognise the 'new spaces' that social actors inhabit and the continuing impact of structures. Williams has adopted this approach in his study of fatherhood. He argues that self-reflexivity is central for the negotiation of fathering identities and practices, downplaying the significance of traditional ideal types, 'fathers create their own individualised roles' (2002: 3). However, he operationalises reflexive modernity as an adaptation to social changes with which fathers are confronted; suggesting that invention takes place within the context of situational circumstances which continue to influence, even sometimes to compel, particular outcomes. This approach is useful because it allows for diversity, while avoiding the other extreme of a mass of free floating options. An increased diversity in fathering situations can be attributed to advances in reproduction technologies, legal developments and new formations in the organisation of families. A multiplicity of living arrangements including large numbers of non-resident fathers and the creation of significant numbers of men parenting as step-fathers, both in blended families and as social fathers without a genetic link to their children, have all contributed to a rethinking of fathering roles. Importantly, this approach allows for alterations in fatherhood, but in response to the practical realities of everyday parenting rather than as abstract principles, and it therefore shifts the problem of assessing the impact of reflexivity onto empirical analysis.

However, there is some confusion about what gets counted as reflexivity. As Adkins (2003) points out in her discussion of gender, the presumption of self-reflexivity as necessarily leading to transformation needs to be challenged: she states that 'reflexivity is part of everyday habit' (Adkins 2003: 34). In other words being self-reflexive defined as 'thinking about', is not always *critical* reflection. Following Adkins, I would argue that existing data shows that much of the 'thinking about' fatherhood results in the adoption of familiar patterns of action rather than radical change. In Bourdieuian terms, the practices of fathers illustrate the inertia of habitus. While some contexts for fathering do prompt critical reflection that can be properly termed self-reflexivity, often the thinking that goes on does not present a challenge to existing modes of behaviour. This difference can be appreciated by examining some specific fathering situations.

The move from non-father to father does not itself entail self-reflexivity, although it is easy to see how this association occurs, since becoming a father means acquiring a new social status and often does involve 'thinking about' a whole range of behaviours and identities. Fathers speak about evaluating the meaning of relationships with family members and friends; they weigh up competing demands for their time in a new light; and they document changes in themselves that are attributed to their new identity. These are evidenced by judgements, for example, about with whom to spend leisure time and the pros and cons of moving house or taking on a new job opportunity. The presence of a child means that different decisions are taken about a whole range of issues and becoming a father is also the catalyst for awareness about, previously unthought of, new possibilities. Deciphering the extent to which individuals are reflexive about their beliefs and behaviours is difficult when relying on interview data since, by their nature, interviews encourage participants to reflect on their personal circumstances and therefore tend to emphasise reflexivity, but it is clear from fathers' accounts that the transition to parenthood is often associated with rethinking relationships, priorities and men's sense of self. However, significantly, these reflections do not necessarily challenge the status quo. The shock of the new is more likely to result in individuals seeking out commonly available patterns of fathering behaviour rather than creating fresh models. The movement from non-parent to parent, although it prompts a renegotiation of the way in which day-to-day life is organised, is not necessarily about reflexivity in its true sense, because this alteration in status is a recognised rite of passage which is associated with well defined modes of behaviour. It may be of interest to explore when 'thinking about' something occurs, but this can be categorised as reflexivity only in a weak, non-transformative form. Men may reflect on their fatherhood as a significant point of transition, but this does not mean that there is critical reflection on the concept of fatherhood.

The veracity of this statement is highlighted by considering the circumstances which do provide an opportunity for more critical reflection. Andrea Doucet's (2006) Canadian primary care giver fathers frequently spoke about how they felt out of place in child-centred environments that are female dominated, 'estrogen-filled worlds'. These fathers were often made conscious of their fatherhood in a way that was more intrusive than for fathers whose performance of the role fits within widespread norms. But this is not just a heightened consciousness, it also necessitates some reflection on the previously unconscious rules of fathering, in a similar fashion to the unease documented by women entering the male dominated terrain of particular professions. Discussions of role reversal fathers who take on the bulk of childcare while their female partners continue in full-time employment continue to receive significant media attention (as examples of two stories see Morrison (2007) 'The parental instinct' and Wilson (2003) 'Stay-at-home fathers hit a record high'). Paradoxically, it is argued that they are increasing in number and so becoming an unexceptional feature of the parenting landscape, at the same time as they continue to be a phenomenon worthy of comment. This contradiction, I would suggest, can be explained by the fact that, while such men are extremely unusual as a proportion of fathers as a whole, those fathers who adopt a form of parenting which is outside common practice are likely to experience their position as not only atypical but as jarring with their preconceptions. Possibilities for critical reflection also occur when men are parenting in allegedly 'fragile' situations, as these more tenuous positions can permit the reformulation of the aims and practices of fatherhood. Genuine reflexivity is a feature of some non-resident fathers' parenting since, if they are to have a meaningful relationship with their children it often means adjusting their view of fathering – 'It was only when I realized that they might not be part of my life that gave me a real shock and it made me more aware' (father quoted in Smart 1999: 103). Likewise the negotiation that is required in becoming a gay father and doing fatherhood, as discussed in Chapter 7, means that these men are more likely to think critically about the meaning and practice of contemporary fatherhood.

Equality, democracy and reciprocity

A key aspect of the transformation in intimacy described by Giddens (1992) is the possibility of more equal and democratic relationships. He suggests that there has been a reduction in structurally based inequalities, including those based on gender. Since relationships are negotiated on an individual basis, they are less influenced by the traditional dimensions along which power is held. For Jamieson however, lives are *not*, in the main, framed by 'disclosing intimacy'. It is clear from descriptions of couple relations that the existence of domestic violence, alongside more mundane inequalities like responsibility for chores and control of finances, mean that equality is the exception not the norm: 'personal relationships are not typically shaped in whatever way gives pleasure without the taint of practical, economic and other material circumstances' (Jamieson 1999: 482). Arguing that equality has not yet been achieved and that many relationships are recognised as falling short of a contemporary ideal could be countered by positing that the transformation process is not yet realised (Giddens himself was cognisant of this fact, arguing that a revolution in personal life was possible rather than complete). However, Jamieson's argument is not limited to this point; she also suggests that relationships which people categorise as 'good' do not necessarily demonstrate equality. An example from research on domestic labour which illustrates this point is that while men and women tend to do unequal amounts of housework they often still perceive them to be fair (Baxter 2000). Further Jamieson argues that where equal relationships do exist, these are sustained not only by disclosing intimacy but by practices of 'mutual practical care' (2005a: 2413) so that equality cannot be seen as emerging simply as a by-product of this form of intimacy. In terms of parent–child relations, the assertion of equality seems especially unsustainable. While an adult child and their parent may have a relationship modelled on friendship, the material dependence of young children on their parents fatally impairs such claims.

Democracy

While it is not difficult to undermine the proposal that personal relationships are now grounded in the idea of equality, Giddens, by focusing attention on the concept of democracy rather than equality – 'a *democratisation* of the private sphere is today not only on the agenda, but is an implicit quality of all personal life' (Giddens 1992: 184, my italics) – has the basis of a more subtle argument. The principle of autonomy which underpins democracy is that individuals are 'free and equal in the determination of the conditions of their own lives' (1992: 184): there are no set rules where one person unilaterally sets the terms of engagement. There are, of course, necessary conditions in order for democracy to operate; there needs to be effective participation which involves discussion in decision making, and equal influence by every individual in outcomes. Giddens states that 'democracy is the enemy of privilege' (1992: 188) but fundamentally democracy does not necessarily imply equality of outcome but rather an equal say, with the ability to consent to inequality. There is an implication in focusing on the personal realm that the decision over what counts as equal is taken by individuals themselves, and so this pursuit of democracy, rather than a more straightforward notion of equality, introduces an element of flexibility in accounting for the experience of personal lives, including allowing for an element of inequality. Nevertheless, the claim of negotiation is still problematic when the focus of attention is parent–child relationships.

Speaking about parent–child relations Giddens argues that 'It is a right of the child to be treated as a putative equal of the adult' (1992: 191), albeit one who is insufficiently autonomous to negotiate with directly. He presents parent–child relations as democracy in waiting, in that, although practical decision-making may fall on the parent, 'It is the quality of the relationship that comes to the fore, with a stress upon intimacy replacing that of parental authoritativeness' (1992: 98). The dominant discourse about parenthood in self-help books (on which Giddens draws) and in manuals on parenting is that of a relationship where children's opinions do have some status. Descriptions of family life also include numerous references to the preferences of children and the way in which these shape family activities, for example a child's involvement in sport will determine how the family weekend is organised. Similarly, the rationale for men spending more time with their children is not only that this has a positive effect on children but that it is what children want. There is also a sense that the parent–child relationship is not one in which parents have all the control beyond internal household negotiations. For example, in discussions about residency and contact after divorce or separation, it is increasingly argued that children's citizenship should be recognised in order that their preferences over welfare are taken seriously (Neale 2004; Smart 2004a).

Ultimately, however, decision-making rests with the adult in parent–child relationships. For example, children may be consulted over the destination for the annual family holiday inasmuch as they make suggestions and express opinions, but they do not have an equal say. Parents have the power to implement their preferences and the ability to draw on other dimensions of power such as access to resources, especially financial, in order to defend their choices. One example of the interaction in decision making between a parental discourse of children's preferences and parents' own priorities is Vincent and Ball's (2006) discussion of the childcare choices made by a group of middle-class parents. They note that 'Parents' prime indicator of a successful placement was the child's happiness' (2006: 138), seemingly demonstrative of parents acting for the child on the basis of what the *child* wants. Yet Vincent and Ball also comment that parents' practical needs influenced choices that were made. Meanwhile the extracts which they include from interviews with mothers actually highlight that these women held views of nursery care and other child activities, based on their perceived benefit to children in terms of their social development, that exemplified the mothers' own particular, classed expectations of what nurseries should provide. A child's preference might therefore be one component in justifying the choice of a nursery placement, but was not sufficient. This example illustrates both the extent to which a nod towards the autonomy of (even very young) children is made by (some) parents, but also the limitations to this democracy. Other authors on parenting have demonstrated that overt attempts to share power are often accompanied and undermined by covert tactics to manage childcare situations and ongoing competition for control (e.g. Solomon *et al.* 2002; Walkerdine and Lucey 1989) and Gabb (2008) notes that one of her interviewees 'crafts a democratic model around deeply entrenched generational power relations'. There is also a question mark over how the wishes of children are brought into play in tense parenting circumstances. When, for example, children are encouraged to voice their opinions in the face of disputes about post divorce or separation parenting, it may be because their views are in alignment with the preference of one parent: allowing children to have a say may be more about 'winning' than promoting a democratic relationship between parents and children. Jamieson argues that any claim to democracy is just gloss:

> Parents cannot start as equals to their children, and no matter how democratic they try to be it will necessarily remain a relationship between superordinate and subordinate for many years.
>
> (1998: 162)

While the suspension of power relations implied in the use of the term democracy may be 'extraordinarily abstracted' from everyday inequalities between an adult and their young child (Jamieson 1998: 73), its presence as a theme in parent child relations does indicate the high value placed on democracy in personal lives in general. An ideal of democracy has become common as a reference point in personal relationships, even in the, perhaps unlikely, realm of parents and children. More importantly, and paradoxically, the recognition that the relationship between a father and their young child is never going to be genuinely equal, since responsibility ultimately lies with the adult, allows other aspects of disclosing intimacy to be maintained more easily. With children, fathers can refer to the trust, communication, love and understanding that is present, while elements such as the wielding of authority, that could cause friction and challenge the idea of intimacy in adult relationships, are viewed as intrinsic and remain therefore unquestioned. Sustaining the idea of intimacy is also easier in circumstances where one individual's capacity for intimacy is unlikely to be called into question by the other party.

Reciprocity

While neither equality or democracy qualify as abiding principles in parent–child relationships, reciprocity, defined as a relationship where each party both gives and receives in some form, is a characteristic of the relationship between fathers and children. Reciprocity need not involve equality, as one party may contribute more than another to the continuation of the relationship. Neither is there necessarily democracy, as the intimate reciprocal relationship is not based on equal contributions to decision making. Gabb, adopting Marion Young's (1997) term 'asymmetrical reciprocity', argues that,

> A model of asymmetrical reciprocity, as the cornerstone of all intimate relationships, not only acknowledges differences between intimates, it makes such differences a creative and dynamic factor within these relationships.
>
> (Gabb 2008)

Instead, reciprocity involves a sense of mutual benefit. Reciprocity may be evidenced by practical demonstrations but is not in itself constituted by these acts, since outwith its material performance, a relationship can still be beneficial in the eyes of both protagonists, existing as an *emotionally* reciprocal relationship.

A note on the boundaries of what can be defined as intimacy is perhaps required here. Using reciprocity – the idea of 'getting something out of it' – rules out activities where the benefit runs in one direction only, for example where an individual perceives an activity as beneficial but the subject is inanimate, say collecting dolls. However, using reciprocity does bring into the frame a range of other relationships that might commonly be considered borderline in terms of the category of intimacy, such as human relationships with pets (non-human animals). It could be added that both parties need in some way to recognise the relationship, though how this should be assessed is not immediately obvious.

In terms of fatherhood, men's involvement is considered positive for their children and men also present themselves as beneficiaries. The material and emotional necessity of parental or equivalent care for children is not in doubt. Fatherhood is also frequently presented as supplying something more than just the interchangeable care that could be provided by any adult, such as the development of self-esteem mentioned by William:

> I see one of my primary functions as a father, as a parent ... is to let my kids know that, at the beginning of the day they are vital, important, independent beings, who know they are absolutely solidly loved and adored and appreciated.

Hence the public discussions which are held about the importance of 'father figures' in situations where fathers are not available to their children. The concept of children as valuable to their parents is not new: historically, children have been seen as providing financial security or care in old age for their kin. The benefits that accrue to parents from children in this model are based on indirect reciprocity; giving 'in the knowledge that good will come back indirectly or in the future' (Jamieson 1998: 84). Contemporary fathers, however, rarely refer to these potential gains, since the status of kinship no longer entails straightforward rights and obligations of this kind so that a presumption of delayed reciprocity is not plausible. The reciprocity that is on offer here, as an aspect of contemporary fatherhood, is not about material goods, and the benefits are immediate and ongoing rather than delayed to some point in the future. Although there are elements of self-sacrifice – comments about initial sleepless nights and a falling away in their social life – fathers are clear about the compensatory gains. What contemporary intimate fatherhood offers men is another chapter within a narrative of self-development – 'I'm a more rounded individual as a result of having children' as one father phrased it to me – promising fathers an ongoing, relationship that is viewed as an important component in the project of the self.

Dyadic intimacy

This emphasis on reciprocity is consistent with the idea of a dyadic relationship and, perhaps because of the dominance of sexual partnerships in thinking about personal relations, it is the 'couple' who are fundamental to intimate relationships.

This 'dyadic turn' is evident in a shift of emphasis from the nuclear family, or the household as a functioning unit, to the relationships between individuals, such as mother and daughter. Indeed, one criticism of Giddens' take on personal relationships is that it downplays the network of social relations to which an individual belongs in favour of an emphasis on couple relationships. The concept of the father–child dyad is prominent in discourse around contemporary fatherhood; it is the relationship between the two that has primary status as fathers are viewed as important for their children and vice versa. This construction sees fatherhood as a standalone relationship, which is therefore inherently equal to motherhood, and downplays other relationships that are integral to the negotiation of fatherhood, such as the role of mothers as both parents and partners. As discussed in Chapter 5, mothers may provide important childcare and have a different kind of relationship with their children but this does not undermine the relationship between father and child. Asserting the value of a one-to-one relationship moves fatherhood away from older versions of good fatherhood, such as the model of father as resource provider, although it does run the risk of unthinkingly, leaving social contexts and influential structural forces unexplored.

Fragility and commitment

Intimacy often appears to be a fragile state. The definition of the pure relationship, the receptacle for transformed intimacy, 'continues only in so far as it is thought by both parties to deliver enough satisfactions for each individual to stay within it' (Giddens 1992: 58), as it is based around 'elective affinities' (Beck-Gernsheim 1998). Intimate relationships are seen as terminable because they are no longer ascribed but chosen, so can be ended at any time. Trust, which is the basis for relationships, cannot be simply assumed (Giddens 2000) and friendship, often used as the exemplar of the pure relationship, has to be worked at rather than taken for granted; in contrast to the kin relations of the past where both obligations and rights were presumed to flow automatically from an ongoing social relationship. Now, it is argued, it is not only friends but all personal relationships that are open to this constant re-evaluation and potential cessation. Marriage, previously 'until death us do part', can be and is often terminated through divorce. For authors, such as Giddens, who are positive about these alleged developments in the nature of intimacy, the ending of unsuccessful, unfulfilling and unequal relationships offers the possibility of greater individual choice. Likewise, Beck-Gernsheim, who sees the 'reinvention' of family life as providing 'more individual choices, more beginnings, more farewells' (2002: 41), mainly focuses on the expanding opportunities that this offers for individuals. It is the possibility of 'families of choice' (Weston 1991) rather than ascribed familial roles which emphasises the increased possibility of creativity in the organisation of personal lives (Weeks *et al.* 2001). For those of a more pessimistic bent, the pressure to achieve a high level of intimacy in relationships is seen as part of a process of increased individualisation which creates expectations that cannot be met (e.g. Craib 1994).

However, the dissolvability of contemporary relationships can be overstated. If the increased fragility of social ties is a reality, it is one that we seem unhappy entirely to embrace. We seek to imbue our relationships with some sense of solidity hence, according to Neil Gross, the continuing importance and popularity of 'social-constitutive traditions' such as marriage (2005). Additionally, to regard obligations as no longer set in concrete for all time is not the same as arguing that they are merely of the moment. Close associations may be dependent on a set of 'cumulative commitments' built up over a period of time: yet while the strength of such a relationship has developed as part of a dynamic process rather than being 'given', this does not mean it can be easily dismantled. The choice about with whom intimate relationships can be developed may be more open but the ability to opt out of these relationships once they are established is not necessarily straightforward. As an example, agony columns which attempt to resolve personal troubles, commonly resort to an appeal to 'talk it through' and 'work on a relationship' in order to save or improve it; while the option of cutting one's losses and moving on does exist, it is only recommended as a last resort. Fragility may therefore be not so much the antithesis to commitment as awareness of the need for nurturing.

Parent–child relations initially seem difficult to fit into the fragility model, 'family and marriage may have become disaggregated, but the question is whether this means that commitment to children and wider kin has also evaporated' (Smart 2005: 550). Parent–child relationships tend, in fact, to be used as the example which undermines the 'only mutual satisfaction holds things together' argument. Jamieson draws on parent–child relations in order to counter the dominance of disclosing intimacy as the orienting principle for our personal lives, and suggests that they provide a particular challenge to arguments that relationships are voluntary (1998: 161). She argues that parent–child relations are voluntary insomuch as they can be broken, but they cannot really be considered optional since in practice they are rarely abandoned and this is not widely perceived as acceptable practice. Alternatively, parent–child relationships are put forward as the exception that highlights the brittleness of other personal relationships. Beck and Beck-Gernsheim argue that, in the face of adult–adult relationships which can only be unreliable, the tie between parent and child may provide 'the ultimate guarantee of permanence' (1995: 73). This vertical relationship becomes more valued as horizontal relationships between peers become more vulnerable. In fact, the permanency of parent–child relationships can have a knock-on effect, disrupting the temporary nature of adult couple relationships. If both parent–child relationships are to endure after a parental separation – as they are encouraged so to do in law (Smart 1999) – then there must also be an ongoing connection between the parents, whether they desire it or not.

What can be added to this picture by looking specifically at father–child relationships? One on level it provides confirmation that the parent–child relationship frequently functions as a constant: being a father is a relationship from which one is not expected to abdicate. Further, the fixed nature of this relationship means that other ties are often negotiated with reference to it: they may develop because of it (e.g. through a child's friendships); be oriented around it (e.g. grandparents); or accommodated because of its status as an ongoing priority (e.g. friendships). Second, the kind of intimate fatherhood which appears to be the goal of the majority of men, and fulfils the cultural expectation of contemporary fatherhood, is fragile in the sense that it often relies on circumstances outside the relationship itself. For example, non-resident fathers may come to recognise the fragility of a relationship that is reliant on the person of the mother to facilitate the father–child relationship and/or the structure of a shared home environment. The label 'father' is not destroyed in the same way as that of friend or partner by a unilateral or even bilateral decision; it is a commitment that the state as well as social networks will normally continue to recognise. However, the father–child relationship, while perhaps less precarious than the pure relationship described by Giddens, does still have its frailties.

Communication

'The imperative of free and open communication is the sine qua non of the pure relationship' (Giddens 1992: 194). The contemporary idea of intimacy is based on a 'dialogic ethos' (Gabb), a dialogue that is about emotional life, as each party in an intimate relationship is required to share with the other their thoughts and feelings. This communication is primarily about opening out to the other person, making feelings available, and so is not necessarily about the detail of everyday goings on but a fundamental authenticity of emotional life. There is a distinction made between mere familiarity and intimacy. Jamieson differentiates between the kind of knowledge and understanding which develops from close associations with another individual, that can originate simply on physical proximity such as through sharing a home, and 'privileged' or 'deep' knowledge and understanding which 'suggests not just cognitive knowledge and understanding but a degree of sympathy or emotional understanding which involves deep insight into an inner self' (1998: 8). It is this 'privileged knowledge' that relies on mutual self-revelation. Intimacy is not only about the 'privileged knowledge' that results from openness but the process: claims to understanding what someone 'is like' must be backed up with reference to ongoing conversations and therefore take time. However, as Jamieson suggests, the emphasis on communication and feelings means that more practical aspects of love and care tend to recede into the background.

In my interviews, the men spoke in ways which suggested that laying the groundwork for successful self-development was their key concern as a father, rather than dealing with day-to-day dilemmas (although certainly they encountered and dealt with these as well). Fathers spoke about the purpose of reading a bedtime story and having a chat in quite abstract terms of 'being there' with the impetus on the child to reveal what they wanted, if they wanted. This highly valued openness was, however, almost entirely one-way – from child to parent. When fathers talked about making sure they allowed time for children to speak, there was little reference to conversation that was not about the child's orbit of interest. It could be argued that the impetus for communication does lead children to some understanding of their parents' worlds. Parents are, for example, encouraged to reveal that children have been adopted and to discuss the process. Children may also, to some degree, become the confidantes of parents, perhaps more commonly if they are an only child and spend more time with adults or if they live in a single parent household. However, while there is a pressure to perform emotional truth at all times (Beck and Beck-Gernsheim 1995), parents do tend to shelter their children from unpleasant information: 'children are to be protected from adult worries and burdens' (Jamieson 1998: 163).

Earlier it was noted that the philosophy of openness advocated by some parents may in practice operate as a unidirectional method of knowledge transfer whereby parents gain information about their children's lives. For example, promoting discussion about subjects such as drugs or sex, opens up the possibility for more direct questioning of a child's own practices. However, evidence of this kind of communication was not dominant in my interviews with fathers and instead there was a sense of a more laissez-faire attitude to parenthood. It may be that with relatively independent teenagers more coercive methods are adopted to find out what is going on, while for the younger, primary school age children whose fathers were interviewed here, using openness to promote the façade of democracy is not required. There is also the possibility that these fathers managed to express the openness ideal while concealing ways in which the information would be used. Yet, the impression was that fathers were less interested in demanding information about their children's lives and were more concerned with providing the opportunity for discussion. Solomon *et al.* claim that 'Information-seeking for the purposes of parental control and information-seeking for the purposes of closeness are competing goals' (2002: 980), and since parents certainly do engage in the former the latter is questioned. Yet, this position is not entirely convincing since the intention of parents may not fit neatly into one of two categories; while closeness may be a general objective, gaining information may be uppermost as a priority in the short-term. It may be that the directional, component of parent–child communication is responsible for the image of conversation as primarily oriented towards information gathering. In practice, conversation may help to develop a close relationship *and* reveal information.

The dynamics of father–child communication do not support the image of intimacy with mutual disclosure at its centre, but openness between fathers and children may match better with disclosing intimacy than the communication strategies of mothers suggested in previous research. According to Giddens, 'Intimacy is not being absorbed by the other, but knowing his or her characteristics' (1992: 94), falling more into the category of 'caring about' than 'caring for'. The communication between father and child based on a close emotional tie is one that promotes a relative degree of autonomy for children because of the absence, in most cases, of expansive everyday involvement that produces knowledge.

Time

Giddens, by focusing on the psychosocial terrain of self-help literature in preference to empirical studies of personal lives, and basing his argument on an understanding of adult relationships rather than those between adults and children, tends to look at the way in which we construct relationships and not the caring that constitutes a significant part of them. In Giddens' account, when time is mentioned it is spent reflecting on relationships rather than performing them (although for him this reflexivity is central to 'doing' intimacy). In Jamieson's critique time is more prominent; since 'knowing and understanding take time' (Jamieson 1998: 166), a time commitment is important in order to achieve 'disclosing intimacy'. Jamieson also argues that when time is spent with young children, caring tasks are likely to be a major activity – 'It is difficult to spend time with young children and not be engaged in practical caring' (1998: 166). In her analysis, time therefore provides the link between caring tasks and the more abstract concept of intimacy.

However, time is mentioned in different ways in accounts of intimacy. Spending time with someone is significant for creating and sustaining intimacy – 'I spend most of my time with my children, one way or another' as one interviewee phrased it – since time spent together allows for shared experiences which are important in constituting a sense of joint-ness. From this, one strand of dominant thought sees time as a quantifiable measure of commitment (paralleling discussions of employment where part-time workers are often considered to be less committed to the labour market – Hakim's (1991) 'grateful slaves'). A noticeable increase in the amount of time fathers spend with their children has been used as evidence of a transformation in fatherhood and a new kind of fathering identity that is more child-centred; and the failure to achieve parity in childcare time between mothers and fathers is used to support the argument for a relative lack of change and fathers who remain predominantly committed to paid work. A more involved fatherhood, grounded in close association between parent and child, is supposed to mesh with a greater time contribution to childcare tasks and a concomitant juggling of time.

The discussion in previous chapters suggests that this distinction misrecognises the relevance of time in negotiating intimate relationships. Intimate fatherhood exists through the building of a relationship that is based on emotional closeness and its expression, which requires time for the sharing of experiences and for sharing feelings about experiences. However, contemporary fathering is a sufficiently fluid concept to allow the total amount of time with children to matter less than the fact that a mutually recognised relationship can be built. Prioritising quality over quantity was advocated in the 1980s as a possible resolution to the dilemma of the stressed 'career woman' who was trying to balance employment and motherhood; the only problem being that the 'quality not quantity' thesis was not internalised by mothers who still expressed guilt about not spending enough time with their children (e.g. Brannen and Moss 1991). The terminology of 'quality time' does though seem applicable to contemporary fatherhood. The *Men, Work and Family Life* study indicates that while knowing and understanding do take up some time, they are not evaluated on the basis of a calculation of time.

> I knew that it was unlikely that I would be around all day, but I knew that at the end of the day, I should put work behind me and should throw myself into whatever is left of the day for the children … given that I have a long journey home from work.
>
> (Greg)

The model of contemporary fatherhood which emerges is, then, closer to the ethic of the pure relationship than an ethic of caring responsibility. *Wanting* to spend time with someone is indicative of the strength of a personal tie: when, for example, fathers speak about a desire to spend time with their kids it is a claim about the value of that relationship to both parties, even if other obligations might get in the way of realising it. 'Making time' for someone is important because it involves a reallocation of this valuable resource for the purpose of maintaining a relationship. Dismissing a relationship on the basis that 'I didn't have time for it' is not primarily a statement about busyness but about where the relationships fits into a set of priorities. Both 'spending time' and 'making time' are principles rather than measurements of quantity. Although a dependent young child requires certain resource provisioning and daily care as an intrinsic and legally defined aspect of parenting, this can be done by someone else. The intimacy perspective instead has the father–child *relationship*, which needs to be supported and accommodated, at its core. This is consistent with the allocation of relatively short periods of time to fathers for leave at the birth of a child where the time is important for what it represents in terms of the relationship rather than for what can be accomplished in practical terms. This commentary should not be taken to mean that the role of father as intimate can be completely disassociated from time as hours and minutes. For fathers who face severe restrictions on the time they can spend with their children, such as men who are incarcerated or those who have only limited access to children after divorce or separation, time may take on a major symbolic status. Equal sharing of time between parents, for example, signifies equal parenthood. This sense of parity can be achieved as long as the *principle* of dividing time between mothers and fathers exists, even if it does not correspond to the practice of parenting.

Time is a valuable resource but, while time limitations may delineate the boundaries of intimacy (Jamieson 2005b) restrictions on time for some fathers make the ideal of contemporary fatherhood impossible to achieve, so it can be thought about flexibly. The complexities of different understandings of time are illustrated by one interviewee who begins by assuming that time can be taken as proxy for involvement, an assumption that becomes problematic when reflecting on his own personal experience.

> I don't see, in any sense, that I did not have time with my father. You know, if I think back to my childhood I have what seems a lot of time with my father. But I'm sure it can't have been because I was at boarding school, apart from anything else, and he was in the Navy. Yet I don't feel any lack of involvement from him as a child.
>
> (Hugh)

Conclusion

Intimacy involves a focus on creative personal relationships. I have suggested that conceptualising contemporary fatherhood as an intimate relationship allows for an emphasis on the aspects of male parenting that fathers themselves view as most significant; emotions, the expression of affection, and the exclusivity of the reciprocal father–child dyad. Contemporary fatherhood is centred on a personal connection at the expense of participation in the work of childcare; because caring activities flow from an emotional connection rather than in themselves constituting the fathering role, the practicalities of 'intimate fatherhood' are fluid and open to negotiation. Consequently, using the idea of intimacy as a framework for thinking about men's parenting provides a way of resolving the apparent gulf between 'culture' and 'conduct'. Understanding this special quality of contemporary fatherhood is necessary in order to move beyond narrow formulations of fathers, either as failing to contribute to, or as sidelined from contemporary family life. Fatherhood is both of interest in itself and as a lens through which to examine personal lives more widely: the intention is that this book contributes to ongoing discussions about fatherhood and provides a new framework in which to conduct these debates.

Appendix

Men, work and family life

Method

Semi-structured interviews were conducted with 25 fathers: interviews were recorded and fully transcribed. Interviews began with a request for the fathers to draw a 'lifeline' consisting of major personal events and then progressed to open-ended questions about their everyday lives, including the impact of becoming a father, typical daily involvement with children, employment, an assessment of their work–life balance, as well as more general views on fatherhood, motherhood and family-friendly policies. Analysis involved close iterative readings of the transcripts in order to note key and recurrent themes.

Access

The men were mainly contacted for interview through a primary school, and this was complemented by some snowballing. The primary school had a large proportion of pupils on free school meals (used as a measure of relative deprivation) but had been very successful in terms of its results. Consequently, the demand for places was high and the catchment area was a desirable location for incomers within which house prices had become inflated. The principal of the primary school agreed to send out a brief questionnaire specifically addressed to fathers of children in the school, along with a covering letter and a note to explain that she had vetted the research. Men were subsequently contacted for interview.

Sample

A subjective definition of 'father' was used, which resulted in a sample of mainly biological fathers, one adoptive father and one man with both biological children and a step-child. Since the interest was on co-residency rather than marital status, both cohabiting and married men were included in the sample. The intention had been to target only men who were cohabiting with a female partner – however, in one case a father who was separated from the mother of his children was interviewed. Frequently the focus in parenthood research has been on the transitional or early phase but in this case interviews were conducted with men who had children of primary school age: all of the fathers had at least one child attending primary school or (in two cases) nursery. As participation in the study was based on the age of children, interviewees had quite a wide age range, from 27 to 54, but the majority were in their early forties. All of the men were in employment and held professional/managerial positions, some as self-employed workers (see table). Two of the fathers were Asian and one interviewee had a Middle-Eastern background. The remainder were of White British/European/American descent. Due to the small sample size, meaningful comparisons based on ethnicity were not possible, though different responses based on ethnicity were not apparent. The location for the research study was in London, UK in the borough of Lambeth. This is an area which continues to be categorised as relatively poor, although it has undergone a recent process of gentrification.

Interviewees

Name	No. of children	Occupation	Employed/ self-employed	Partner's employment status
Alan	2	Accountant	E	P/T
Bill	2	Accountant	E	F/T
Vik	2	Lawyer	E	F/T
Chris	1*	Business manager	E	P/T
Derek	2	Vicar	E	F/T
Duncan	2	IT manager	E	No (recently redundant, previously F/T)
Euan	3	Camera operator	S/E	P/T
Gareth	2	IT manager	E	P/T
George	2	Civil servant	E	F/T
Greg	2*	Television producer	S/E	No (maternity leave, previously P/T)
Hugh	4	Lawyer	E	No
Ivan	2	Advertising executive	E	P/T
Jack	2	Teacher	E	P/T
Jim	1	Civil servant	E	F/T
Joe	2*	Business manager	E	No
John	1	Writer/photographer	S/E	P/T + student
Ken	2	Lecturer	E	F/T
Marcus	2	Company director	S/E	F/T
Michael	2	Civil servant	E	F/T
Patrick	3	Researcher	S/E	F/T
Phil	1*	Personnel manager	E	P/T
Raj	2	Editor	E	?
Simon	2	Behavioural support officer	E	P/T + student
Tony	2	Teacher	E	No (temporary)
William	2	Lawyer	E	No

*Indicates that one child was not yet attending school.
All original names have been changed and some employment details have been slightly altered to help preserve anonymity

Notes

Introduction

1 Rachel Thomson is Professor of Social Research, Open University, UK. 'Making of Modern Motherhoods: Fatherhood Seminar' 8 June 2007, Open University, Milton Keynes.

1 Paradoxes of contemporary fatherhood

1 As Crow has argued (2005), the focus on identifying and resolving paradoxes is a method of developing sociological arguments which has proved especially popular in family sociology. He suggests that this is the case because family research has as its central focus emotions and positions that often appear oppositional: love and hate, altruism and self-interest, rights and responsibilities.
2 The Act applies in England and Wales: similar legislation was passed in Scotland in 2006.

2 Fatherhood as breadwinning

1 It is worth noting that this pattern is not so pronounced in Europe as a whole. Across the EU15 the gap between full-time hours for men and women was only 2.2 hours per week in 2002 and the arrangement for couples with children of male full-time worker plus female part-time worker is not dominant (Crompton 2006).
2 Respondents in the NCDS were all aged 41/42 at the time of interview in 1999/2000 in the wave of data used here.
3 More detailed discussion of these findings are available in Dermott (2006b).
4 A recent conversation with a self-proclaimed 'stay-at-home dad' revealed that he actually worked full-time but defined himself in this way because he did childcare during the day, when his partner was at work, and did his paid job in the evenings. If this definition is widespread it might explain why stay-at-home dads appear to be more numerous than statistics usually suggest.

3 Fathering activities and the meaning of time

1 The same survey also found that a majority of children would like the footballer David Beckham as their dad.
2 Interestingly, the study by Gray (2006), which also uses the category 'family time', only quotes mothers as viewing it positively rather than a chore.
3 Based on a measure developed by Hawkins *et al.* (2002).

4 Performing emotion

1 Calculating the timing of this move is difficult: referring back to the US of the 1930s, Griswold (1993) notes how experts on parenting had already begun to declare that love and involvement had taken over from discipline and authority as the hallmarks of the modern father.

5 Linking fatherhood and motherhood

1 See appendix for details of how interviewees were contacted.
2 The intention with this sample of fathers had been to speak only to men who were co-resident with their children and partner. Raj was approached for an interview because he had not fully completed the initial questionnaire and his circumstances only became apparent during the interview.
3 See appendix.

6 Policy: defining and accommodating fathers

1 This may be unfounded since, while there remains a considerable shortage in donors, the figures for the year after the introduction of the new legislation has not shown a reduction (Human Fertilisation and Embryology Authority 2007). However, publicity around the issue may have been responsible for prompting some additional donors to come forward, thereby mitigating the negative effects of the law change.
2 This publication was by the left-leaning think tank, the Institute for Public Policy Research which was influential for New Labour policy. The lead author, Baroness Blackstone was a Labour peer in the House of Lords and two other authors went on to take up positions in subsequent Labour governments.
3 In 2003 Gordon Brown (who at the time was Chancellor of the Exchequer) followed suit and also took two weeks of paternity leave after the birth of his son.
4 Memoranda and oral representations to the Select Committee on Social Security from a number of organisations and individuals made this point, including The Fawcett Society, Parental Leave Campaign, Parents at Work, Transport and General Workers Union and the GMB.
5 This was extended in 2007 to include carers of adults.

7 Fragile fathering

1 A significant proportion of these men will eventually move into a joint home with the mother and their child: in a sample of over 3,500 fathers who were a non-resident parent at the time of birth, 24 per cent were living with the mother and their child by the time the child was nine months old (Kiernan 2006).
2 http://www.fathers-4-justice.org/f4j/.
3 http://www.realfathersforjustice.org/.
4 http://www.fnf.org.uk.
5 The original Fathers 4 Justice manifesto (2003) declared that one problem they wished to counter was that of 'children growing up with multiple surrogate fathers but being denied access to their natural father' to read 'After disbanding in 2006, Fathers4Justice was relaunched in 2007. The original manifesto is no longer available from the new website.

References

Adam, B. (1995) *Timewatch*. Cambridge: Polity Press.

Adkins, L. (2003) 'Reflexivity: Freedom or Habit of Gender?', *Theory, Culture and Society* 20(6): 21–42.

Ambert, A-M. (1994) 'An International Perspective on Parenting: Social Change and Social Constructs', *Journal of Marriage and the Family* 56(3): 529–43.

Amis, M. (2000) *Experience*. London: Jonathan Cape.

Arendell, T. (1995) *Fathers and Divorce*. Thousand Oaks, CA: Sage.

Arendell, T. (2000) 'Conceiving and Investigating Motherhood: The Decade's Scholarship', *Journal of Marriage and the Family* 62(4): 1192–207.

Ariès, P. (1962) *Centuries of Childhood*. New York: Vintage Books.

Atkinson, M.P. and Blackwelder, S.P. (1993) 'Fathering in the 20th Century', *Journal of Marriage and the Family* 55(4): 975–86.

Babb, P., Butcher, H., Church, J. and Zealey, L. (2006) (eds) *Social Trends No. 36*. Office for National Statistics. Basingstoke: Palgrave Macmillan.

Backett, K. (1987) 'The Negotiation of Fatherhood', in Lewis, C. and O'Brien, M. (eds) *Reassessing Fatherhood*. London: Sage.

Bainham, A. (2002) 'Can we Protect Children and Protect their Rights?', *Family Law* 32(4): 279–89.

Barnes, H., Day, P. and Cronin, N. (1998) *Trial and Error: A Review of UK Child Support Policy*. London: Family Policy Studies Centre.

Baxter, J. (2000) 'The Joys and Justices of Housework', *Sociology* 34(4): 609–31.

BBC (2003) 'Blood Claims IVF Paternity Victory'. 28 February. http://news.bbc.co.uk/1/hi/health/2807707.stm (last accessed 30/7/07).

BBC (2004) 'Aggrieved Dads Stage Bridge Protest. 2 February. http://news.bbc.co.uk/1/hi/england/bristol/3450415.stm (last accessed 30/7/07).

BBC (2007) 'Eddie Murphy Confirms Paternity'. 4 August http://news.bbc.co.uk/1/hi/entertainment/6931037.stm (last accessed 30/7/07).

Beck, U. and Beck-Gernsheim, E. (1995) *The Normal Chaos of Love*. Cambridge: Polity Press.

Beck-Gernsheim, E. (1998) 'On the Way to a Post-familial Family: From a Community of Need to Elective Affinities', *Theory, Culture and Society* 15(3/4): 53–70.

Beck-Gernsheim, E. (2002) *Reinventing the Family: In Search of New Lifestyles*. Cambridge: Polity Press.

Bell, A., Kazirmirski, A. and La Valle, I. (2006a) *An Investigation of CSA Maintenance Direct Payments – Qualitative Study*. London: National Centre for Social Research.

Bell, A., Bryson, C., Southwood, H. and Butt, S. (2006b) *An Investigation of CSA Maintenance Direct Payments – Quantitative Study*. London: National Centre for Social Research.

Berkowitz, D. and Marsiglio, W. (2007) 'Gay Men: Negotiating Procreative, Father and Family Identities', *Journal of Marriage and the Family* 69(2): 366–81.

Bernard, J. (1981) 'The Good-Provider Role: Its Rise and Fall', *American Psychologist* 36(1): 1–12.

Bertoia, C. and Drakich, J. (1993) 'The Fathers' Rights Movement: Contradictions in Rhetoric and Practice', *Journal of Family Issues* 14(4): 592–615.

Bianchi, S. (2000) 'Maternal Employment and Time With Children: Dramatic Change or Surprising Continuity?', *Demography* 37(4): 401–14.

Bittman, M. (2004) 'Parenting and Employment: What Time-Use Surveys Show', in Folbre, N. and Bittman, M. (eds) *Family Time: The Social Organization of Care*. London: Routledge.

Bittman, M., Craig, L. and Folbre, N. (2004) 'Packaging Care: What Happens when Children Receive Non-Parental Care?', in Folbre, N. and Bittman, M. (eds) *Family Time: The Social Organization of Care*. London: Routledge.

Björnberg, U. (1992) 'Parenting in Transition', in Björnberg, U. (ed.) *European Parents in the 1990s*. New Brunswick, NJ: Transaction Publishers.

Björnberg, U. (1995) 'Family Orientation among Men: Fatherhood and Partnership in a Process of Change', in Brannen, J. and O'Brien, M. (eds) *Childhood and Parenthood*. London: Institute of Education.

Blackstone, T., Cornford, J., Hewitt, P. and Miliband, D. (1992) *Next Left: An Agenda for the 1990s*. London: IPPR.

Blakenhorn, D. (1995) *Fatherless America: Confronting our Most Urgent Social Problem*. New York: Basic Books.

Boyd, S.B. (2006) 'Robbed of their Families? Fathers' Rights Discourses in Canadian Parenting Law Reform Processes', in Collier, R. and Sheldon, S. (eds) *Fathers' Rights Activism and Law Reform in Comparative Perspective*. Oxford: Hart.

Bradley, H., Erickson, M., Stephenson, C. and Williams, C. (2000) *Myths at Work*. Cambridge: Polity Press.

Bradley, H., Frost, J., Levitas, R., Smith, L. and Garcia, J. (2002) *Women's Experience of Early Pregnancy Loss*. Final Report to: National Health Service Executive Research and Development Directorate.

Bradshaw, J. and Millar, J. (1991) *Lone-Parent Families in the UK*. London: HMSO.

Bradshaw, J., Stimson, C., Skinner, C. and Williams, J. (1999) *Absent Fathers?* London: Routledge.

Brandth, B. and Kvande, E. (1998) 'Masculinity and Childcare: The Reconstruction of Fathering', *The Sociological Review* 46(2): 293–313.

Brandth, B. and Kvande, E. (2001) 'Flexible Work and Flexible Fathers', *Work, Employment and Society* 15(2): 251–67.

Brannen, J. (2002) 'The Work Family Lives of Women: Autonomy or Illusion?', paper presented to the Gender Institute Seminar, LSE, 25 October.

Brannen, J. and Moss, P. (1991) *Managing Mothers*. London: Unwin Hyman.

Brannen, J. and Nilsen, A. (2006) 'From Fatherhood to Fathering: Transmission and Change among Fathers in Four-generation Families', *Sociology* 40(2): 335–52.

British Association for Adoption and Fostering (2007) *First Questions*. http://www.baaf.org.uk/info/firstq/adoption.shtml#tell   http://www.baaf.org.uk/info/firstq/adoption.shtml#contact (last accessed 28/8/07).

Brannen, J., Dodd, K., Oakley, A. and Storey, P. (1994) *Young People, Health and Family Life*. Buckingham: Open University Press.

Bronstein, P. and Cowan, C.P. (1988) *Fatherhood Today: Men's Changing Role in the Family*. New York: John Wiley and Son.

Brown, F. H. (1989) 'The Impact of Death and Serious Illness on the Family Life Cycle' in Carter, B. and McGoldrick, M. (eds) *The Changing Family Life Cycle* (2nd edition). Boston, MA: Allyn and Bacon.

Budgeon, S. and Roseneil, S. (2004) 'Beyond the Conventional Family', *Current Sociology* 52(2): 127–34.

Bunting, L. and McAuley, C. (2004) 'Research Review: Teenage Pregnancy and Parenthood: The Role of Fathers', *Child and Family Social Work* 9(3): 295–303.

Burgess, A. (1997) *Fatherhood Reclaimed: The Making of the Modern Father*. London: Vermilion.

Burghes, L., Clarke, L. and Cronin, N. (1997) *Fathers and Fatherhood in Britain*. London: Family Policy Studies Centre.

Calderwood, L. (2004) 'Patterns of Parenthood at the Beginning of the 21st Century', Paper presented at Family Futures Conference, London, 17 June.

Calderwood, L., Kiernan, K., Joshi, H., Smith, K. and Ward, K. (2005) 'Parenthood and Parenting', in Dex, S. and Joshi, H. (eds) *Children of the 21 Century*. Bristol: Policy Press.

Carsten, J. (2007) 'Recognising Relations', paper presented at Extended and Extending Families Centre for Research on Families and Relationships International Conference, 27–29 June.

Castelain-Meunier, C. (2002) 'The Place of Fatherhood and the Parental Role: Tensions, Ambivalence and Contradictions', *Current Sociology* 50(2): 185–201.

Christiansen, S.L. and Palkovitz, R. (2001) 'Why the "Good Provider" Role Still Matters: Providing as a Form of Paternal Involvement', *Journal of Family Issues* 22(1): 84–106.

Clarke, L., Cooksey, E.C. and Verropoulou, G. (1998) 'Fathers and Absent Fathers: Socio-Demographic Similarities in Britain and the United States', *Demography* 35(2): 217–28.

Cohen, T.F. (1993) 'What Do Fathers Provide? Reconsidering the Economic and Nurturant Dimensions of Men as Parents' in Hood, J.C. (ed.) *Men, Work and Family*. Newbury Park, CA: Sage.

Collier, R. (1999) 'Men, Heterosexuality and the Changing Family: (Re)constructing Fatherhood in Law and Social Policy' in Jagger, G. and Wright, C. (eds) *Changing Family Values*. London: Routledge.

Collier, R. (2005) 'Fathers 4 Justice, Law and the New Politics of Fatherhood', *Child and Family Law Quarterly* 17(4): 1–29.

Collier, R. (2006) ' "The Outlaw Fathers Fight Back": Fathers' Rights Groups, Fathers 4 Justice and the Politics of Family Law Reform – Reflections on the UK Experience', in Collier, R. and Sheldon, S. (eds) *Fathers' Rights Activism and Law Reform in Comparative Perspective*. Oxford: Hart.

Collier, R. and Sheldon, S. (2006) 'Fathers' Rights, Fatherhood and Law Reform – International Perspectives', in Collier, R. and Sheldon, S. (eds) *Fathers' Rights Activism and Law Reform in Comparative Perspective*. Oxford: Hart.

Collier, R. and Sheldon, S. (forthcoming 2008) *Fatherhood: A Socio-Legal Study*. Oxford: Hart.

Coltrane, S. (1996) *Family Man: Family, Housework and Gender Equality*. New York: Oxford University Press.

Coltrane, S. (2004) 'Fathers' in *Sloan Work and Family Research Network Overviews and Briefs*. http://wfnetwork.bc.edu/encyclopedia_template.php?id=236 (last accessed 30/8/07).

Commons Select Committee on Social Security (1999) 'Social Security Implications of Parent Leave'. http://www.publications.parliament.uk/pa/cm200001/cmselect/cmliaisn/321/321v223.htm (last accessed 8/8/07).

Connell, R.W. (1998) 'Men in The World: Masculinities and Globalisation', *Men and Masculinities* 1(1): 3–23

Connell, R.W. (2000) *The Men and the Boys*. Los Angeles: University of California Press.

Coughlan, S. (2006) 'Should I Stay or Should I Go?' *BBC* 1 March http://news.bbc.co.uk/1/low/magazine/4758354.stm (last accessed 29/7/07).

Cowdery, R.S. and Knudson-Martin, C. (2005) 'The Construction of Motherhood: Tasks, Relational Connection, and Gender Equality', *Family Relations* 54(3): 335–45.

Craib, I. (1994) *The Importance of Disappointment*. London: Routledge.

Craig, L. (2006a) 'Does Father Care Mean Fathers Share? A Comparison of How Mothers and Fathers in Intact Families Spend Time with Children', *Gender and Society* 20(2): 259–81.

Craig, L. (2006b) 'Parental Education, Time in Paid Work and Time with Children: an Australian Time-diary Analysis', *British Journal of Sociology* 57(4): 553–75.

Craig, L. (2006c) 'Children and the Revolution: A Time Diary Analysis of the Impact of Motherhood on Daily Workload', *Journal of Sociology* 42(2): 125–43.

Crewe, B. (2003) *Representing Men: Cultural Production and Producers in the Men's Magazine Market*. Oxford: Berg.

Crompton, R. (1993) *Class and Stratification*. Cambridge: Polity Press.

Crompton, R. (2006) *Employment and the Family*. Cambridge: Cambridge University Press.

Crompton, R. and Lyonette, C. (2007) 'Are We all Working too Hard? Women, Men, and Changing Attitudes to Employment', in Park, A., Curtice, J., Thomson, K., Phillips, M. and Johnson, M. (eds) *British Social Attitudes: The 23rd Report – Perspectives on a Changing Society*. London: Sage.

Crompton, R., Brockmann, M. and Wiggins, R.D. (2003) 'A woman's place ... Employment and Family Life for Men and Women' in Park, A., Curtice, J., Thomson, K., Jarvis, L. and Bromley, C. (eds), *British Social Attitudes: The 20th Report*. London: Sage.

Crosbie-Burnett, M. and Helmbrecht, L. (1993) 'A Descriptive Empirical Study of Gay Male Stepfamilies', *Family Relations* 42(3): 256–62.

Crow, G. (2005) *The Art of Sociological Argument*. Basingstoke: Palgrave.

Cunningham-Burley, S. (1984) ' "We Don't Talk About It ..." Issues of Gender and Method in the Portrayal of Grandfatherhood', *Sociology* 18(3): 325–38.

Daily Telegraph (The) (2001) 'False DNA Test Led Father to Reject Daughter', 19 June. http://www.telegraph.co.uk/news/main.jhtml?xml=/news/2001/02/11/ndna11.xml (last accessed 22/8/07).

Daily Telegraph (The) (2002) 'Why Does He Want to Destroy His own Flesh and Blood?', 15 September. http://www.telegraph.co.uk/news/main.jhtml?xml=/news/2002/09/15/nembry15.xml (last accessed 30/7/07).

Daily Telegraph (The) (2007) 'Woman loses Final Frozen Embryo Appeal', 11 April. http://www.telegraph.co.uk/news/main.jhtml?xml=/news/2007/04/10/nembryo110.xml (last accessed 30/7/07).

Daly, K.J. (1995) 'Reshaping Fatherhood: Finding the Models', in Marsiglio, W. (ed.) *Fatherhood; Contemporary Theory, Research and Social Policy*. Newbury Park, CA: Sage.

Daly, K.J. (1996) 'Spending Time with the Kids: Meaning of Family Time for Fathers', *Family Relations* 45(4): 466–76.

Dalzell, A. (2007) 'The Expectation Has Always Been That I'll Not Have Kids' – the Narratives of Childless Gay Men'. Unpublished MEd dissertation, University of Bristol.

Davidoff, L. and Hall, C. (1987) *Family Fortunes: Men and Women of the English Middle-Class 1780–1850*. London: Hutchinson.

Dench, G. (1996) *The Place of Men in Changing Family Culture*. London: Institute of Community Studies.

Dennis, N. and Erdos, G. (1992) *Families without Fatherhood*. London: Institute of Economic Affairs.

Department of Trade and Industry (2007) *Additional Paternity Leave and Pay Administration Consultation*. London: DTI.

Department of Work and Pensions (2005) *Individual Incomes of Men and Women 1996/97 to 2003/04*. London: Women and Equality Unit.

Dermott, E. (2002) 'Fathers' Orientations to Paid Employment', *Gender Institute New Working Paper Series* No.6. London: LSE.

Dermott, E. (2006a) 'What's Parenthood Got To Do With It?: Men's Hours of Paid Work', *British Journal of Sociology* 57(4): 619–34.

Dermott, E. (2006b) *The Effect of Fatherhood on Men's Employment*. Swindon: ESRC.

Deven, F and Moss, P. (2002) 'Leave Arrangements for Parents: Overview and Future Outlook', *Community, Work and Family* 5(3): 237–55.

Deven, F., Inglis, S., Moss, P. and Petrie, P. (1998) *A State of the Art Review on the Reconciliation of Work and Family Life for Men and Women and the Quality of Care Services*. Research Report 44. London: Department for Education and Employment.

Dex, S. and Smith. C. (2002) *The Nature and Patterns of Family-Friendly Employment Policies in Britain*. York: York Publishing Services.

Dex, S. and Ward, K. (2007) *Parental Care and Employment in Early Childhood*. Working Paper Series No.57. London: EOC.

Dey, I. and Wasoff, F. (2006) 'Mixed Messages: Parental Responsibility, Public Attitudes and the Reform of Family Law', *International Journal of Law, Policy and the Family* 20(2): 225–48.

Dienhart, A. (1998) *Reshaping Fatherhood: The Social Construction of Shared Parenting*. Thousand Oaks, CA: Sage.

Doherty, W.J., Kouneski, E.F. and Erickson, M.F. (1998) 'Responsible Fathering: An Overview and Conceptual Framework', *Journal of Marriage and the Family* 60(2): 277–92.

Donovan, C. (2000) 'Who Needs A Father? Negotiating Biological Fatherhood in British Lesbian Families Using Self-Insemination', *Sexualities* 3(2): 149–64.

Doucet, A. (2006) '"Estrogen-filled worlds": Fathers as Primary Caregivers and Embodiment', *The Sociological Review* 54(4): 696–716.

Dowd, N.E. (2000) *Redefining Fatherhood*. New York: New York University Press.

Draper, J. (2002) '"It's the First Scientific Evidence": Men's Experience of Pregnancy Confirmation', *Journal of Advanced Nursing* 39(6): 563–70.

Duncan, S. (2005) 'Mothering, Class and Rationality', *Sociological Review* 53(2): 50–76.

Duncan, S., Edwards, R., Reynolds, T. and Alldred, P. (2003) 'Motherhood, Paid Work and Partnering: Values and Theories', *Work, Employment and Society* 17(2): 309–30.

Dunn, J., Cheng, H., O'Connor, T.G. and Bridges, L. (2004) 'Children's Perspectives on their Relationships with their Nonresident Fathers: Influences, Outcomes and Implications', *Journal of Child Psychology and Psychiatry* 45(3): 553–66.

Dunne, G.A (2001a) 'The Different Dimensions of Gay Fatherhood: Exploding the Myths', Gender Institute Discussion Paper no. 8. http://www.lse.ac.uk/collections/genderInstitute/pdf/gayfatherhood.pdf

Dunne, G.A. (2001b) 'The Lady Vanishes? Reflections on the Experiences of Married and Divorced Non-Heterosexual Fathers', *Sociological Research Online* 6(3). http://www.socresonline.org.uk/6/3/dunne.html.

Edley, N. and Wetherell, M. (1999) 'Imagined Futures: Young Men's Talk about Fatherhood and Domestic Life', *British Journal of Social Psychology* 38(2): 181–94.

Edwards, R. and Gillies, V. (2005) *Resources in Parenting: Access to Capitals Project Report*. Families and Social Capital Research Group Working Paper No.14. London: London South Bank University.

Edwards, R., Bäck-Wiklund, M., Bak, M. and Ribbens-McCarthy, J. (2002) 'Step-fathering: Comparing Policy and Everyday Experience in Britain and Sweden', *Sociological Research Online* 7(1). http://www.socresonline.org.uk/7/1/edwards.html.

Ehrensaft, D. (1985) 'Dual Parenting and the Duel of Intimacy' in Handel, G. (ed.) *The Psychosocial Interior of the Family*. New York: Aldine.

Ehrensaft, D. (1987) *Parenting Together*. New York: The Free Press.

Elliott, H. (2007) 'Becoming A Mother: Emergent Findings', *Making of Modern Motherhoods Fatherhood Seminar*, Open University 8 June 2007.

EOC (2003) *Fathers: Balancing Work and Family*. London: EOC.

Fagan, C. (2001) 'Time, Money and the Gender Order: Work Orientations and Working-Time Preferences in Britain', *Gender, Work and Organization* 8(3): 239–66.

Fagan, J. (2003) 'Prenatal Involvement of Adolescent Unmarried Fathers', *Fathering: A Journal of Theory, Research and Practice* 1(3): 283–302.

Families Need Fathers (2007) 'Families Need Fathers: About Us'. http://www.fnf.org.uk/about-us (last accessed 30/7/07).

Fathers 4 Justice (2003) *Fathers 4 Justice Manifesto*, http://www.fathers-4-justice.org.

Fathers Direct (2001) 'Children Want More Time With Dad'. http://www.fathersdirect.com/index.php?id=3&cID=61 (last accessed 8/7/2007).

Finch, J. and Mason, J. (1993) *Negotiating Family Responsibilities*. London: Routledge.

Firestone, S. (1970) *The Dialectic of Sex*. New York: William Morrow and Company.

Fisher, K., McCulloch, A. and Gershuny, J. (1999) 'British Fathers and Children', *Institute for Social and Economic Research Working Paper*. University of Essex.

Flouri, E. (2005) *Fathering and Child Outcomes*. Chichester: John Wiley and Sons.

Forth, J., Lissenburgh, S., Callender, C. and Millward, N. (1996) *Family-Friendly Working Arrangements in Britain*. DfEE Research Report No.15. London: DfEE.

Freeman, T. (2002) 'Loving Fathers or Deadbeat Dads: The Crisis of Fatherhood in Popular Culture', in Earle, S. and Letherby, G. (eds) *Gender, Identity and Reproduction: Social Perspectives*. London: Palgrave.

Furstenburg, F.F. (1988) 'Good Dads-bad Dads: Two Faces of Fatherhood', in Cherlin, A. J. (ed.) *The Changing American Family and Public Policy*. Washington, DC: Urban Institute Press.

Furstenburg, F.F. (1995) 'Fathering in the Inner City: Paternal Participation and Public Policy', in Marsiglio, W. (ed.) *Fatherhood. Contemporary Theory, Research and Social Policy*. Newbury Park, CA: Sage.

Gabb, J. (forthcoming 2008) *Researching Intimacy and Sexuality*. Basingstoke: Palgrave Macmillan.

Gattrell, C. (2005) *Hard Labour. The Sociology of Parenthood*. Maidenhead: Open University Press.

Gattrell, C. (2007) 'Whose Child is it Anyway? The Negotiation of Paternal Entitlements within Marriage', *The Sociological Review* 55(2): 352–72.

Gauthier, A.H., Smeeding, T.M. and Fursternberg, F.F. (2004) 'Are Parents Investing Less Time in Children? Trends in Selected Industrialized Countries', *Demography* 30(4): 647–71.

Gavanas, A. (2002) 'The Fatherhood Responsibility Movement: The Centrality of Marriage, Work and Male Sexuality in Reconstructions of Masculinity and Fatherhood' in Hobson, B. (ed.) *Making Men Into Fathers: men, masculinities and the social politics of fatherhood*. Cambridge: Polity Press.

Geldof, B. (2002) 'Interview by Jonathan Maitland', *ITV 'Tonight'* 17 June.

Gershuny, J. (2001) *Changing Times*. New York: Oxford University Press.

Gershuny, J. and Sullivan, O. (1998) 'The Sociological Uses of Time-use Diary Analysis', *European Sociological Review* 14(1): 69–85.

Gershuny, J. Godwin, M. and Jones, S. (1994), 'The Domestic Labour Revolution: A Process of Lagged Adaptation', in Anderson, M., Bechhofer, F. and Gershuny, J. (eds) *The Social and Political Economy of the Household*. Oxford: Oxford University Press.

Giddens, A. (1992) *The Transformation of Intimacy*. Cambridge: Polity Press.

Giddens, A. (2000) *Runaway World: How Globalization is Reshaping Our Lives*. London: Routledge.

Gill, R. (2003) 'Power and the Production of Subjects: A Genealogy of the New Man and the New Lad'. http://www.lse.ac.uk/collections/genderInstitute/pdf/powerAndProduction. pdf (last accessed 16/7/2007).

Gillies, V. (2007) *Marginalised Mothers*. London: Routledge.

Gillis, J. (2000) 'Marginalization of Fatherhood in Western Countries', *Childhood* 7(2): 225–38.

Goleman, D. (1995) *Emotional Intelligence: Why It Can Matter More Than IQ*. New York: Bantam Books.

Golombok, S., Cook, R., Bish, A. and Murray, C. (1995) 'Families Created by the New Reproductive Technologies: Quality of Parenting and Social and Emotional Development of the Children', *Child Development* 66(2): 285–98.

Golombok, S., Murray, C., Brinsden, P. and Abdalla, H. (1999) 'Social versus Biological Parenting: Family Functioning and the Socioemotional Development of Children Conceived by Egg or Sperm Donation', *Journal of Child Psychology* 40(4): 519–27.

Government Consultation Document (Green Paper) (1998) *Supporting Families*. London: The Stationery Office.

Government Consultation Document (Green Paper) (2000) *Work and Parents: Competitiveness and Choice*. London: The Stationery Office.

Government Consultation Document (Green Paper) (2003) *Every Child Matters*. London: The Stationery Office.'

Government Consultation Document (White Paper) (1998) *Fairness at Work*. London: The Stationery Office.

Gray, A. (2006) 'The Time Economy of Parenting', *Sociological Research Online* 11(3). http://www.socresonline.org.uk/11/3/gray.html.

Greif, G.L. (1985) *Single Fathers*. Lexingon, MA: Lexington Books.

Griswold, R.L. (1993) *Fatherhood in America*. New York: Basic Books.

Gross, N. (2005) 'The Detraditionalization of Intimacy Reconsidered', *Sociological Theory* 23(3): 286–311.

Grundy, E. (2005) 'Reciprocity in Relationships: Socio-Economic and Health Influences on Intergenerational Exchanges between Third Age Parents and their Adult Children in Great Britain', *British Journal of Sociology* 56(2): 233–55.

Guinness, L. (ed.) (1998) *The Vintage Book of Fathers*. London: Vintage.

Hakim, C. (1991) 'Grateful Slaves and Self-Made Women: Fact and Fantasy in Women's Work Orientations', *European Sociological Review* 7(2): 101–21.

Harkness, S., Machin, S. and Waldfogel, J. (2004) *The Decline of the Male Breadwinner*. London: STICERD, London School of Economics.

Harman, H. (2007) *The Hidden Heroes of International Development: Remittances from the Southwark African Diaspora to families and villages in Africa*. London: House of Commons.

Harrington, M. (2006) 'Sport and Leisure as Contexts for Fathering in Australian Families', *Leisure Studies* 25(2): 165–83.

Harrison, F. (1985) *A Father's Diary*. London: Fontana.

Hatten, W., Vinter, L. and Williams, R. (2002) *Dads on Dads: Needs and Expectations at Home and at Work*. London: EOC.

Hawkins, A.J., Bradford, K.P., Palkovitz, R., Christiansen, S.L., Day, R.D. and Call, V.R.A. (2002) 'The Inventory of Father Involvement: A Pilot Study of a New Measure of Father Involvement', *Journal of Men's Studies* 10(2): 183–96.

Hays, S. (1996) *The Cultural Contradictions of Motherhood*. New Haven, CT: Yale University Press.

Henwood, K. (2005) *Masculinities, Identities and the Transition to Fatherhood*. Swindon: ESRC.

Henwood, K.L. and Procter, J. (2003) 'The "Good Father": Reading Men's Accounts of Paternal Involvement during the Transition to First Time Fatherhood', *British Journal of Social Psychology* 42(3): 337–55.

Himmelweit, S. (1995) 'The Discovery of Unpaid Work: The Social Consequences of the Expansion of Work', *Feminist Economics* 1(2): 1–20.

Himmelweit, S. and Sigala, M. (2004), 'Choice and Relationship between Identities and Behaviour for Mothers with Pre-School Children: Some Implications for Policy from a UK study', *Journal of Social Policy* 33(3): 455–78.

Hobson, B. (ed.) (2002) *Making Men Into Fathers: Men, Masculinities and the Social Politics of Fatherhood*. Cambridge: Polity Press.

Hobson, B. and Morgan, D. (2002) 'Introduction' in Hobson, B. (ed.) *Making Men Into Fathers: Men, Masculinities and the Social Politics of Fatherhood*. Cambridge: Polity Press.

Hochschild, A. (1995) 'Understanding the Future of Fatherhood: The "Daddy Hierarchy" and Beyond', in Van Dongen, M.C.P., Frinking, G.A.B. and Jacobs, M.J.G. (eds.) *Changing Fatherhood: A Multidisciplinary Perspective*. Amsterdam: Thesis Publishers.

Højgaard, L. (1997) 'Working Fathers – Caught in the Web of the Symbolic Order of Gender', *Acta Sociologica* 40(3): 245–61.

Hood, J.C. (1986) 'The Provider Role: Its Meaning and Measurement', *Journal of Marriage and the Family* 48(2): 349–59.

Hook, J.L. (2006) 'Care in Context: Men's Unpaid Work in 20 countries, 1965–2003', *American Sociological Review* 71(4): 639–60.

Hornby, N. (1998) *About A Boy*. London: Gollancz.

Human Fertilisation and Embryology Authority (2007) 'Number of Sperm Donors up Following Anonymity Law Changes'. http://www.hfea.gov.uk/en/1523.html (last accessed 24/7/07).

Hunt, J. and Roberts, C. (2004) 'Child Contact With Non-Resident Parents', *Family Policy Briefing No. 3*. Oxford: Department of Social Policy and Social Work, University of Oxford.

Hutton, J. (2006) 'Statement on Child Support Redesign. Department for Work and Pensions', 24 July. http://www.dwp.gov.uk/aboutus/2006/24-07-06.asp (last accessed 8/8/07). Cited on P180

Income Data Services (2000) *Maternity and Parental Leave* No. 688, London: IDS

Irwin, S. (2005) *Reshaping Social Life*. Abingdon: Routledge.

Ishii-Kuntz, M., Makino, K., Kato, K. and Tsuchiya, M. (2004) 'Japanese Fathers of Preschoolers and Their Involvement in Child Care', *Journal of Marriage and Family* 66: 779–91.

Jackson, B. (1984) *Fatherhood*. London: Allen and Unwin.

Jamieson, L. (1998) *Intimacy: Personal Relationships in Modern Society*. Cambridge: Polity Press.

Jamieson, L. (1999) 'Intimacy Transformed? A Critical Look at the "Pure Relationship"', *Sociology* 33(3): 477–94.

Jamieson, L. (2005a) 'Intimacy', in Ritzer, G. (ed.) *Encyclopedia of Sociology*. Oxford: Blackwell.

Jamieson, L. (2005b) 'Boundaries of Intimacy', in McKie, L. and Cunningham-Burley, S. (eds) *Families in Society: Boundaries and Relationships*. Bristol: Policy Press.

Jamieson, L., Morgan, D., Crow, G. and Allan, G. (2006) 'Friends, Neighbours and Distant Partners: Extending or Decentring Family Relationships?', *Sociological Research Online* 11(3). http://www.socresonline.org.uk/11/3/jamieson.html.

Jayakody, R. and Kalil, A. (2002) 'Social Fathering in Low-Income, African American Families with Preschoolers', *Journal of Marriage and the Family* 64(2): 504–16.

Jensen, A-M. (1998) 'Partnership and Parenthood in Contemporary Europe: A Review of Recent Findings', *European Journal of Population* 14(1): 89–99.

Jensen, A-M. (1999) 'Partners and Parents in Europe: A Gender Divide', in Leira, A. (ed.) *Comparative Social Research Vol. 18: Family Change: Practices, Policies and Values*. Stanford, CA: JAI Press.

Johnson, M.P. and Puddifoot, J.E. (1998) 'Miscarriage: Is Vividness of Visual Imagery a Factor in the Grief Reaction of the Partner?', *British Journal of Health Psychology* 3(2): 137–46.

Jones, G. (2004) *The Parenting of Youth: Social Protection and Economic Dependence*. Swindon: ESRC.

Keane, F. (1996) *Letter to Daniel: Dispatches from the Heart*. London: Penguin.

Kielty, S. (2005) 'Mothers Are Non-Resident Parents Too: A Consideration of Mothers' Perspectives on Non-residential Parenthood', *Journal of Social Welfare and Family Law* 27(1): 1–16.

Kiernan, K. (2004) 'Changing European Families: Trends and Issues', in Scott, J., Treas, J. and Richards, M. (eds) *The Blackwell Companion to the Sociology of Families*. Oxford: Blackwell.

Kiernan, K. (2006) 'Non-residential Fatherhood and Child Involvement: Evidence from the Millennium Cohort Study', *Journal of Social Policy* 35(4): 651–69.

Kiernan, K. and Smith, K. (2003) 'Unmarried Parenthood: New Insights from the Millennium Cohort Study', *Population Trends* 114(Winter): 26–33.

Kitterød, R.H. and Lyngstad. J. (2007) 'Fathering from a Distance – Are Wealthy Fathers More Successful? The Effects of Fathers' Socio-economic Characteristics on Contact with Non-resident Children', paper presented at Extended and Extending Families, Centre for Research on Families and Relationships International Conference, 27–29 June.

Knijn, T. (1995) 'Towards Post-paternalism? Social and Theoretical changes in Fatherhood', in van Dongen, M., Frinking, G. and Jacobs, M. (eds) *Changing Fatherhood: A Multidisciplinary Perspective*. Amsterdam: Thesis Publishers.

La Rossa, R. (1988) 'Fatherhood and Social Change', *Family Relations* 37(4): 451–7.

La Rossa, R. (1997) *The Modernization of Fatherhood: A Social and Political History*. Chicago, IL: University of Chicago Press.

La Rossa, R. (2005) ' "Until the Ball Glows in the Twilight": Fatherhood, Baseball, and the Game of Playing Catch', in Marsiglio, W., Roy, K. and Litton Fox, G. (eds) *Situated Fathering: A Focus on Physical and Social Space*. Oxford: Rowman and Littlefield.

La Valle. I., Arthur, S., Millward, C., Scott, J. and Clayden, M. (2002) *Happy Families? Atypical Work and its Influence on Family Life*. Bristol: Policy Press.

Lamb, M.E. (1993) 'Review: Fatherhood in America: A History, Fathers and Families: Paternal Factors in Child Development', *Journal of Marriage and the Family* 55(4): 1047–9.

Lamb, M.E., Pleck, J.H., Charnov, E.L. and Levine, J.A. (1987) 'A Biosocial Perspective on Paternal Behaviour and Involvement', in Lancaster, J.B., Altmann, J., Rossi, A.S. and Sherrod, L.R. (eds) *Parenting Across the Lifespan: Biosocial Perspectives*. New York: Academic Press.

Larder, D., Short, S. and Gershuny, J. (2006) *Time Use Study 2005: How We Spend our Time*. London: ONS.

Lash, S. (1994) 'Reflexivity and its Doubles: Structure, Aesthetics, Community', in Beck, U., Giddens, A. and Lash, S. (eds) *Reflexive Modernization*. London: Polity Press.

Leroy, M. (1988) *Miscarriage*. London: Miscarriage Association.

Letherby, G. (1994), 'Mother or Not, Mother or What? Problems of Definition and Identity', *Women's Studies International Forum* 17(5): 525–32.

Letherby, G. and Williams, C. (1999) 'Non-Motherhood: Ambivalent Autobiographies', *Feminist Studies* 25(3): 719–28.

Levitas, R. (1998) *The Inclusive Society? Social Exclusion and New Labour*. Basingstoke: Macmillan.

Lewis, C. (1986) *Becoming a Father*. Milton Keynes: Open University Press.

Lewis, C. (1995) 'Comment on Van Dongen, M. "Men's Aspirations Concerning Child Care: The Extent to which They Are Realised" ', in Van Dongen, M., Frinking G. and Jacobs, M. (eds) *Changing Fatherhood: A Multidisciplinary Perspective*. Amsterdam: Thesis Publishers.

Lewis, C. (2000) *A Man's Place: Fathers and Families in the UK*. York: Joseph Rowntree Foundation.

Lewis, C. and Lamb, M.E. (2003) 'Fathers' Influences on Children's Development: the Evidence from Two-parent Families', *European Journal of Psychology of Education* 18(2): 211–28.

Lewis, C. and Lamb, M.E. (2006) *Fatherhood: Connecting the Strands of Diversity across Time and Space*. York: Joseph Rowntree Foundation.

Lewis, C. and O'Brien, M. (1987) (eds) *Reassessing Fatherhood: New Observations on Fathers and the Modern Family*. Newbury Park, CA: Sage.

Lewis, C. and Warin, J. (2001) 'What Good Are Dads?' Fathers Direct. http://www.fathersdirect.com/index.php?id=3&cID=59 (last accessed 29/7/07).

Lewis, C., Papacosta, A. and Warin, J. (2002) *Cohabitation, Separation and Fatherhood*. York: Joseph Rowntree Foundation.

Lewis, J. (1992) 'Gender and the Development of Welfare Regimes', *Journal of European Social Policy* 2(3): 159–73.

Lewis, J. (2001) 'The Decline of the Male Breadwinner Model: Implications for Work and Care', *Social Politics* 8(2): 152–69.

Lewis, J. (2002) 'Policy and Behaviour in Britain', in Hobson, B. (ed.) *Making Men Into Fathers: Men, Masculinities and the Social Politics of Fatherhood*. Cambridge: Cambridge University Press.

Lewis, J. (2007) 'Balancing Work and Family: The Nature of the Policy Challenge and Gender Equality', *Gender Equality Network Newsletter* No. 2. http://www.genet.ac.uk/newsletter/newsletter_feb07.pdf (last accessed 10/7/2007).

Lewis, J. and Campbell, M. (2007) 'Work/Family Balance Policies in the UK since 1997: A New Departure?', *Journal of Social Policy* 36(3): 365–81.

Lewis-Stempel, J. (2001) *Fatherhood: An Anthology*. London: Simon and Schuster.

Lin, I-F. and McLanahan, S. (2007) 'Parental Beliefs about Nonresident Fathers' Obligations and Rights', *Journal of Marriage and Family* 69(2): 382–98.

Lummis, T. (1982) 'The Historical Dimension of Fatherhood: A Case Study 1890–1914', in McKee, L. and O'Brien, M. (eds) *The Father Figure*. London: Tavistock Publications.

Lundberg, S. and Rose, E. (2000) 'Parenthood and the Earnings of Married Men and Women', *Labour Economics* 7(6): 689–710.

Lupton, D. (2000) ' "A Love/Hate Relationship": The Ideals and Experiences of First-time Mothers', *Journal of Sociology* 36(1): 50–63.

Lupton, D. and Barclay, L. (1997) *Constructing Fatherhood: Discourses and Experiences*. London: Sage.

McGlone, F., Park, A. and Roberts, C. (1996) 'Kinship and Friendship: Attitudes and Behaviour in Britain, 1986–1995', in Jowell, R., Curtice, J., Park, A., Brook, L. and Thomson, K. (eds) *British Social Attitudes Survey: The 13th Report*. Aldershot: Dartmouth.

McGlone, F., Park, A. and Smith, K. (1998) *Families and Kinship*. York: Family Policy Studies Centre/Joseph Rowntree Foundation.

McKie, L., Bowlby, S. and Gregory, S. (2001) 'Gender, Caring and Employment in Britain', *Journal of Social Policy* 30(2): 233–58.

McMahon, A. (1999) *Taking Care of Men*. Cambridge: Cambridge University Press.

Mander, R. (2004) *Men and Maternity*. Abingdon: Routledge.

Marsiglio, W. (1993) 'Contemporary Scholarship on Fatherhood: Culture, Identity and Conduct', *Journal of Family Issues* 14(4): 484–509.

Marsiglio, W. (1998) *Procreative Man*. New York: New York University Press.

Marsiglio, W. (2004) *Stepdads: Stories of Love, Hope, and Repair*. Lanham, MD: Rowman and Littlefield.

Marsiglio, W. and Cohan, M. (2000) 'Contextualizing Father Involvement and Paternal Influence: Sociological and Qualitative Themes' *Marriage and Family Review* 29(2/3): 75–95.

Marsiglio, W., Amato, P., Day, R.D. and Lamb, M.E. (2000) 'Scholarship on Fatherhood in the 1990s and Beyond', *Journal of Marriage and the Family* 62(4): 1173–91.

Masardo, A. (2007) 'Managing Shared Residence: Fathers' Dilemmas and the Challenges for Law, Policy and Practice', paper presented at Extended and Extending Families, Centre for Research on Families and Relationships International Conference, 27–29 June.

Matheson, J. and Summerfield, C. (eds) (2001) *Social Focus on Men*. London: The Stationery Office.

Maushart, S. (2002) *Wifework: What Marriage Really Means for Women*. London: Bloomsbury.

Morgan, D.H.J. (1992) *Discovering Men*. London: Routledge.

Morgan, D.H.J. (1996) *Family Connections*. Cambridge: Polity Press.

Morgan, D.H.J. (1998) 'Risk and Family Practices: Accounting for Change and Fluidity in Family Life', in Silva, E.B. and Smart, C. (eds) *The New Family?* London: Sage.

Morgan, D.H.J. (2003) 'Fathers, Fatherhood, Fathering: Exploring and Unpacking Distinctions', paper presented at Father Figures: Gender and Paternity in the Modern Age, Liverpool John Moores University, 30 June–2 July.

Morgan, D.H.J. (2004) 'Men in Families and Households', in Scott, J., Treas, J. and Richards, M. (eds) *The Blackwell Companion to the Sociology of Families*. Oxford: Blackwell.

Moriarty, H.J., Carroll, R. and Cotroneo, M. (1996) 'Differences in Bereavement Reactions within Couples Following Death of a Child', *Research in Nursing and Health* 19(6): 461–9.

Morrison, B. (1993) And *When Did You Last See Your Father?* London: Granta.

Morrison, B. (2007) 'The Paternal Instinct', *The Guardian* 16 June. http://www.guardian.co.uk/family/story/0,,2103165,00.html (last accessed 30/6/07).

Municio-Larsson, I. and Pujol Algans, C. (2002) 'Making Sense of Fatherhood: The Non-Payment of Child Support in Spain', in Hobson, B. (ed.) *Making Men Into Fathers: Men, Masculinities and the Social Politics of Fatherhood*. Cambridge: Polity Press.

Murphy, F.A. (1998) 'The Experience of Miscarriage from a Male Perspective', *Journal of Clinical Nursing* 7(4): 325–32.

National Health Service (2005) *NHS Maternity Services Quantitative Research*. London: Department of Health.

Neale, B. (2004) 'Privately Ordered Arrangements for Contact after Divorce: The Dynamics of Child-parent Relationships', ESRC/Scottish Executive Public Policy Seminar. http://www.crfr.ac.uk/Reports/ESRC-SE.pdf (last accessed 30/7/07).

Neale, B. and Smart, C. (1997) 'Experiments with Parenthood', *Sociology* 31(2): 210–19.

New Ways to Work (1999) 'Memoranda Submitted to the Select Committee on Social Security', http://www.parliament.the-stationery-office.co.uk/pa/cm1999899/cmselect/cmsocsec/543/54302.htm (last accessed 29/7/07).

Nolan, J. and Scott, J. (2006) 'Gender and Kinship in Contemporary Britain', in Ethan, F., Lindley, B. and Richards, M. (eds) *Kinship Matters*. Oxford: Hart.

O'Brien, M. (2005) *Shared Caring: Bringing Fathers into the Frame*. London: EOC.

O'Brien, M. and Jones, D. (1995) 'Young People's Attitudes to Fatherhood', in Moss, P. (ed.) *Father Figures: Fathers in the Families of the 1990s*. Edinburgh: HMSO.

O'Brien, M. and Schemilt, I. (2003) *Working Fathers – Earning and Caring*. London: EOC.

Oakley, A. (1979) *From Here to Maternity*. Oxford: Martin Robertson.

Observer (The) (2002) 'The Right to An Identity', 16 June. http://observer.guardian.co.uk/comment/story/0,,737777,00.html (last accessed 22/8/07).

Observer (The) (2006) 'Andrew Flintoff: This Much I Know', 14 May. http://sport.guardian.co.uk/cricket/theobserver/story/0,,1774150,00.html (last accessed 29/7/07).

Oláh, L. Sz. Bernhardt, E.M. and Goldscheider, F.K. (2002) 'Coresidential Paternal Roles in Industrialised Countries: Sweden, Hungary and the United States' in Hobson, B. (2002) (ed.) *Making Men into Fathers: Men, Masculinities and the Social Politics of Fatherhood*. Cambridge: Polity Press.

Pahl, R. (2000) *On Friendship*. Cambridge: Polity Press.

Palkovitz, R. (1985) 'Fathers' Birth Attendance, Early Contact and Extended Contact with their Newborns: A Critical Review' *Child Development* 56: 392–406.

Palkovitz, R. (1997) 'Reconstructing "Involvement": Expanding Men's Conceptualizations of Men's Caring in Contemporary Families', in Hawkins, A.J. and Dolerite, D.C. (eds) *Generative Fathering: Beyond Deficit Perspectives*. Thousand Oaks, CA: Sage.

Parsons, T. (1999) *Man and Boy*. London: Harper Collins.

Patterson, C.J. and Chan, R. W. (1997) 'Gay Fathers', in M.E. Lamb (ed.) *The Role of the Father in Child Development* (3rd edition). New York: Wiley and Sons.

Perälä-Littunen, S. (2007) 'Gender Equality or Primacy of the Mother? Ambivalent Descriptions of Good Parents', *Journal of Marriage and Family* 69(2): 341–51.

Peters, E. and Day, R.D. (eds) (2000) *Fatherhood: Research, Inventions and Policies*. New York: Haworth.

Phoenix, A. and Woolett, A. (1991) 'Motherhood: Social Construction, Politics and Psychology', in Phoenix, A., Woolett, A. and Lloyd, E. (eds) *Motherhood. Meanings, Practices and Ideologies*. London: Sage.

Pleck, E. and Pleck, J.H. (1997) 'Fatherhood Ideals in the United States: Historical Dimensions', in M. Lamb (ed.) *The Role of the Father in Child Development* (3rd edition) New York: John Wiley and Sons.

Pleck, J.H. (1993) 'Are Family-Supportive Policies Relevant to Men?', in Hood, J.C. (ed.) *Men, Work and Family*. Newbury Park, CA: Sage.

Pleck, J.H. and Masciadrelli, B.P. (2004) 'Paternal Involvement by US Residential Fathers: Levels, Sources and Consequences', in Lamb, M.E. (ed.) *The Role of the Father in Child Development* (4th edition) New York: John Wiley and Sons.

Popenoe, D. (1996) *Life Without Father*. New York: Free Press.

Pryor, J. and Trinder, L. (2004) 'Children, Families and Divorce', in Scott, J., Treas, J. and Richards, M. (eds) *The Blackwell Companion to the Sociology of Families*. Oxford: Blackwell.

Puddifoot, J.E. and Johnson, M.P. (1997) 'The Legitimacy of Grieving: The Partner's Experience at Miscarriage', *Social Science and Medicine* 45(6): 837–45.

Queniart, A. (2004) 'A Profile of Young Fatherhood Among Young Men', *Sociological Research Online* 9(4). http://www.socresonline.org.uk/9/4/queniart.html.html.

Quinton, D., Pollock, S. and Golding, J. (2002) *The Transition to Fatherhood in Young Men*. Swindon: ESRC.

Ranson, G. (2001) 'Men At Work: Change – Or no Change? – In the Era of the "New Father"', *Men and Masculinities* 4(1): 3–26.

Reynolds, T. (2005) *Caribbean Mothers: Identity and Experience in the UK*. London: Tufnell Press.

Richards, M. (2004) 'Assisted Reproduction, Genetic Technologies, and Family Life', in Scott, J., Treas, J. and Richards, M. (eds) *The Blackwell Companion to the Sociology of Families*. Oxford: Blackwell.

Riley, S.C.E. (2003) 'The Management of the Traditional Male Role: A Discourse Analysis of the Constructions and Functions of Provision', *Journal of Gender Studies* 12(2): 99–113.

Risman, B.J. and Johnson-Sumerford, D. (1998) 'Doing It Fairly: A Study of Post-gender Marriages', *Journal of Marriage and the Family* 60(1): 23–40.

Roberts, Y. (2006) 'When Lads Become Dads', *The Guardian* 10 June. http://www.guardian.co.uk/family/story/0,,1794041,00.html (last accessed 16/7/2007).

Rodgers, B. and Pryor, J. (1998) *Divorce and Separation: The Outcomes for Children*. York: Joseph Rowntree Foundation.

Roper, M. (1994) *Masculinity and the British Organization Man since 1945*. Oxford: Oxford University Press.

Roseneil, S. and Budgeon, S. (2004) 'Cultures of Intimacy and Care Beyond "the Family": Personal Life and Social Change in the Early 21st Century', *Current Sociology* 52(2): 135–59.

Rotundo, E. A. (1993) *American Manhood: Transformations in Masculinity from the Revolution to the Modern Era*. New York: Basic Books.

Ruspini, E. (2000) 'Longitudinal Research in the Social Sciences', *Social Research Update* 20. http://sru.soc.surrey.ac.uk/SRU28.html (last accessed 1/10/07).

Ryan-Flood, R. (2005) 'Contested Heteronormativities: Discourses of Fatherhood among Lesbian Parents in Sweden and Ireland', *Sexualities* 8(2): 189–204.

Sandberg, J.F. and Hofferth, S.L. (2001) 'Changes in Children's Time with Parents: US 1981–1997', *Demography* 38(3): 423–36.

Sayer, L.C., Bianchi, S.M. and Robinson, J.P. (2004) 'Are Parents Investing Less in Children? Trends in Mothers' and Fathers' Time with Children', *American Journal of Sociology* 110(1): 1–43.

Scott, J. (1999) 'Family Change: Revolution or Backlash?', in McRae, S. (ed.) *Changing Britain: Families and Households in the 1990s*. Oxford: Oxford University Press.

Scott, J. (2006) 'Family and Gender Roles: How Attitudes Are Changing', *GeNet Working Paper No. 21*. http://www.genet.ac.uk/workpapers/GeNet2006p21.pdf.

Scott, J., Braun, M. and Alwin, D. (1998), 'Partner, Parent, Worker: Family and Gender Roles' in Jowell, R., Curtice, J., Park, A., Brook, L., Thomson, K. and Bryson, C. (eds) *British and European Social Attitudes: The 15th BSA Report*. Aldershot: Aldgate.

Seidler, V.J. (1997) *Man Enough: Embodying Masculinities*. London: Sage.

Seidler, V.J. (2006) *Transforming Masculinities*. Abingdon: Routledge.

Seltzer, J. A. (1991) 'Relationships between Fathers and Children Who Live Apart: The Father's Role After Separation', *Journal of Marriage and the Family* 53(1): 79–101.

Seward, R.R., Yeatts, D.E., Zottarelli, L.K. and Fletcher, R.G. (2006) 'Fathers Taking Parental Leave and their Involvement with Children', *Community, Work and Family* 9(1): 1–9

Sheldon, S. (2004) 'Natallie Evans' Case: Some Lessons for the Parliamentary Review of the Human Fertilisation and Embryology Act (1990)'. http://www.prochoiceforum.org.uk/irl_rep_tech_3.asp (last accessed 24/7/07).

Sheldon, S. (2005a) 'Fragmenting Fatherhood: The Regulation of Reproductive Technologies', *The Modern Law Review* 68(4): 523–53.

Sheldon, S. (2005b) 'Reproductive Technologies and the Legal Determination of Fatherhood', *Feminist Legal Studies* 13(3): 349–62.

Sigle-Rushton, W. (2005) 'Young Fatherhood and Subsequent Disadvantage in the United Kingdom', *Journal of Marriage and the Family* 67(3): 735–53.

Siltanen, J. (1994) *Locating Gender: Occupational Segregation, Wages and Domestic Responsibilities*. London: University College of London Press.

Simpson, B., McCarthy, P. and Walker, J. (1995) *Being There: Fathers After Divorce*. Newcastle: Relate Centre for Family Studies.

Simpson, B., Jessop, J.A. and McCarthy, P. (2005) 'Fathers after Divorce', in Bainham, A., Lindley, B., Richards, M. and Trinder, L. (eds) *Children and Their Families: Contact, Rights and Welfare*. Oxford: Hart.

Singleton, A. (2003) 'Men Getting Real? A Study of Relationship Change in Two Men's Groups', *Journal of Sociology* 39(2): 131–47.

Skevik, A. (2006) ' "Absent Fathers" or "Reorganized Families"? Variations in Father–Child Contact after Parental Break-up in Norway', *The Sociological Review* 54(1): 114–32.

Smart, C. (1997) 'Wishful Thinking and Harmful Tinkering? Sociological Reflections on Family Policy', *Journal of Social Policy* 26(3): 301–21.

Smart, C. (1999) 'The "New" Parenthood: Fathers and Mothers after Divorce', in Silva, E.B. and Smart, C. (eds) *The New Family?* London: Sage.

Smart, C. (2004a) 'Equal Shares: Rights for Fathers or Recognition for Children?', *Critical Social Policy* 24(4): 484–503.

Smart, C. (2004b) 'Retheorising Families', *Sociology* 38(5): 1037–42.

Smart, C. (2005) 'Textures of Family Life: Further Thoughts on Change and Commitment', *Journal of Social Policy* 34(4): 541–56.

Smart, C. (2006) 'Preface', in Collier, R. and Sheldon, S. (eds) *Fathers' Rights Activism and Law Reform in Comparative Perspective*. Oxford: Hart.

Smart, C. and May, V. (2004) 'Why Can't They Agree? The Underlying Complexity of Contact and Residence Disputes', *Journal of Social Welfare and Family Law* 26(4): 347–60

Smart, C. and Neale, B. (1999) *Family Fragments?* Cambridge: Polity Press.

Smeaton, D. (2006) *Dads and their Babies: A Household Analysis*. Manchester: EOC.

Smeaton, D. and Marsh, A. (2006) *Maternity and Paternity Rights and Benefits: Survey of Parents 2005*. DTI Employment Relations Research Series No.50. London: Policy Studies Institute.

Smeeding, T.M. and Marchand, J.T. (2004) 'Family Time and Public Policy in the United States', in Folbre, N. and Bittman, M. (eds) *Family Time: The Social Organization of Care*. London: Routledge.

Smith, A.J. (2004) 'Who Cares? Fathers and the Time They Spend Looking After Children', *Sociology Working Papers 2004–05*, Oxford: University of Oxford.

Smith, A.J. (2007) *Working Fathers in Europe: Earning and Caring?* Centre for Research on Families and Relationships, Research Briefing No.30. Edinburgh: CRFR.

Solomon, Y., Warin, J., Lewis, C. and Langford, W. (2002) 'Intimate Talk Between Parents and Their Teenage Children: Democratic Openness or Covert Control?', *Sociology* 36(4): 965–83

Southerton, D. (2006) 'Analysing the Temporal Organisation of Daily Life: Social Constraints, Practices and their Allocation', *Sociology* 40(3): 435–54.

Speak, S., Cameron, S. and Gilroy, R. (1997) *Young Single Fathers: Participation in Fatherhood – Bridges and Barriers*. London: Family Policy Studies Centre.

Spencer, L. and Pahl, R. (2006) *Rethinking Friendship: Hidden Solidarities Today*. Princeton, NJ: Princeton University Press.

Stacey, J. (2006) 'Gay Parenthood and the Decline of Paternity as We Knew It', *Sexualities* 9(1): 27–55.

Stannard, M. (2002) 'Head to Head: Fatherless Families', BBC 29 April. http://news.bbc.co.uk/1/hi/uk/1958237.stm (last accessed 8/7/2007).

Straw, J. (2007) BBC Radio 4 'Today', 21/8/07.

Sullivan, O. (2000) 'The Division of Domestic Labour: Twenty Years of Change?', *Sociology* 34(3): 437–56

Sunderland, J. (2000) 'Baby Entertainer, Bumbling Assistant and Line Manager: Discourses of Fatherhood in Parentcraft Texts', *Discourse and Society* 11(2): 249–74.

Tasker, F.L. and Golombok, S. (1997) *Growing Up in a Lesbian Family: Effects on Child Development*. New York. The Guildford Press.

Terkel, S. (1974) *Working*. New York: Pantheon Books.

Thompson, C. (2001) 'Strategic Naturalizing: Kinship in an Infertility Clinic', in Franklin, S. and McKinnon, S. (eds) *Relative Values. Reconfiguring Kinship Studies*. Durham, NC: Duke University Press.

Thompson, M., Vinter, L. and Young, V. (2005) *Dads and their Babies: Leave Arrangements in the First Year*. Manchester: EOC.

Times (The) (2007a) 'Hi, I'm your Biological Son', 21 August. http://www.timesonline.co.uk/tol/life_and_style/men/article2293863.ece (last accessed 22/8/07).

Times (The) (2007b) 'Gay British Men Pay Fertility Clinic £33,000 for Designer Babies', 25 March. http://www.timesonline.co.uk/tol/news/uk/science/article1563914.ece (last accessed 30/7/07).

Tosh, J. (1996) 'Authority and Nurture in Middle-Class Fatherhood: The Case of Early and Mid-Victorian England', *Gender and History* 8(1): 48–94.

Townsend, N. (2002) *The Package Deal: Marriage, Work, and Fatherhood in Men's Lives*. Philadelphia, PA: Temple University Press.

Trinder, L., Beek, M. and Connolly, J. (2002) *Making Contact: How Parents and Children Negotiation and Experience Contact after Divorce*. York: Joseph Rowntree Foundation.

University of Essex. Institute for Social and Economic Research, *British Household Panel Survey: Waves 1-15, 1991–2006* [computer file]. 3rd Edition. Colchester, Essex: UK Data Archive [distributor], June 2007. SN: 5151.

University of London. Institute of Education. Centre for Longitudinal Studies, *National Child Development Study: Sweep 6, 1999–2000* [computer file]. Joint Centre for Longitudinal Research, [original data producer(s)]. Colchester, Essex: UK Data Archive [distributor], January 2007. SN: 5578.

Van Dongen, M.C.P. (1995) 'Men's Aspirations Concerning Childcare: The Extent to which They are Realised', in Van Dongen, M.C.P., Frinking, G.A.B. and Jacobs, M.J.G. (eds) *Changing Fatherhood: A Multidisciplinary Perspective*. Amsterdam: Thesis Publishers.

Vance, J.C., Boyle, F.M., Najman, J.M. and Thearle, J.M. (1995) 'Gender Differences in Parental Psychological Distress Following Perinatal Death or Sudden Infant Death Syndrome', *British Journal of Psychiatry* 167(6): 806–11.

Vincent, C. and Ball, S. (2006) *Childcare, Choice and Class Practices*. London: Routledge.

Walby, S. (1990) *Theorizing Patriarchy*. Oxford: Blackwell.

Walkerdine, V. and Lucey, H. (1989) *Democracy in the Kitchen: Regulating Mothers and Socialising Daughters*. London: Virago.

Wall, G. and Arnold, S. (2007) 'How Involved is Involved Fathering? An Exploration of the Contemporary Culture of Fatherhood', *Gender and Society* 21(4): 508–27.

Walling, A. (2004) 'Families and Work', *Labour Market Trends* 113(7): 275–83.

Warin, J., Solomon, Y., Lewis, C. and Langford, W. (1999) *Fathers, Work and Family Life*. London: Family Policy Studies Centre.

Warren, T. (2003) 'Class- and Gender-based Working Time? Time Poverty and the Division of Domestic Labour', *Sociology* 37(4): 733–52.

Warren, T. (2007) 'Conceptualizing Breadwinning', *Work, Employment and Society* 21(2): 317–86.

Wasoff, F. (2004) 'Private Arrangements for Contact With Children: the Scottish perspective', ESRC/Scottish Executive Public Policy Seminar. http://www.crfr.ac.uk/Reports/ESRC-SE.pdf (last accessed 30/7/07).

Weeks, J., Heaphy, B. and Donovan, C. (2001) *Same Sex Intimacies*. London: Routledge.

Welsh, E., Buchanan, A., Flouri, E. and Lewis, J. (2004) *'Involved' Fathering and Child Well-being: Fathers' Involvement with Secondary School Age Children*. York: Joseph Rowntree Foundation.

Weston, K. (1991) *Families We Choose: Lesbians, Gays, Kinship*. New York: Columbia University Press.

Westwood, S. (1996) ' "Feckless Fathers": Masculinity and the British State', in Mac an Ghaill, M. (ed.) *Understanding Masculinities*. Buckingham: Open University Press.

Williams, S.M. (2002) 'Reflexive Fathering: The Individualisation of Fathering'. Unpublished PhD thesis, University of Glamorgan.

Willott, S. and Griffin, C. (1997) 'Wham Bam, am I a Man? Unemployed Men Talk about Masculinities', *Feminism & Psychology* 7(1): 107–28.

Wilson, G. (2003) 'Stay-at-home Fathers Hit a Record High', *The Scotsman on Sunday*, 26 October. http://news.scotsman.com/scotland.cfm?id=1180332003 (last accessed 30/6/07).

Wilson, G.B., Gillies, J.B. and Mayes, G.M. (2004) 'Fathers as Co-Parents: How Non-Resident Fathers Construe Family Situations', *Social Research Legal Studies*. Research Findings No. 52. Edinburgh: Scottish Executive.

Yaxley, D., Vinter, L. and Young, V. (2005) *Dads and Their Babies: The Mothers' Perspective*. London: EOC.

Yeung, W.J., Sandberg, J.F., Davis-Kean, P.E. and Hofferth, S.L. (2001) 'Children's Time with Fathers in Intact Families', *Journal of Marriage and Family* 63(1): 136–54.

Young, I.M. (1997) *Intersecting Voices: Gender, Political Philosophy, and Policy*. Princeton, NJ: Princeton University Press.

Zelizer, V. (1985) *Pricing the Priceless Child*. New York: Basic Books.

Zelizer, V. (2005) *The Purchase of Intimacy*. Princeton, NJ: Princeton University Press.

Zick, C.D. and Bryant, W.K. (1996) 'A New Look at Parents' Time Spent in Child Care: Primary and Secondary Time Use', *Social Science Research* 25(3): 260–80.

Index